LATINO COMMUNITIES

Emerging Voices

Political, Social, Cultural, and Legal Issues

edited by

ANTOINETTE SEDILLO LOPEZ
University of New Mexico

LATINOS AND LOCAL REPRESENTATION

Changing Realities, Emerging Theories

FLORENCE ADAMS

Routledge
Taylor & Francis Group
LONDON AND NEW YORK

Published in 2000 by
Garland Publishing Inc.

Published 2016 by Routledge
2 Park Square, Milton Park, Abingdon, Oxfordshire OX14 4RN
711 Third Avenue, New York, NY 10017

First issued in paperback 2016

Routledge is an imprint of the Taylor and Francis Group, an informa business

Library of Congress Cataloging-in-Publication Data

Library of Congress Cataloging-in-Publication Data is available from the Library of Congress.

ISBN 13: 978-1-138-97944-4 (pbk)
ISBN 13: 978-0-8153-3370-8 (hbk)

In Memoriam
George S. Blair
Teacher, Scholar, Colleague, Friend

Contents

Figures

Tables

Acknowledgments

I must acknowledge the generous support of the Earhart Foundation, which provided support for my work on local districting at the Rose Institute of State and Local Government at Claremont McKenna College. Three mentors at the Rose Institute, George Blair, Leroy Hardy and Alan Heslop, introduced me to the arcana of reapportionment and redistricting. I owe a special debt to Professor Hardy's extraordinary bibliographical knowledge in these areas and to his fund of wisdom on the practice of line drawing. Professor Jack Pitney introduced me to the advantages of the Internet and helped me perceive the significance of some of my own work. George Felkenes most kindly agreed to step into the void left by the untimely death of George Blair.

The legal mysteries of the Voting Rights Act first became clear to me when expounded by Marguerite Leoni, who was also my Cicerone through the politics of several Central Valley communities. I am also grateful to Antoinette Sedillo Lopez for her insightful suggestions.

No one who writes about the innermost political processes of more than twenty jurisdictions can fail to be impressed by the dedication of the elected and appointed officials with whom she works. I need to record particular indebtedness to: Marion Porch, Intergovernmental Relations Coordinator of the City of Glendale and Jan Graziano, City Clerk of Peoria, Arizona.

I must acknowledge, also, the Rose Institute students with whom I have worked for the past twenty years. Their cheerful company and their ability to help a representative of an older generation understand the uses of advanced geographic information systems were important at many points along the way. I am especially indebted to Chris Skinnell, whose assistance in the final preparation of tables and maps was invaluable. And I acknowledge, too, my friend, Peter Petri, who rescued me from a GIS quagmire.

Last, but far from least, are my family (Norm, Jeff and Emily) and my friends, who never gave up on me.

Introduction

This study addresses the interplay of electoral structures and the political behavior of ethnic minorities. Specifically, it examines recent trends in enforcement of the Voting Rights Act. It traces the development of certain kinds of at-large and single-member-district forms of election in selected jurisdictions; and reviews the history of minority participation under these forms in those jurisdictions. The geographic focus of the study is California and Arizona; and, with one or two exceptions, it describes districting and redistricting processes that involved this writer as a principal technician or "political cartographer."

The literature of American political science on voting rights has focused at the level of congressional and state legislative districting. Our focus here is on districting in cities and special districts. Citizen concern with issues of local representation is often greater than it is at higher levels; and the political pressures of incumbent and group ambition in the line-drawing process are hardly less intense. It is our hope, therefore, that this study will shed as much light on the character of local politics as similar studies have achieved for state legislative and congressional politics.

Nearly all redistricting fights, at any level of politics, are expensive and labor intensive; unlike state legislatures, however, municipalities often lack the resources to conduct such fights. Many of the contests that we describe placed enormous burdens on the budgets and energies of city or special district staffs and elected politicians alike; they constituted, in effect, major crises in the political life of the jurisdictions; and, in some cases, litigation threatened literally to bankrupt the city or special district. Unlike congressional and state legislative redistrictings, therefore, the intervention of the U.S. Justice Department in local actions has enormous impact, even threatening the continuing viability of the jurisdiction. Few studies in the political science literature have concerned themselves with these unequal contests.

Much of the political science literature in this area is taken up with changes in the laws affecting voting, whether in the form of congressional amendments to the Voting Rights Act or decisions of the U.S. Supreme Court. This general literature is replete, also, with theoretical discussions of the perceived gains and losses from different decisions, with close exegesis of the language of statutes and judicial rulings, and with statistical measures of vote dilution and polarization. Such an emphasis, of course, is vital to understanding many aspects of the field. In the case of the present study, however, we go beyond that focus to an examination of the practical political consequences of changes in the law. We look behind the language of statutes and judicial rulings to the actual drawing of district lines and to the effects of those lines on minority politics.

Many of the jurisdictions that we deal with experienced (and continue to experience) dramatic changes in their population: rapid growth in total population, enormous expansion of territory through annexation, and huge changes (both increases and decreases proportionate to total population) in minority population. Today, no state experiences such dramatic changes over so short a period: their boundaries are fixed, their populations never double or triple within a single decade (as was the case with several of our jurisdictions), and in few states do minorities constitute more than a fraction of the population. Thus, the challenge of drawing local boundaries is often much more complicated than at the state or congressional level, because percentage changes in populations can be much sharper and the proportions of minority population may be much greater. Perhaps, therefore, there is more to be learned from local redistrictings; yet, few political science studies have focused their interest at this level.[1]

With rare exceptions,[2] the political science literature on racial gerrymandering has focused in the southern states. In part, this is so because most of the judicial action has occurred in southern jurisdictions; and, moreover, the problem of African American representation has attracted most of the attention and sympathy of the discipline. Yet, both Section 2 and Section 5 of the Voting Rights Act have been targeted increasingly at jurisdictions in the Southwest and

Western United States; and there is a swelling number of cases involving problems of Hispanic representation. This study deals with some of the most interesting of such cases; and, as such, it makes a contribution to an embryonic professional literature.

In the literature on redistricting in the U.S., there is no attention to situations where non-white populations have reached majority status. Yet, in several of the jurisdictions with which we deal here, minorities are approaching that status or actually form a numerical majority. In two jurisdictions, indeed, minorities constitute a majority of the voting age electorate. For us, then, it is not a merely theoretical concern, but a practical one, to ask whether voting rights concepts, such as the "majority minority" district and the push to replace at-large with single member districts, will remain relevant when "minorities" become majorities. This study is the first to deal with a situation that will be increasingly frequent in some areas of the United States.

The contribution that this study makes to the literature, then, is its focus on local districtings and redistrictings, its concern with issues of Hispanic rather than with African American representation, its concentration on the actual processes of implementation rather than with legal and judicial policy and theory, and its development of issues and concerns that are prompted by the dramatically changing character of local demographics. The study is written with clear sympathy for the aims of broadening and expanding the inclusion of minorities in the political process; but it subjects some of the standard concepts of voting rights theory to a realistic appraisal of their actual consequences for minorities and for the political process as a whole.

NOTES

1. Studies here include: Mary P. Beeman, "Implementing Equality: The Voting Rights Act and Its Impact on Municipal Government," Paper delivered at Southwestern Political Science Association Annual Meeting, Dallas, March 1987; Brett W. Berri, "Annexation and Municipal Voting Rights," *Washington University Journal of Urban and Contemporary Law* 35 (Spring 1989): 237-48; Charles S. Bullock, III, "Symbolics or Substance: A Critique to the At Large Election Controversy," *State and Local Government Review* 21 (Fall 1989): 91-99; Chandler Davidson and George Korbel, "At-Large Elections and Minority Group Representation: A Reexamination of Historical and Contemporary Evidence," *Journal of Politics* 43 (1981): 982-1005; Robert G. Dixon, Jr., "Local Representation: Constitutional Mandates and Apportionment Options,"

George Washington Law Review 36 (May 1968): 693-712 and "Rebuilding the Urban Political System: Some Heresies Concerning Citizen Participation, Community Actions, Metros, and One-Man-One Vote," *Georgetown Law Journal* 58 (March-May 1970): 955-958; Malcolm E. Jewell, "Local Systems of Representation: Political Consequences and Judicial Choices," *George Washington Law Review* 36 (May 1968): 790-807; Susan A. MacManus, "City Council Elections Procedures and Minority Representation: Are they Related?" *Social Science Quarterly* 59 (June 1978): 153-161 and "Mixed Electoral Systems: The Newest Reform Structure," *National Civic Review* 74 (November 1985): 484-490; Frank J. Machiarola and Joseph G. Diaz, "The 1990 New York City Districting Commission: Renewed Opportunity for Participation in Local Government or Race-Biased Gerrymandering?" *Cardozo Law Review* 14 (April 1993): 1175-235; John E. McDermott and Bernard Grofman, "Pro/Con: Should City Councils be Elected by District?" *Western City* (March 1987): 4-8, 24-31, 44; Howard D. Neighbor, *City Council Districting in the 1980s* (New York: National Municipal League, 1980); and Timothy G. O'Rourke, "City and County At-large Elections and the Problem of Minority Representation," *University of Virginia Newsletter* 55 (February 1979).

2. Exceptions include: Rufus P. Browning, Dale Rogers and David H. Tabb, "Blacks and Hispanics in California City Politics: Changes in Representation," *Public Affairs Report* 20 (June 1979): 1-9; Aide Cristina Cabeza, "Total Population: A Constitutional Basis for Apportionment Reaffirmed in *Garza v. Los Angeles County* (918 F.2d 763 (1990))," *Chicano-Latino Law Review* 13 (Summer 1993): 74-95; Charles L. Cotrell and Arnold Fleishmann, "The Change from At-Large Representation and Political Participation of Minority Groups in Fort Worth and San Antonio Texas," *Urban Affairs Quarterly* 10 (September 1974): 17-39; Chandler Davidson, "The Voting Rights Act: Protecting the Rights of Racial and Language Minorities in the Electoral Process," *Chicano Law Review* 13 (Summer 1993); Rodolfo O. De la Garza and Louis Desipio, "Save the Baby, Change the Bathwater, and Scrub the Tub: Latino Electoral Participation After Seventeen Years of Voting Rights Act Coverage," *Texas Law Review* 71 (June 1993): 1479-539; Richard E. DeLeon, "Race and Politics in San Francisco," Delivered at the Annual Meeting of the Western Political Science Association, San Franciso, CA, March 10-12, 1988; John F. Gallagher, "Apportionment in California Counties," *State Government* 37 (Winter 1964): 36-41; Luis Fraga, "Policy Consequences of the Changes From At Large Elections to Single Member Districts in Three Texas Cities," A paper presented at the annual meeting of the Western Political Science Association, March 1991; Bernard Grofman, "Voting Rights In a Multi-Ethnic World," *Chicano Law Review*

(Summer 1993); Rodney Hero, "The Election of Hispanics in City Government: An Examination of the Election of Federico Pena as Mayor of Denver," *Western Political Quarterly* 40 (March 1987): 93-105; Bob Johnson, Watsonville's New Crop: A Court Decision is Changing the Way Local Elections are Held," *Golden State Report* (September 1989): 17-31; "One Man, Less Than One Vote: How Certain Methods of Electing City Councilmen Result in Significant Under-Representation of Minorities in Major California Cities" (Sacramento, CA: Senate Majority Caucus, June 1971); *Political Participation of Mexican Americans in California* (Washington, D.C.: Government Printing Office, 1971); James A. Regalado, "Racial Gerrymandering in Los Angeles, California: Redistricting and the Question of Latino Representation," Paper presented at the Western Political Science Association Annual Meeting, Eugene, Oregon, March 2-5, 1986; Gloria Romero, "The Challenge to At-Large Elections in California: *Romero, et. al. v. The City of Pomona*," Paper delivered at Western Political Science Association Annual Meeting, Anaheim, CA, March 1987; Carole Uhlaner, Bruce Cain and D. Roderick Kiewiet, "Patterns of Political Participation Among Ethnic Minorities in California," Paper delivered at a meeting of Western Political Science Association, March 1986; and Susan Welch, "The Impact of At-Large Elections on the Representation of Blacks and Hispanics," *Journal of Politics* 52 (November 1990): 1050-76.

Latinos and Local Representation

CHAPTER 1

Minority Voting and Voting Rights: Congress and the Courts

The historical context of this study begins with the Fifteenth Amendment of 1870, which provided that "the right of citizens of the United States to vote shall not be denied or abridged by the United States or by any state on account of race, color, or previous condition of servitude." Under Section 2 of the Amendment, Congress gained the right to enforce the Amendment through legislation—a right that was promptly exercised through the Enforcement Act of 1870 and the Force Act of 1871.

It is well beyond the focus of this study to retrace the history of efforts to evade both the spirit and the letter of the Fifteenth Amendment and the successor laws affirming the rights of black citizens to vote. Suffice it to say that neither the Enforcement Act nor the Force Act proved effective. After the withdrawal of military supervision under the Compromise of 1877, innumerable measures were used to intimidate, to deter or even, by violence, to prevent blacks from casting ballots; and that, by 1876, the U.S. Supreme Court had drained both Acts of their potency.[1] Our story really begins after 1877.

With the ending of Reconstruction and with the collapse of the enforcement legislation, the only remaining barrier to Southern efforts to crush black suffrage was the Fifteenth Amendment itself. It was to the undermining of the Fifteenth Amendment that the South now turned its attention. During the next half-century, Southern Democrats developed techniques for reducing the numbers of black voters:[2] literacy tests, poll taxes, requirements for proofs of long residence (or, even, proofs that a grandfather had fought in the War Between the

States, the "Fighting Grandfather Clause"), and "White Primaries."[3] Other techniques were more sophisticated, for they sought to exclude blacks by manipulation of electoral arrangements: replacing district or ward elections with at-large systems; annexing or de-annexing territory for the purpose of bolstering the white vote or reducing the black vote; and, of course, various kinds of racial gerrymandering.

Southern Democrats' success in excluding blacks from suffrage helped to develop their Party's national power, for they secured for it a solid regional base. With the election of Woodrow Wilson, the federal government itself became an agency for implementing Jim Crow. Thus, in less than a half-century, the Fifteenth Amendment had lost all vitality.

Even the United States Supreme Court took part. Passively, the Court accepted much of the disfranchising machinery: in *Grovey v. Townsend* (1935) the Court upheld the White Primary; in *Breedlove v. Suttles* (1937) the Court upheld the poll tax; and literacy tests survived throughout the period. (It should be noted, however, that the Supreme Court did strike down the use of grandfather clauses in *Guinn v. United States* in 1915; and in *Lane v. Wilson* in 1939, the Court forbade extraordinary time limits on the ability to register to vote.)

Not until World War II did the Court strike down the most effective means of electoral discrimination, the White Primary: a series of four Texas cases, concluding in 1944 with *Smith v. Allwright*, refused to regard the Democratic Party as merely a private organization and, thus, eliminated this means of restricting the franchise. Yet, the result was little more than to give additional urgency to efforts to maintain the racial purity of the electoral process. The period after World War II saw a continuation, even an escalation, of discriminatory electoral arrangements, restrictions on black registration, and various kinds of racial gerrymandering.

Thus, the United States entered the second half of the Twentieth Century with one of its regions—accounting at mid-century for more than a quarter of its population—effectively confined to one-party rule. Although the most blatant measure—the White Primary—had fallen, other devices remained as means of restricting black suffrage.

FEDERAL VOTING RIGHTS LEGISLATION

Perhaps we are still too close to the civil rights revolution to identify the prime mover in the efforts to enforce black rights of suffrage. Some maintain that civil rights demonstrations of the period fueled the movement for voting rights. Others see cynical competition between Republicans and Democrats for the loyalty of black voters. Whatever the explanation, the Eisenhower, Kennedy and Johnson administrations all advanced efforts to remedy the problem.

The 1957 Civil Rights Act was the Eisenhower administration's effort to prove that the Party of Lincoln was ready finally to assert itself on behalf of blacks against the Southern Democratic barons.[4] The legislation, which passed over a filibuster by Southern Democrats, provided that an assistant attorney general in the U.S. Department of Justice would be responsible for intervening in civil suits by individuals, and could file suits in federal court in cases of violation of the Fifteenth Amendment. A further civil rights act passed in 1960 in an effort to give support to this approach to civil and voting rights.[5]

In 1964, Lyndon Johnson again broke with his Southern colleagues to lead the fight for the Civil Rights Act of that year, an extraordinarily ambitious statute that struck at many different kinds of discrimination. Yet, the right of blacks to register and to vote in southern jurisdictions remained largely unimproved by these three federal acts. Relatively few additional blacks joined the registration lists as a result of litigation under these new laws. As Chief Justice Earl Warren noted in *South Carolina v. Katzenbach* in 1966, registration of voting age blacks had been barely affected: "In Alabama (registration) rose only from 14.2 percent to 19.4 percent between 1958 and 1964; in Louisiana it barely inched ahead from 31.7 to 31.8 percent between 1956 and 1965; and in Mississippi it increased only from 4.4 percent to 6.4 percent between 1954 and 1964."[6]

The breach in the solid wall of southern resistance to black enfranchisement came only in 1965. Immediately following his 1964 landslide, Lyndon Johnson instructed attorney general Nicholas Katzenbach, to write "The Goddamndest, toughest voting rights act that you can devise."[7] Johnson's Voting Rights Act, dispensing with the reliance on litigation of earlier legislation, began with a forceful restatement of the Fifteenth Amendment, prohibiting any techniques that would "deny or abridge the right of any citizen of the United States to vote on account of race or color."[8] Strengthened powers of enforcement of the right to vote were granted to the Justice Department and to federal courts in various ways: preclearance provisions, federal examiners, federal observers, and suspension of electoral tests and arrangements could be ordered by courts if the right to vote was threatened.[9] The most revolutionary feature of the legislation—the one that drew most of the ire of the southern establishment—was the formula used to target the southern jurisdictions.[10] The special provisions of the Act could come into effect under two conditions:

> First, if the jurisdiction maintained any tests or devices as preconditions for or obstacles to registering to vote or voting as of November 1, 1964; and
> Second, if less than half the voting age population was registered to vote on that date, or if less than half the voting age population actually had voted in the November presidential election of that year.[11]

Although the legislation was supposedly national, the triggering criteria focused upon the South. The criteria resulted in the selection of only seven entire states: Alaska, Alabama, Georgia, Louisiana, Mississippi, South Carolina, and Virginia. As allowed under Section 4a of the Act, Alaska soon filed a declaratory judgment action and excluded itself from coverage, leaving only states of the old Solid South. (Two states, Hawaii and Idaho, included jurisdictions or individual counties that were covered under the Act). These jurisdictions, and those added by subsequent amendments to the triggering formula of the Voting Rights Act, were subject to the preclearance provisions of Section 5 of the Act.[12]

In 1966, the Supreme Court upheld the Act in *South Carolina v. Katzenbach*. Justice Black, a former United States senator from Alabama, was the lone dissenter, protesting that the Act treated the southern states like "conquered provinces." Writing for the majority, Chief Justice Warren admitted that the legislation was "an uncommon exercise of congressional power," but affirmed that "exceptional conditions can justify legislative measures not otherwise appropriate."[13] Evidently, Warren believed—as the Congressional sponsors of the legislation themselves seem to have believed—that the legislation would be temporary and would end as soon as suffrage had been restored to southern black citizens.

Expansion of Voting Rights Enforcement from the South to the Southwest and West

The 1965 Act was scheduled to expire after five years, in August of 1970. Congress did not let the legislation lapse, however. As expiration approached, it passed a renewal of the Act that would continue it in effect until August of 1975. The new legislation expanded the coverage of the Act to include states or jurisdictions in which less than half the population of voting age was registered to vote or had actually voted in the November 1968 presidential election. This new triggering formula brought under coverage non-Southern areas: five counties in Arizona; local governments in Connecticut; two counties in California; local governments in Maine; local governments in Massachusetts; local governments in New Hampshire; three counties in New York; and a county in Wyoming.

In August of 1975, Congress again extended the Act. Joining southern black groups in pressing for its extension were Hispanics,[14] who argued that their voting rights were in jeopardy, as indicated by the inclusion of California and Arizona under the triggering formula.[15] At first, many black leaders, including Clarence Mitchell, of the National Association for the Advancement of Colored People (NAACP), opposed inclusion of Hispanics. But the strength of the Chicano political groups was decisive and the 1975 Voting Rights Act expanded coverage to language minorities (Alaskan natives, Asian Americans, Hispanics and native Americans). The Act broadened the triggering formula to include jurisdictions that used English only materials for the ballot but that included substantial numbers of language minorities. In this way, the 1975 Act reached outside the South to the Southwest and the West.

It reached, as well, beyond the provisions of the Fifteenth Amendment to provide for bilingual election arrangements. The Act established that, if 5 percent or more of a jurisdiction's voting age (18-plus) citizens belonged to a single language minority, and if that language minority's illiteracy rate was greater than the national illiteracy rate, then bilingual election materials and assistance must be provided to that language minority. (These protections were based by Congress on the Equal Protection clause of the 14th Amendment, rather than on the power to enforce the Fifteenth Amendment.) As a result of these changes, all of Alaska, all of Arizona, four counties in California, and parts of Colorado, and South Dakota, plus the whole state of Texas were brought into coverage. (The provisions also brought additional jurisdictions in the South under coverage, including five counties in Florida).

Voting Rights and the Question of Intention to Discriminate

It is commonplace for political studies to note the extraordinary effectiveness of the Voting Rights Act in bringing southern black voters into the political system. In 1965 alone, the U.S. Department of Justice listed the names of nearly 80,000 black voters for addition to registration rolls in southern states. By 1967, more than a half-million new black voters had been listed in the southern states and no southern state had registered less than 50 percent of its black voting age population. Not only black registration, but black turnout had shown sharp improvement; and in election after election, blacks began to prove the power of a bloc vote.

The great gains in black participation occurred in the first five years of the legislation—1965-1970. It was then that federal intervention struck down the poll taxes, literacy tests and other restrictive registration procedures. More generally, it was then that the threat of federal intervention played its most significant part in deterring white intimidation of black voters. By the 1970s the path of black suffrage was cleared of the worst obstructions. In the late 1970s, therefore, the focus of voting rights litigation and of federal intervention began to turn from the overt barriers to the more subtle manipulation of electoral arrangements to dilute minority votes.

One cause of the shift was recognition by minority group leaders that the formal rights were not enough to assure full minority participation, particularly the election of minority candidates. Voting rights enforcement targeted racial gerrymandering: either concentration of minority voters in too few districts (racial packing) or use of boundary lines to disperse minority voters among too many districts ("racial cracking"). Another focus was the use of at-large elections or multi-member districts to "swamp" minority voters (whose candidates might otherwise win in a single-member district). Other structural devices have also come under challenge. These include exclusive slating practices that reduce minority influence in the selection of candidates; anti-single shot ordinances, which prevent minority groups from mobilizing to vote for their own candidate in multi-candidate elections; reductions in the size of elective bodies in order to increase the population of districts, which again swamps the minority vote; and replacement of elective with appointive officials.[16]

It can be seen, then, that a dramatic expansion was under way in the reach and scope of the Voting Rights Act. It no longer focused on the South, but embraced other regions as well, particularly the west and southwest with their many Hispanic voters. It no longer rested solely on Congress's power to enforce the Fifteenth Amendment, but had found an additional basis in the Equal Protection clause of the Fourteenth Amendment. And, it no longer targeted just active discrimination, but had widened its sweep to encompass practices that, *whether by intention or not*, had the *effect* of reducing minority influence.

As the 1980s opened, courts were deciding "vote dilution" cases on a wide variety of facts. *Zimmer v. McKeithen*, a case decided by the Fifth Circuit Court of Appeals,[17] involved a "totality of Circumstances" ruling. The Court held that successful constitutional challenges could be based on a number of different facts.[18] It was a standard that, although placing a considerable burden of proof on plaintiffs, resulted in a swelling number of rulings overturning official procedures and structures that were held supportive of unconstitutional dilution of minority voting power.

Suddenly, however, the Supreme Court appeared to throw up a roadblock to continuation of this development. The apparent change of direction came in *City of Mobile v. Bolden,*[19] a case involving a challenge to the Alabama city's at-large system for election of its three-member city commission. Since establishment of the system in 1911, no black had won election to the commission, although one-third of the population was black and although black leaders saw the commission as unresponsive to their community's needs. Applying the *Zimmer* standard, the trial and appeals court rulings had supported the plaintiffs' challenge and had held that *Mobile* had unconstitutionally diluted their vote. In a divided opinion, however, a plurality on the Supreme Court ruled that the Fourteenth Amendment protects against dilution only when it can be proved that the diluting structure or procedure was adopted expressly for racially discriminatory purposes.

Essentially, the *Mobile* ruling held that where the character of a law is readily explainable on grounds apart from race, disproportionate impact alone cannot be decisive, and courts must look to other evidence to support a finding of discriminatory purpose. Thus, to show discriminatory *effect*, even across a range of several different circumstances, was no longer sufficient; now, plaintiffs would have to show discriminatory *purpose* in order to sustain an effective challenge. In Congress, the Court's change of course produced a sharp political response and turned the direction of the civil rights lobby to renewal of Section 5 of the Voting Rights Act, scheduled to expire in August of 1982, and to amendment of Section 2 of the Act. The 1982 amendments, representing a significant victory for the civil rights lobby, were a direct response to the *Mobile* decision. Section 2a, as amended in 1982 reads as follows:

> a. No voting qualifications or prerequisite to voting or standard, practice, or procedure shall be imposed or applied by any State or political subdivision in a manner which results in a denial or abridgment of the right of any citizen of the United States to vote on account of race or color, or in contravention of the guarantees set forth in section 1973b(f)(2) of this title, as provided in subsection (b) of this section.
> b. A violation of subsection (a) of this section is established if, based on the totality of the circumstances, it is shown that the political processes leading to nomination or election in the State or political subdivision are not equally open to participation by members of a class of citizens protected by subsection (a) of this section in that its members have less opportunity than other members of the electorate to participate in the political process and to elect representatives of their choice. The extent to which members of a protected class have been elected to office in the State or political subdivision is one circumstance which may be considered: Provided, That nothing in this section establishes a right to have members of a protected class elected in numbers equal to their proportions in the population.[20]

The Senate Judiciary Committee majority report, which accompanied the bill to amend Section 2 of the Voting Rights Act, specified seven "typical factors" that might indicate a voting rights violation. A listing of those factors follows:

1. the extent of any history of official discrimination in the state or political subdivision that touched the right of the members of the minority group to register, to vote, or otherwise to participate in the democratic process;

2. the extent to which voting in the elections of the state or political subdivision is racially polarized;
3. the extent to which the state or political subdivision has used unusually large election districts, majority vote requirements, anti-single shot provisions, or other voting practices or procedures that may enhance the opportunity for discrimination against the minority group;
4. if there is a candidate slating process, whether the members of the minority group have been denied access to that process;
5. the extent to which members of the minority group in the state or political subdivision bear the effects of discrimination in such areas as education, employment and health, which hinder their ability to participate effectively in the political process;
6. whether political campaigns have been characterized by overt or subtle racial appeals;
7. the extent to which members of the minority group have been elected to public office in the jurisdiction.[21]

In *Thornburg v. Gingles*,[22] a case decided in 1986, the Court elucidated its interpretation of the 1982 amendments. The Court held that "while many or all of the factors listed in the Senate Report may be relevant to a claim of vote dilution through submergence in multimember districts, unless there is a conjunction of the following circumstances, the use of multimember districts generally will not impede the ability of minority voters to elect representatives of their choice."[23] The Court then enumerated three basic circumstances or tests that would support a claim of vote dilution through submergence in multimember districts.

> First, the minority group must be able to demonstrate that it is sufficiently large and geographically compact to constitute a majority in a single-member district. If it is not, as would be the case in a substantially integrated district, the multimember form of the district cannot be responsible for minority voters' inability to elect its candidates. . . .
> Second, the minority must be able to show that it is politically cohesive. If the minority group is not politically cohesive, it cannot be said that the selection of a multimember electoral structure thwarts distinctive minority group interests. . . .

> Third, the minority must be able to demonstrate that the white majority votes sufficiently as a bloc to enable it—in the absence of special circumstances, such as the minority candidate running unopposed—usually to defeat the minority's preferred candidate.[24]

The Court affirmed the finding of the lower court of discriminatory purpose in four out of the five districts that were appealed to the Supreme Court.

The findings in *Thornburg* were applied in a landmark California voting rights case, *Gomez v. City of Watsonville*.[25]

The City of Watsonville, although it had a Hispanic population of 36 percent in the 1980 Census, had never elected a Hispanic to the city council under the at-large system that had been established in 1952. Nine Hispanic candidates had run for council between 1971 and 1985, but none had won. In 1985, Dolores Cruz Gomez, a Latina community worker, challenged the City's at-large electoral system under Section 2 of the Voting Rights Act, as amended in 1982. The case was not decided until early 1987, in the wake of *Thornburg*.

Although the district court found that racially polarized voting did exist in Watsonville, it also found Watsonville's Hispanic population "insufficiently geographically compact to meet the requirements of a Section 2 claim."[26] Further, it found that the plaintiffs did not demonstrate "sufficient political cohesiveness"[27] among the Hispanics in Watsonville. The court based this judgment, not on the fact that many registered Hispanics in Watsonville had failed to vote alike, but on a refusal to assume that the large proportion of unregistered Hispanics would vote like those who were registered. The court believed that the non-registration of Hispanics demonstrated a lack of interest in the Hispanic candidates. The Ninth Circuit, U.S. Court of Appeals, however, reversed the district court's decision, holding that the actual pattern of voting of registered Hispanics was the relevant test and not whether those Hispanics who were eligible had registered to vote. Watsonville's move from at-large to a single-member district system is one of the case histories in this study.[28]

Recent Rulings: A Change of Course?

An important ruling, perhaps indicating a further change in the Court's handling of voting rights issues, came in *Shaw v. Reno* in 1993.[29] North Carolina's legislature had drawn a congressional district that ran, ribbon-like, along Interstate 85 for nearly 160 miles, with the obvious and officially admitted purpose of concentrating enough blacks to assure the election of a black representative.[30] The bizarre shape of the district produced a sharp reaction to race-based districting. Associate Justice Sandra Day O'Connor, writing for the majority, noted: "Racial gerrymandering, even for remedial purposes, may balkanize us into competing racial factions; it threatens to carry us further from the goal of a political system in which race no longer matters."[31] Apparently, the Court was developing important second thoughts about the use of racial classifications in the development of electoral arrangements.

The Court went a step further in June of 1995 with its ruling in *Miller v. Johnson*.[32] In this case, too, a serpentine congressional district—this time in Georgia—drew the Court's anger. Associate Justice Anthony Kennedy, writing for the majority, announced that the Court would use "strict scrutiny" in voting rights cases to decide whether districts were tailored narrowly to achieve a compelling state interest. Race, Justice Kennedy insisted, must not be "the predominant factor" motivating the legislature's decision to put a significant number of voters into a particular district. Kennedy was unimpressed by the argument that Georgia's 11th District had the benefit of uniting African Americans: he found that the district "tells a tale of disparity not community," linking African Americans in rural Savannah to those in metropolitan Atlanta, groups who were "worlds apart in culture." Taking the rulings in *Shaw* and *Miller* together, the Court now seems intent on applying strict scrutiny when "traditional districting principles, such as compactness, contiguity, and respect for political subdivisions" are disregarded in the design of districts.

In 1996, in *Bush v. Vera*,[33] the Court returned to these themes in a case involving majority-minority districts in Texas: the 30th District in Dallas, with a black majority; the 18th District in Houston, also with a black majority; and the 29th District in Houston, with an Hispanic majority. The Court ruled that Texas had focused too much on ethnicity, too little on "traditional districting principles." On the same day, in *Shaw v. Hunt*,[34] the Court struck down the black-majority 12th District of North Carolina on the same grounds. The rulings were widely held to put at risk majority-minority districts in New York, Illinois and Virginia that are subjects of pending court challenges.

SUMMARY

Three decades of interplay between Congress and the courts have produced far-reaching changes in voting rights law:

1965 The Voting Rights Act applied exclusively to Southern states and to African Americans.
1970 The Act was expanded, via new triggering formulae, to certain counties in Alaska, Arizona, California, Connecticut, Maine, Massachusetts, New Hampshire, New York and Wyoming.
1975 Hispanics and other language minorities were brought under coverage of the Act, which was thus expanded to cover states of the Southwest, West and parts of Florida.
1980 *City of Mobile v. Bolden*. By requiring a showing of "discriminatory intent" the Court removed from challenge a wide range of practices with discriminatory effects (including at-large elections in many jurisdictions).
1982 Congress, in amendments to the Act, returned to a "totality of circumstances" test.
1986 In *Thornburg v. Gingles* the Court enumerated three tests that must be met to support claims of vote dilution (i.e., size and compactness of minority groups; their political cohesion; and evidence of racial bloc voting. The application of the Thornburg tests sustains several challenges to at-large elections (e.g., *Gomez v. City of Watsonville*).
1993 In *Shaw v. Reno* the Court refuses to permit "racial gerrymandering" even for remedial purposes. Later cases also (e.g., *Miller v. Johnson, Bush v. Vera*) point to the use of "strict scrutiny" in voting rights cases and hostility to the use of race or ethnicity as dominant factors in the design of districts.

Although no-one can be sure of the future course of voting rights law, "majority-minority" districts and their use in place of at-large elections will be central issues.

NOTES

1. See *United States v. Reese*, 92 U.S. 214 (1876) and *United States v. Cruikshank*, 92 U.S. 542 (1876).

2. C. Vann Woodward has chronicled many of these techniques in his book, *The Strange Career of Jim Crow* (Second Revised Edition. Oxford: Oxford University Press, 1966). Also see the same author's *Origins of the New South* (Baton Rouge: Louisiana University Press, 1971); and J. Morgan

Kousser, *The Shaping of Southern Politics* (New Haven: Yale University Press, 1974).

3. An internal mechanism used by the Democratic Party as a means of exclusion, the White Primary was based on the Party's claim that it was a private rather than an official organization.

4. The 1957 Act would not have passed without Lyndon B. Johnson's support: he wished both to maintain the support of liberals in his own caucus and to make himself viable as a national candidate.

5. See the discussion in Bernard Grofman, Lisa Handley, and Richard G. Niemi, *Minority Representation and the Quest for Voting Equality* (Cambridge: Cambridge University Press, 1992), 12-15.

6. See *South Carolina v. Katzenbach*, 383 U.S. 301 (1966) 313.

7. See Howell Raines, *My Soul is Rested* (New York: Putnam, 1977), 337.

8. See Section 2 of the *Voting Rights Act*, 1965. It is under this section that the majority of legal claims are made against jurisdictions that do not fall under the triggering formula of Section 4b, and which are, therefore, not subject to the preclearance provisions of Section 5.

9. Ibid, Section 3.

10. Ibid, Section 4b.

11. It did not escape the attention of Southern conservatives--although the fact was ignored by the media--that the triggering formulae were carefully devised to exclude Texas.

12. The purpose of Section 5 is stated in the Federal Register: "(a) Section 5 of the Voting Rights Act of 1965, as amended, 42 U.S.C. 1973c, prohibits the enforcement in any jurisdiction covered by section 4(b) of the Act, 42 U.S.C. 1973b(b), of any voting qualification or prerequisite to voting, or standard, practice, or procedure with respect to voting different from that in force or effect on the date used to determine coverage until either: (1) A declaratory judgment is obtained from the U.S. District Court for the District of Columbia that such qualification, prerequisite, standard, practice or procedure does not have the purpose and will not have the effect of denying or abridging the right to vote on account of race, color, or membership in a language minority group, or (2) It has been submitted to the Attorney General and the Attorney General has interposed no objection within a 60-day period following submission."

13. *South Carolina v. Katzenbach*, 334.

14. The official term in the U.S. Census for persons with a Spanish language background or who are of Spanish descent is Hispanic. This is an ethnic, not a racial category. More specific terms such as Latino, Chicano and Mexican American have been used by some groups to define themselves and

the reader will note that some of the data tables use the term Latino rather than Hispanic. If the citizens of a particular jurisdiction felt strongly about terminology, the consultant would respect their concern. In Arizona, for example, the term Hispanic is preferred; while in California, where much of the Spanish speaking population comes from Mexico or from Latin America, Mexican American or Latino is often preferred. Those who wish to follow the contemporary controversy over identity and terminology of "Hispanics" should consult Peter Skerry, "Many American Dilemmas: The Statistical Politics of Counting by Race and Ethnicity," *The Brookings Review*, Vol. 14, No. 3, Summer, 1996.

15 See David Hunter, "The 1975 Voting Rights Act and Language Minorities," *Catholic University Law Review* 25 (1976): 250-270.

16. Even today, the practice—common to the U.S. Congress and to most other legislative bodies—of allowing population growth to increase the size of districts and thereby to complicate the task of minorities in winning office, has not come under attack.

17. *Zimmer v. McKeithen*, 485 F.2d 1297(5th Cir. 1973)(en banc). This ruling followed the Supreme Court decision in *White v. Regester*, 412 U.S. 755 (1973). In *White* the Supreme Court had held that a finding of unconstitutional dilution must rest on evidence to support findings: that the political processes leading to nomination and election were not equally open to participation by the group in question—that its members had less opportunity than did other residents in the district to participate in the political processes and to elect legislators of their choice.

18. These facts included a history of official discrimination, low levels of minority group success in elections, poor official responsiveness to minority group needs, poor socio-economic status of minorities, majority vote requirements, primary or special election obstacles and lack of access to candidate slating, anti single-shot requirements, large district size, and other factors. The ruling required that courts assess each case after considering all the relevant factors.

19. *City of Mobile v. Bolden*, 446 U.S. 55 (1980).

20. 42 U.S.C. 1973, as amended, 96 Stat. 134.

21. S.Rep., at 28-29, *U.S. Code Cong. & Admin. News* 1982, 206-207.

22. *Thornburg v. Gingles*, 478 U.S. 30 (1986).

23. Ibid., 2765.

24. Ibid., 2766.

25 *Gomez v. City of Watsonville*, 863 F.2d 1407 (9th Cir. 1988), *cert. denied* 489 U.S. 1080 (1989).

26. Ibid., 1410.

27 Ibid., 1410.

28. A number of other cities were watching the Watsonville case. The City of Salinas chose to escape expensive litigation by adopting a district system. The Redlands City Council and the Cerritos Community College District used ballot measures to switch to district systems. In 1990, the City of Ontario, with a Hispanic population of 41.70 percent, formed an advisory committee to study the possibility of moving to a district system but rejected the concept at that time. In 1996, the City formed a new committee to study reforms to city government, including the move to a district system. And the City of San Diego reached an agreement with a Hispanic group to perform a redistricting that would be more equitable to Hispanics. Watsonville was also an important influence in several of the case histories in this study, including Hanford and Corcoran.

29. *Shaw v. Reno*, 113 U.S. 2816 (1993).

30. There is a continuing controversy regarding the role of the Bush administration's appointees in the U.S. Department of Justice in encouraging, even requiring, development of such "ethnically representative" congressional districts. One view is that the Republicans fully understood that a by-product of such affirmative action gerrymandering would be the enhancement of Republican chances in neighboring districts.

31. Ibid., 2832.

32. *Miller v. Johnson*, 115 S.Ct. 2475 (1995).

33. *Bush v. Vera*, Docket No. 94-805, June 1996 (U.S. Reports citation not yet available).

34. *Shaw v. Hunt*, Docket No. 94-923, June 1996 (U.S. Reports citation not yet available).

CHAPTER 2

Minority Voting and Voting Rights: Practice and Problems

The brief history in the preceding chapter[1] canvassed major changes in voting rights law. The focus now turns to the practical political consequences of such changes, looking behind the statutes and judicial rulings to districting practices and their effects on minority politics. This chapter begins to examine problems of interpreting and implementing the law.

WHICH MINORITY? HOW MANY MINORITIES? MAJORITY-MINORITY DISTRICTS AND INFLUENCE DISTRICTS

Even before the reapportionment cases of 1962-4, the United States Supreme Court confronted racial gerrymandering in the form of a legislatively-drawn 28-sided figure that described the town boundaries of Tuskegee, Alabama. The polygon had been drawn to exclude all but a handful of African Americans from voting in the town's elections. The case, *Gomillion v. Lightfoot*,[2] in which the blatant gerrymander was struck down, represented the Court's first major involvement in the issue of minority vote dilution by manipulation of electoral boundaries. In 1973, the Court again confronted the issue, this time in the Texas case, *White v. Regester*,[3] where two urban counties had used multi-member districts to dilute the votes of African Americans (Dallas County) and Hispanics (Bexar County). In Dallas, where African Americans had long suffered from discrimination, they had been by-passed by a white slating group that essentially controlled the system of numbered places on the ballot, and they could point to campaign messages that invoked to anti-black prejudice. The Hispanics in Bexar County were also able to prove discrimination and the use of language barriers to limit their access to city government. The Court unanimously found that the use of a "totality of circumstances" test justified striking down the multi-member districts of both counties to protect both minorities.

In 1977, however, the Court faced a situation that pitted minorities against minorities. Hasidic Jews in New York challenged the power of the New York State Legislature to divide their community in order to draw remedial "ethnically representative districts" for African Americans. The NAACP had brought an action to apply the Voting Rights Act to urban counties of New York;[4] and the United States Department of Justice instructed the Legislative committee to develop districts in these counties that would improve black access to the political system. Apparently, the Justice Department also insisted that a 65 percent proportion of black voters was required to produce an ethnically representative black district. In a further curious decision, the Department accepted Puerto Rican voters as "non-whites" who could be counted toward the black percentage.[5] The State Legislature redrew the district lines in 1974 and increased the black percentage of two assembly districts, with the consequence that the Hasidic community (which had elected an Hasidic Jew to the assembly) was divided into two.[6]

Despite protests by the Hasidics—as well as by Irish, Italian and Polish groups—the Attorney General of the United States cleared the new districts, declaring that the Voting Rights Act was intended to protect against vote dilution on the basis of race, not ethnic origin or religious belief. The U.S. District Court affirmed that race could be considered when it was necessary to correct previous racial discrimination; and the Appeals Court followed with a finding that race could be used as a positive criterion in correcting past wrongs (and, moreover, that the preservation of "ethnic community unity" would be an impossible task in New York's polyglot and polyethnic community).

In the District Court process, the executive director of the Legislative committee that had drawn the district lines had stated that the Justice Department's insistence on a 65 percent proportion of black voters was "the sole reason" that two assembly districts had divided the Hasidic community. Thus, the United States Supreme Court, forced to adjudicate a contest between a racial minority and a religious or ethnic minority, also had to revisit its rulings in *Gomillion* and *White*, which had overturned districts drawn on the basis of race.

The Supreme Court ruled that the New York districts were constitutional as drawn, that the Voting Rights Act was "broadly remedial," and that "neither the Fourteenth nor the Fifteenth Amendment mandates any *per se* rule against using racial factors in districting and apportionment." The justices made clear that they anticipated that the use of racial criteria—even racial minimums of the type of the 65 percent requirement, or other such standards of racial "critical mass"—would be necessary to achieve the aims of the Act.[7] This ruling committed the Court to the concept of the "majority-minority district" and the theory that racial minorities make political progress by electing candidates of their own choice from districts in which their group is a voting majority.[8] Brushed aside in this decision is the quandary mentioned by John Marshall Harlan in *Allen v. Board of Elections*:

> It is not clear to me how a court would go about deciding whether an at-large system is to be preferred over a district system. Under one system, Negroes have *some* influence in the election of *all* officers; under the other, minority groups have *more* influence in the selection of *fewer* officers.[9]

In the *United Jewish Organizations* (UJO) case, the Court determined that it is better that one district be formed that is 65 percent black than that several be formed in which blacks could play the role of an influential minority.

The problems with this position have become clearer over time. One has to do with the districting techniques that concentrate racial minorities: given the power of computer Geographic Information Systems (GIS), it is possible to achieve a concentration of widely dispersed minority populations, but within district boundaries so contorted that the Tuskegee polygon seems almost a model of compactness. How heroic must the effort be to concentrate minorities? A later section analyzes this problem.

Another problem involves situations in which no degree of concentration can form a majority district, but where it is possible to establish a near-majority. If the political effectiveness of a racial majority might grow through such a degree of concentration, should a "minority influence district" be formed? And, if so, how large does a minority population have to be to claim the benefits of an "influence district?" If it is possible to draw a district with a 40 percent minority population, is it mandatory to do so? What about 35 percent, 30 percent, or 25 percent? If only minorities that can approach the 50 percent level are to be concentrated in influence districts, then larger minorities always will be advantaged over smaller minorities. Can such a result jibe with the protection of minority voting rights?

A further problem is the definition of "a majority-minority district." Does the word "majority" refer to *total minority population*? And if so, is that the total counted in the last decennial census or can it be an estimate of the total minority population at the time of the districting? Or does it refer to *total voting age minority population*? And if so, does that include all minority persons of 18 years of age and older, or only those who are eligible as citizens to vote? Or does it refer only to *total registered minority population*? And if so, to what extent should one look to actual turnout?

Obviously, there are many ways of defining the term "majority-minority," but if the aim is the actual election of a minority candidate, then more complex considerations also come into play. For example, what are the facts of minority political organization in the area, and who are the likely candidates? Candidates, whether minority or non-minority, always jockey for position in districtings and redistrictings, and the lines that will advantage or disadvantage them can be calculated by almost any political insider. Should districts be drawn, then, to include the residence and political base of leading minority candidates and to enhance their chances of victory? And if so, should districts be drawn so as to exclude the residence and political base of others whose candidacy could divide the minority vote and allow the election of a non-minority? Or must one seek to maintain a fiction of being blind to the geographical ambitions of minority candidates?

An additional complication has to do with the non-minority electorate. After all, in nearly every district, except only those that are overwhelmingly stacked with minority voters, the successful minority candidate will need some non-minority votes. Indeed, the lack of racial cohesion among white voters is often at least as important as the racial cohesion of the minority voters in enabling the election of minority candidates. Thus, if a particular minority candidate can appeal across racial or ethnic lines to pick up non-minority votes in a district, is it permissible to concentrate a lower level of minority voters in that district? Or do the definitions "majority-minority district" and "minority candidate" exclude districts in which a member of a minority group wins election with much less than a majority of minority votes and with substantial numbers of non-minority votes? Say, for example, that white Republican voters will cast ballots for a Republican Hispanic candidate, but not for a Democratic Hispanic candidate; in that case, a Republican-leaning district with a relatively small Hispanic population may produce the election of a minority candidate, and the unneeded Hispanic voters can be used to build another "minority influence district." Or does the involvement of white Republican voters somehow change the calculation?

Yet another complication emerges from other differences among minority populations. In many areas, African American population has been outpaced by the rapid growth of Hispanic and Asian populations; but the majority-minority districts created for and won by African Americans are now an important part of the political landscape, and their incumbents are often leading members of the political establishment. At what point, then, do the rights of the other minorities begin to outweigh those of the African American power elite? The issue becomes most intense when—as seems to be the case in several areas of California—Hispanic and African American voting behavior is increasingly polarized. Do Hispanics have the same rights against African American gerrymanders as they do against Anglo[10] gerrymanders?

A particularly sensitive issue has to do with the very term "minority group member." Who qualifies? And in what group? In the UJO case Puerto Ricans counted as blacks, a procedure that would be deeply controversial in today's New York. Should Cuban Americans be counted toward Hispanic totals, when their voting behavior often sharply differs from that of Mexican Americans? Should Filipinos be counted as Asian or as Hispanic? (California's large Filipino population divides about equally between those who describe themselves as Asian and those who prefer to be known as Hispanic). What if a significant number of Hispanics dispute the need for an ethnically representative district and claim that racial concentration is discriminatory? And what of the rapidly growing and increasingly self-conscious "mixed race" population that resists inclusion in any existing minority group categorization?

A final issue concerns the development of minority power. At what stage does the apparatus of majority-minority and influence districts become irrelevant to the protection of minority voting rights? Is it at the point when as many majority-minority districts as can be created have each elected a minority candidate? Or is it only when minority candidates win in proportion to the minority group share of the total population? Is it permissible for a minority incumbent of a majority-minority district to redistrict in order to decrease the percentage of minority population? What if such a reduction would assist the design of an influence district elsewhere? Or is that "retrogression?" Already, there are some jurisdictions where "minority" populations have grown to a point where they constitute the dominant numerical majority: do districts then become irrelevant or do they even handicap the full-scale assertion of minority voting power?

Several of the case studies in later chapters give examples of these difficulties as experienced in districtings and redistrictings in California and Arizona jurisdictions.

Annexations and Districts

The exercise by cities of their power to add neighboring unincorporated areas to their territory has obvious implications for minority voting power. By extending its boundaries to include white voters, but exclude minority voters, a city can adjust the racial or ethnic proportions of its electorate. In 1971, in *Perkins v. Matthews*, the United States Supreme Court decided that Section 5 extended to annexations.[11]

A year later, in *City of Richmond v. United States*, the Court confronted an annexation that had already taken place and on which the City had spent many millions of dollars.[12]

Although the District Court ordered Richmond to abandon its at-large electoral arrangements and to submit to districting, the Supreme Court allowed the annexation to stand and refused to sustain the District Court's order.

A similar case, *City of Petersburg, Virginia v. United States et al*[13] pointed in a different direction. Petersburg had annexed 14 square miles of land in Dinwiddie and Prince George's Counties, thus increasing the white population by nearly 10 percent in a jurisdiction that held at-large elections.[14] The District Court for the District of Columbia, although finding that the annexation was intended to expand the City's tax base, focused on evidence of the City's "long history of racial segregation and discrimination" and held that the annexation would only be approved if the at-large electoral scheme were discontinued and replaced by election of councilmembers by district. The Supreme Court affirmed the District Court's decision.

Yet another case presented annexation in a slightly different perspective. In 1972 the City of Richmond approached the Court seeking approval for the 1970 annexation (to which the Attorney General of the United States had twice denied pre-clearance). The City's nine-member council, elected at-large in 1970 from the newly enlarged, post-annexation (but unprecleared) city territory, included only one black councilman. The elections had been contested as illegal, since neither the annexation nor the election within the post-annexation city had been precleared. The District Court for the District of Columbia held that the city council had been illegally elected. In 1973, therefore, the City instituted a single-member district system in place of its city-wide elections. The District Court also found this change illegal and condemned it as "discriminatory in purpose and effect" and thus violative of Section 5's substantive standards as well as the Section's procedural command that prior approval be obtained from the Attorney General or the Court.[15] In 1975, however, the U.S. Supreme Court overruled the District Court. Noting that the districting plan would give blacks a near two-thirds majority in four of the nine districts and a two-fifths minority in a fifth "influence" district, the high court refused to give priority to the concern over dilution of the pre-annexation black vote. Instead, the Court made its priority the "fair representation" of blacks on the city council following annexation. The decision involved a distinction between the *Petersburg* and *Richmond* cases and noted the use in *Petersburg* of the district system as a remedy for the consequences of annexation. The majority opined as follows:

> *Petersburg* was correctly decided. On the facts here presented, the annexation of an area with a white majority, combined with at-large councilmanic elections and racial voting, created or enhanced the power of the white majority to exclude Negroes totally from participation in the governing of the city through membership on the city council. We agreed, however, that the consequence would be satisfactorily obviated if at-large elections were replaced by a ward system of choosing councilmen. . . . We cannot accept the position that such a single-member ward system would nevertheless have the effect of denying or abridging the right to vote because Negroes would constitute a lesser proportion of the population after the

annexation than before, and given racial bloc voting, would have fewer seats on the city council.[16]

In this way, the Court committed itself to the principle that the remedy for minority vote dilution by annexation is the imposition of district systems. Before long, the Justice Department was scrutinizing all annexations of Section 5 municipalities and, in many cases, using the threat of a refusal to preclear to force imposition of districts.

Problems and questions posed by this approach soon appeared. For example, are districts to be imposed even if it is impossible to create a majority-minority district? And, if so, for what purpose and according to what criteria? What if minority candidates won in the existing at-large scheme and oppose districts as a threat to their political survival? What if the jurisdiction is so small that the districts may be dysfunctionally minuscule? What if the annexations are long-standing and their residents have already voted in city elections? What if the imposition of districts divides the community along racial lines and so polarizes voting behavior that non-minority voters withhold their votes from minority candidates?

Again, the case histories in later chapters provide examples of these difficulties in California and Arizona jurisdictions.

Retrogression Tests and District Development

In 1976, in *Beer v. United States*, the Supreme Court first advanced the concept of "retrogressive effect on minority voting strength." The Court, confronting a New Orleans city redistricting plan that divided the black community among five districts, held that the "effects" language of Section 5 was intended merely to protect minority voters from changes that would dilute their voting power. Under the existing districting plan, none of the five city districts had a black majority; and the new plan, although fragmenting the areas of black concentration, nevertheless gave blacks majorities in two districts. The Court approved the plan finding that it would not adversely affect black voting strength.

The *Beer* ruling suggested that any redistricting plan, which is not otherwise violative of the Constitution, will not violate Section 5 of the Voting Rights Act unless it is retrogressive in its effects on minority voting strength.[17] The key part of the ruling reads: "In other words, the purpose of Section 5 has always been to insure that no voting procedure changes would be made that would lead to a retrogression in the position of racial minorities with respect to the effective exercise of the electoral franchise."[18]

In enunciating the test, the Court presumably hoped to establish a measure that would advance minority voting rights. What, however, if redistrictings become exercises in reinforcement of the status quo by jurisdictions that have long frustrated minority aspirations? Or, what if such jurisdictions make only the smallest, merely cosmetic changes? The retrogression test in those cases could actually reward rogue jurisdictions.[19]

Before long, such problems cropped up with the retrogression test. In *Wilkes County v. United States* in 1978,[20] a jurisdiction using a severely malapportioned plan as the base measure appealed to the retrogression standard in advancing a discriminatory redistricting. In *Mississippi v. United States* in 1979[21] another jurisdiction tried to use the retrogression test to support movement from a racially discriminatory multi-member plan to a racially discriminatory single-member district plan.

Some commentators saw the *Beer* retrogression test as an effort to advance voting rights without moving further in the direction of quotas or proportional representation.[22] The district court in *Beer* had used a numerical test to judge the New Orleans redistricting, calculating that, on the basis of their proportion of the registered electorate, blacks should be able to elect 2.4 city councilmembers. In practice, however, the test did not reduce the dependency on statistical measures of race: the effect of the retrogression test was further to encourage the Justice Department to use various quantitative indices in the pre-clearance process.

The 1982 amendments to the Voting Rights Act seemed to modify the *Beer* retrogression test. Section 2 of the Act now incorporated a "results" test:

> No voting qualification or prerequisite to voting or standard, practice or procedure shall be imposed or applied by any state or political subdivision in a manner which results in a denial or abridgment of the right of any citizen of the United States to vote on account of race or color. . . .[23]

A reading of the legislative history of the 1982 Amendments suggested to many experts[24] that the new dilution "results" standard of Section 2 had been incorporated in the Section 5 pre-clearance determination and in such a way as to expand the *Beer* rule. Retrogression might now be proved if a plan had the result of producing any decline in minority representation. As of 1986—and formalized in new regulations issued in that year and adopted in 1987—the U.S. Department of Justice refused pre-clearance to plans that resulted in Section 2 violations.

At the level of local redistrictings, the effort to design non-retrogressive redistricting plans in Section 5 jurisdictions can face many practical difficulties. Take, for example, the situation—not infrequent in suburban Arizona—of a community whose non-minority population has outpaced the growth of its minority population. How does "retrogression" apply if the minority community now lacks the numbers to constitute a majority-minority district? Or, take the case of a city that underpopulated its minority districts in the old redistricting.[25] Then, in the wake of the new census, when the area is shown to have lost population, suppose that its majority-minority character can be retained only by doubling the deviation to possibly unconstitutional levels or by questionably constitutional contortions of its boundaries. Or, to take the case—hearteningly common throughout suburban California and Arizona—of Hispanics who are rapidly assimilating and dispersing through the community. If the old barrio-like concentration at the heart of the majority-minority district is losing population to up-scale suburbs, how does the districter meet the non-retrogression test?

Compactness, Geography and Political Subdivisions

Does shape matter in districting? The two mandatory requirements that the United States Supreme Court imposed on the reapportionment process in the 1960s and 1970s—equality of population and minority representation—say nothing directly about shape. By giving priority to numerical standards (whether of total population or of minority population), however, those requirements gradually opened the door to very strangely-shaped districts. In the immediate wake of *Reynolds* and *Wesberry*, districters all over the country discovered the freedom to ignore county boundaries, to cut through cities, and to jiggle boundaries to maximum political advantage: so long as the resultant districts were equipopulous, they could pass judicial muster. Then, as the Court moved to impose single member districts as remedies for racially discriminatory multi-member districts and the at-large electoral arrangements of Southern jurisdictions, voting rights activists began to demand lines that would concentrate African American voters in minority "control" districts. Again, with no geographical limits the result produced progressively stranger shapes.

Bizarre districts proliferated. Compactness, contiguity, respect for political subdivisions—these traditional standards of redistricting were pushed to one side by the more easily quantified, supposedly more objective criteria of population equality and minority representation.

The case histories in this study span a transitional period: the first cases occurred when all the evidence pointed to an escalating federal concern with the development of majority-minority districts of whatever shape and with little regard for geography or existing jurisdictional lines; and the last cases occurred in the wake of *Shaw v. Reno*,[26] when the Court began what appears to be a return to "traditional redistricting standards," including "compactness." The *Shaw* plaintiffs had specifically attacked shape: they complained that "the plan, which contains district boundary lines of dramatically irregular shape, constitutes an unconstitutional racial gerrymander." Even more recently,[27] the Court, again expressing a concern with geographical issues, has struck down a series of oddly shaped districts.

One theme of our case studies, then, is to examine the ways in which the changing requirements of federal law—or, more precisely, districters' expectations of likely responses from the U.S. Department of Justice—have affected the design of district lines. Perhaps more important than the changing detail of shape, however, is the role of political geography in the districting process. Does "effective political representation" contain any geographical components? Is there a sense in which "functional compactness" is a standard for the development of districts? Should district lines be (to use Bernard Grofman's neologism) "cognizable,"[28] and to what extent is the use of existing jurisdictional lines an aid to "cognizability?" The experience of this writer in designing district lines in different jurisdictions may shed light on these issues.

Districts as Panacea

Running through all the case histories that form the central portion of this study is the effort by some groups to impose and others to resist districts. The issue of replacing at-large electoral arrangements with single-member districts is one that touches many aspects of politics in California and other western states.[29]

The use of at-large electoral schemes purportedly deprives minorities (racial, ethnic or linguistic) of an equal opportunity to elect candidates of their choice (whether minority candidates or minority-supported candidates). The alleged flaw of at-large systems is that they allow a majority group, acting as a bloc, to defeat minority group candidates—even when the minority has a sufficient share of the population to "deserve" its "own representation." By contrast, single-member districts, because they do not "submerge" minority votes, make it easier for minorities to elect their own candidates: that is, geographically compact minorities, acting as voting blocs, can elect candidates in their own districts. (The corollary, of course, is that the districts must not be gerrymandered to divide the minority group population.)

From an early point in its entry into the political thicket of redistricting, the United States Supreme Court embraced districts as the sovereign remedy for vote dilution. The commitment to districts may be traced to the challenges, originating in southern jurisdictions, to multi-member districts and at-large arrangements, many of which were of recent origin and which stemmed directly from deliberate efforts to prevent or limit black participation in the political process.[30] According to one commentator, "the creation of the doctrine of minority vote dilution was fashioned largely in the context of challenges either to multi-member legislative districts or local at-large elections" and the Court "has been as much concerned with perfecting geographic districting as guaranteeing fair treatment." As the doctrine evolved, "the Court came to see single-member districting as the remedy for racially discriminatory multi-member schemes."[31] Cases in the 1970s[32] not only endorsed single member districting as a solution, but required federal judges to rely on single-member arrangements when crafting redistricting remedies.

The advantages of single-member districts to African American voters in many Southern jurisdictions seem unquestionable: the election of Southern blacks to state legislatures, county boards and city councils has been directly and massively assisted by such arrangements. The issue, however, is not as clear in *Western* jurisdictions where Hispanic voters and candidates are concerned. First, at-large electoral arrangements in California and Arizona typically pre-date the development of large concentrations of Hispanic voters, and the use of such arrangements is rarely linked to deliberate efforts to restrict their access to the political process. Secondly, the Hispanic population in many Western jurisdictions is so dispersed through the community that Hispanic majority districts can be created only with difficulty. And, finally, Hispanic assimilation in many communities in California and Arizona has reached the point where Hispanic candidates can appeal across racial lines and secure election in at-large elections: to such candidates, many of whom have quite realistic aspirations for higher office, election districts are either a doubtful advantage or may actually put their electoral ambitions at hazard.

As a practical matter, the replacement of at-large systems with single-member districts often raises troubling questions in Western jurisdictions; and, as we shall see in several of our case histories, there is often only a doubtful gain for Hispanic representation from districts. Moreover, and it is, again, a feature of several of the case histories, district lines, especially when they concentrate a substantial voting majority of minorities, may serve to stimulate competition among minority candidates: thus, Anglos are often elected even in the most carefully tailored "control" districts.

To summarize these practical concerns, we may group them as follows:

Problems of Concentration. For example: What minorities are to be concentrated (e.g., all minorities or only those that vote together)? What percentages of concentration should be counted (e.g., total minority population, voting age population, registrants, voters)? If a majority-minority district cannot be formed, what degree of concentration should be attempted to form an "influence district?" How should "retrogression" in the degree of concentration be calculated in areas of shrinking minority population or in cases of rapidly growing Anglo population?

Problems of Candidacies. For example: Should districts be drawn with an eye to assisting minority candidacies? Should black incumbents be protected in areas of rapidly growing Hispanic population? Should districts be designed to minimize rivalry among minority candidates?

At-Large v. Single Member Districts. Should at-large schemes be replaced in situations where it is impossible to create single-member districts? What if minority candidates have been elected in at-large systems and the imposition of districts might defeat them?

It is time to move from such general problems and hypothetical concerns to the actual facts of local redistrictings. Often, such facts are "messy," failing to fit neatly into analytic categories. Yet, by carefully tracing the districting process—from plan design to election results—we may be able to see behind the theoretical concepts of law and political science to some of the changing realities of race and politics today.

NOTES

1. The reader who wishes to go beyond that account should consult: K. Abrams, "'Raising Politics Up': Minority Political Participation and Section 2 of the Voting Rights Act," *New York University Law Review* 63 (June 1988): 449-531; Gordon E. Baker, "Judicial Determination of Political Gerrymandering: A 'Totality of Circumstances' Approach," *Journal of Law and Politics* 3 (Winter 1986): 1-19; Howard Ball, Dale Krane and Thomas P. Lauth, *Compromised Compliance: Implementation of the 1965 Voting Rights Act* (Westport, CT: Greenwood Press, 1982); Bierstein, Andrea, "Millennium Approaches: The Future of the Voting rights Act After *Shaw* (*Shaw v. Reno*, 113 S. Ct. 2816 (1993), *De Grandy* (*Johnson V. De Grandy*, 114 S. Ct. 2647 (1994), and *Holder* (*Holder v. Hall*, 114 S. Ct. 2581 (1994))," *The Hastings Law Journal* 46 (July 1995): 1457-531; Kimball Brace, et. al., "Minority Voting Equality: The 65 Percent Rule in Theory and Practice," *Law and Policy* 10 (January 1988): 43-62; Chandler Davidson, ed., *Minority Vote Dilution* (Washington, D.C.: Howard University Press, 1984); D. R. Eichenthal, "Voting Rights, Political Gerrymandering, and Proportional Representation," *Annual Survey of American Law* 1987 (June 1988): 93-116; "The Future of Voting Rights After *Shaw v. Reno* (113 S. Ct. 2816 (1993)): Symposium," *Michigan Law Review* 92 (December 1993): 482-682; "Gerrymandering and the Courts: a Symposium," *UCLA Law Review* 33 (October 1985): i-ii, 1-281; Bernard M. Grofman and Chandler Davidson, eds., *Controversies in Minority Voting: A 25 Year Perspective on the Voting Rights Act of 1965* (Washington, D.C.: Brookings Institution, 1992); Bernard Grofman and Lisa Handley, "Identifying and Remedying Racial Gerrymandering," *The Journal of Law & Politics* 8 (Winter 1992): 345-404; Bernard Grofman, Lisa Handley and Richard G. Niemi, *Minority Representation and the Quest for Voting Equality* (Cambridge: Cambridge University Press, 1992); Bernard M. Grofman, Arend Lijphart, Robert McKay and Howard Scarrow, eds., Representation and Redistricting Issues (Lexington Books, 1982); Lani Guinier, "Group Representation and Race-Conscious Districting: A Case of the Emperor's Clothes," *Texas Law Review* 71 (June 1993): 1589-642 and "(E)racing Democracy: The Voting Rights Cases," *Harvard University Law Review* 108 (November 1994): 109-37;

Morgan J. Kousser, "Beyond *Gingles*: Influence Districts and the Pragmatic Tradition in Voting Rights Law," *University of San Francisco Law Review* 27, no. 3 (Spring 1993): 551; Richard H. Pildes, "The Politics of Race," *Harvard Law Review* 108 (April 1995): 1359-92; "The Supreme Court, Racial Politics, and the Right to Vote: *Shaw v. Reno* (113 S. Ct. 2816 (1993)) and the Future of the Voting Rights Act (Conference)," *The American University Law Review* 44 (October 1994): 1-126; Abigail M. Thernstrom, "The Odd Evolution of the Voting Rights Act," *Public Interest* (Spring 1979): 49-76 and *Whose Vote Counts? Affirmative Action and Minority Voting Rights* (Cambridge, MA: Harvard University Press, 1987); "Voting Rights After *Shaw v. Reno* (113 S. Ct. 2816 (1993)): Symposium," *Rutgers Law Journal* 26 (Spring 1995): 517-773; "Voting Rights and Elections," *University of Chicago Legal Forum* (1995): 1-599; "Voting Rights Law: Symposium," *University of San Francisco Law Review* 27 (Summer 1993); "Voting Rights Symposium," *Howard Law Journal* 28 (1985): 393-601; "Voting Rights Symposium," *Mississippi Law Journal* 65 (Winter 1995); "Voting Rights Symposium," *Stetson Law Review* 21 (Summer 1992). Largely absent from this literature, however, are close examinations of the interplay of law and politics—that is, the actual *practice* of districtings and redistrictings—in the jurisdictions affected by the Voting Rights Act. The present study attempts to fill this lacuna.

2. *Gomillion V. Lightfoot*, 364 U.S., 339 (1960).

3. *White v. Regester*, 412 U.S. 755 (1973).

4. Bronx, Kings (Brooklyn), and New York (Manhattan) Counties. These counties came under Sections 4 and 5 of the Voting Rights Act, since a literacy test had been used by them and fewer than 50 percent of voting age residents had voted in the 1968 presidential election. See the excellent account of the background to the Hasidic Jews case in Joseph F. Zimmerman, "Election Systems and Representative Democracy: Reflections on the Voting Rights Act of 1965," *National Civic Review*, Vol. 84, No. 4, Winter 1995.

5. One of the mysteries of the case was that no official would admit responsibility for the 65 percent requirement.

6. See Emanuel Perlmutter, "Hasidic Groups File Suit to Bar Districting as 'Gerrymander,'" *The New York Times*, June 12, 1974, 28. Also see Linda Greenhouse, "Hasidic Jews are Called 'Victims of a Racial Gerrymander' at Hearing on Suit," *The New York Times*, June 21 1974, 19.

7. *United Jewish Organizations of Williamsburg, Inc. v. Wilson*, 377 F.Supp.1164 (1974).

8. In one version, the theory is that political progress is made only when groups elect members of their own community because only members of their own community understand their needs. Another, less racially exclusive version

of the theory and the position that the Court takes in the UJO decision is that the group can elect members of their own choosing, whatever their race and ethnicity. It is notable, however, that very few non-minority representatives of majority minority districts seem to find favor with minority group activists. The classic example of this is L.A. City Councilman Art Snider who was repeatedly reelected to a predominately Hispanic district in spite of the protests of the Hispanic activists.

9. 393 U.S. 544 at 586 (1969).

10. Like the term Hispanic, use of the term Anglo may present problems for some readers. In this instance the writer has chosen to avoid the census term "white," since many in the Hispanic ethnic category also consider themselves white. The group in the census represented here by the term Anglo includes those identified as "non-Hispanic white."

11. *Perkins v. Matthews*, 400 U.S. (1971), 379-89. This ruling came in the wake of *Allen v. State Board of Elections*, a case in which the court had concluded that it was Congress's intent to give the Voting Rights Act "the broadest possible scope" to reach "any state enactment which altered the election law of a covered state in even a minor way." *Allen v. State Board of Elections*, 393 U.S. 544 (1969), 566-67. *Perkins* involved annexations by the City of Canton, Mississippi, of territory populated by 331 white voters and only 82 black voters. A special three-judge district court had dismissed a complaint against the annexation in 1969 on the ground that black voters still had a majority of not less than 600 after the annexations were effected. (*Perkins*, 565.) The U.S. Supreme Court overturned the district court and struck down the annexation, insisting that "annexations that enlarge the City's number of eligible voters" also constituted the change of a "standard, practice, or procedure with respect to voting." The Court noted that annexations, by including certain voters within city boundaries and omitting others, can determine who votes; and that annexations may "dilute the weight of the voters to whom the franchise was limited before annexation." The Court concluded that Section 5 of the Voting Rights Act "was designed to cover changes having a potential for racial discrimination in voting, and such potential inheres in a change in composition of the electorate affected by an annexation." (*Perkins*, 388-89.)

12. *Holt v. City of Richmond*, 459 F.2d 1093 at 1099 (4th Cir., 1972, *cert. denied*, 408 U.S. 931 (1972). A group of black residents in the City protested its 1970 annexation of an area whose residents were 97 percent white. About half of Richmond's pre-annexation population of 202,000 was black; the annexation lowered that percentage to 42 percent by adding 45,705 whites but only 1,557 blacks. The plaintiffs alleged that the annexation was designed to dilute their

weight in the City's at-large elections, thereby violating their rights under the Fourteenth and Fifteenth Amendments and Section 5 of the Voting Rights Act. The U.S. District Court for the Eastern District of Virginia found in favor of the black plaintiffs, ruling that vote dilution was covered by the Fourteenth Amendment's prohibition on deprivation of voting rights by reason of race. Because Richmond had already spent huge sums to improve the annexed area, the court admitted that de-annexation was not an appropriate remedy, but declared instead that the City must abandon at-large electoral arrangements and be districted for future councilmanic elections. In ordering the districting, the District Court distinguished between the original pre-annexation area of the city and the annexed territory: seven members would be elected from the former and two from the latter, with a small overlap area shared between the two. The U.S. Court of Appeals reversed the District Court and held that Richmond had undertaken its annexations "for perfectly valid reasons;" and the U.S. Supreme Court denied certiorari.

13. *City of Petersburg, Virginia v. United States*, 354 F.supp. 1021 (1972).

14. The City of Petersburg's five-member council, which adopted the annexation ordinance in 1971, included two black members.

15. *City of Richmond v. United States*, 376 F.Supp. 1344 at 1351 (1974).

16. *City of Richmond v. United States,* 422 U.S. 358 at 370-71 (1975).

17. *Beer V. United States* 425 U.S. 130 (1976).

18. For commentary on *Beer* see: Richard L. Engstrom, "Racial Discrimination in the Electoral Process: The Voting Rights Act and the Vote Dilution Issue," *Party Politics in the South*, ed. Robert P. Steed, Lawrence W. Moreland, and Todd A. Baker (New York: Praeger, 1980), 207-209; also, Chandler Davidson, "Minority Vote Dilution," 16-17, Frank R. Parker "Racial Gerrymandering and Legislative Reapportionment," 104-105, in *Minority Vote Dilution*, ed. Chandler Davidson (Washington D.C.: Howard University Press, 1989).

19. This is the view, for example, of Gail Binion, who is quoted by Engstrom, supra, 209, as insisting that the test has "the serious consequence of rewarding those jurisdictions with a history of the worst dilution of black electoral strength."

20. 450 F.Supp. 1171 1178 (D.D.C. 1978).

21. 490 F. Supp. 569 (D.D.C. 1979).

22. This is the view of Frank R. Parker: "The Supreme Court's *Beer* decision dealt minority voting rights a severe setback. Under the *Beer* retrogression standard, if the prior plan is 90 percent discriminatory, and the new plan is only 80 percent discriminatory, the new plan must be precleared (in the absence of discriminatory purpose) because it constitutes a 10 percent

enhancement of black voting strength and is not discriminatory. The apparent basis of this retrogression holding may have been the Court's fear that Section 5 could be interpreted to require racial quotas or proportional representation." Parker, 105.

23. The un-amended statute had read: "No voting qualification or prerequisite to voting or standard, practice or procedure shall be imposed or applied by any state or political subdivision to deny or abridge the right of any citizen of the United States to vote on account of race or color. . . . " See Section 2(a)Public Law 97-205, 96 Stat. 131 (1982).

24. See, for example, Armand Derfner, "Voting Dilution and the Voting Rights Act Amendments of 1982," in Chandler, 146.

25. Advocated by many as a means of making minority votes go further, majority-minority districts with negative deviations were created in many communities.

26. *Shaw v. Reno*.

27. *Bush v. Vera* and *Shaw v. Hunt*.

28. Not only recognizable in a simple sense but composed in line with clearly stated criteria.

29. As of 1990, California's 453 cities included only 21 that used true single-member district systems. Of the 1,028 school boards in California, only 41 elected board members by district. This great preponderance of at-large systems (over 95 percent) has been under challenge. Most of the at-large districting systems in California cities require all candidates to compete against one another for votes in city-wide elections: then, the five highest vote-getters (or seven or nine, depending on the size of the council) are elected. Some cities, however, employ variants of the true at-large system. In several cities, two separate elections are used to elect to "numbered post" seats. In other cities, residency in individual districts is required of candidates, but the voting is city-wide. In yet others, a primary election is held in individual districts, but the general election is city-wide. And there are even cities where some councilmembers are elected at large, others in individual districts. In the course of the past two decades, challenges to the use of at-large elections in California cities have mounted. One source of discontent is the belief that at-large arrangements discriminate against minorities (especially racial and ethnic minorities). Another source is the belief that at-large systems gave advantage to established interests (for example, "the downtown group") at the expense of new, more diverse and rapidly growing populations.

30. See Timothy G. O'Rourke, Constitutional and Statutory Challenges to Local At Large Elections," 17 *Richmond Law Review*, (1982) 39.

31. Timothy O'Rourke, "The Shape of Things to Come," *Rutgers Law Journal*, Vol. 26, No. 3, Spring 1995, 723-770 at 735.

32. See, in particular, *Connor v. Johnson*, 402 U.S. 690, (1971) and *Connor v. Finch*, 431 U.S. 407, (1977).

CHAPTER 3

The Beginning of the Push from At-Large to Single-Member Districts: Watsonville and Pomona

In California, the movement by activists to replace at-large with single-member district elections begins with two voting rights suits, *Gomez v. City of Watsonville*[1] and *Romero v. City of Pomona.*[2] Watsonville, a tiny market town on California's central coast, lies some 400 miles away from Pomona, a long established suburb of Los Angeles County's San Gabriel Valley. The two cities had very different records of involving Latinos in their civic life; the cases produced sharply different results; and, the experience of the two cities in implementing district systems has also diverged.

WATSONVILLE

In 1960, the City of Watsonville had a total population of 11,572, including only 1,001 Latinos. By 1980, Watsonville's total population had climbed to 23,543 residents, of whom 11,509 were Latino. Latinos, however, made up only 40 percent of the voting age population; and because of the large proportion of non-citizens among the Latino population, they constituted only 37.0 percent of Watsonville's citizens. Watsonville had a city council of six members and a mayor elected at-large: three councilmembers were elected in each odd-numbered year, and the candidates with the highest number of votes were elected.

Between 1971 and 1985, the years that saw most of the extremely rapid growth in the Latino population, eight Latino candidates ran unsuccessfully for city council positions and, in 1975, one Latino lost a race for mayor. In the early- and mid-1980s, Latino activists in Watsonville, tiring of this record, began efforts to change the city's electoral system.

In 1985, a labor dispute brought several thousand Latino workers out on strike against two local food processing plants, the Watsonville Cannery and Shaw Frozen Foods. The dispute, which centered on cuts in wages and health and benefit programs, brought in a union organizer, an El Salvador native named Oscar Rios, from San Francisco's Mission District. Rios stayed in Watsonville to continue organizing the city's Latino workers. The City Council sided with the cannery owners and spent funds policing the strike and protecting strike breakers brought in from outside. The strike ended in 1987 with the Watsonville Cannery going out of business and Shaw Frozen Foods settling with the unions: some hundreds of jobs were lost, a result that Rios and other Latino activists blamed on the City's intervention.

Gomez v. City of Watsonville

Cruz Gomez, a Latina leader of the movement in support of the strike, and a co-founder of a low-income health clinic, was prominent in the effort to change the city's electoral system. Having campaigned unsuccessfully for a seat on the Council in 1983, she joined with Patricia Leal and Waldo Rodriquez in a suit filed in May of 1985 against the city's at-large mayoral and city council elections. In November of 1986, the plaintiffs filed a motion to enjoin the mayoral and city council elections of May 1987; and after the latter motion was dismissed, a trial was held in the United States District Court for the Northern District of California in 1987.

In *Gomez vs. the City of Watsonville*, the district court, although finding that there had been racially polarized voting in the city, refused to conclude that the Latino community was sufficiently cohesive politically or sufficiently compact geographically to meet Section 2 tests. Although finding that Latinos had the potential to win two single-member districts in the City, the court noted that a majority of the City's Latinos would still live in Anglo-controlled districts, in which their group vote would be ineffective. Similarly, although the court recognized that 95 percent of Latino voters had voted for the same candidates, it gave greater prominence to the facts of low voter registration and turnout among Latinos. Reasoning from the apparent political apathy of Latino non-voters and of Latino non-registrants, the court concluded that there had been only low levels of enthusiasm for past Latino candidates and that this was another demonstration of the Latino community's lack of political cohesion.

In 1989, the U.S. Court of Appeals for the Ninth Circuit, in an opinion written by Judge Dorothy Nelson, overturned the district court's findings. The appeals court held that the district court had focused improperly on low Latino voter registration and turnout as evidence for a lack of political cohesion; that the lower court had also improperly considered the fact that three-fifths of eligible Latino voters would live outside the two heavily Latino districts in its holding that there was a lack of geographical compactness. Judge Nelson also wrote that the district court had wrongly relied on socioeconomic disparities and differences of political opinion within the Latino community to suggest a likely failure to vote together as a community; and, that the lower court could have considered discrimination by parties other than the city. In one of the most widely quoted statements from the opinion, Judge Nelson indicated that it would be appropriate to take judicial notice of pervasive discrimination against Latinos in California. Latinos in California had been the victims of "ubiquitous" discrimination, Judge Nelson opined, and need not prove current discriminatory practices. "Low voter turnout levels are indicative of lingering effects of past discrimination," she wrote. "Discrimination against Latinos in California and the southwest has pervaded nearly all aspects of public and private life," she said.[3] In March of 1989, the U.S. Supreme Court upheld the appeals court ruling.

The Aftermath of *Gomez v. City of Watsonville*

Joaquin G. Avila, a Fremont-based attorney, formerly president of the Mexican- American Legal Defense and Education Fund, and the lead counsel in the Watsonville case, emphasized the political importance of the ruling not only in Watsonville, but for California's Latino community in general. "[I]t will be important to integrate the Latino community at all levels. The Watsonville decision will assist in the political integration of the community." Many Latino leaders predicted that Watsonville would begin a movement to enfranchise Latino voters in cities throughout California and that a new generation of Latino candidates would be elected. The model for such predictions was Texas. Thus, Assemblyman Peter Chacon argued that district elections would increase Latino voter turnout at the local level just as they had done in the Lonestar State: "From 1976 to 1984, at-large elections in Texas were replaced by district elections in most cities. Latino voter turnout increased by 75% during that period while voter turnout for the population as a whole increased by only 32%."[4] Chacon predicted that the Watsonville case would persuade the California legislature to take a more sympathetic view of his proposal to require district elections for most large cities and school districts.[5]

The most immediate consequence of the *Gomez* ruling, however, was that Watsonville's neighboring city, Salinas, voted to scrap its at-large elections to avoid a lawsuit it could not afford.[6] Joaquin Avila met with Latino leaders in Salinas and, in August of 1988 filed suit against the City's at-large system. After negotiations between Avila and City officials, however, the City put the issue to a vote on December 6, 1988, asking voters to decide on three measures—to change to district elections, to increase the size of the city council, and to alter the method of filling vacancies. All three measures passed, mostly because of a higher than usual Latino turnout. Three out of four Anglo voters voted against the measure to create districts, but the Latino voters of Salinas were drawn into the issue in large part by the activities of Simon Salinas, an elementary school teacher and a plaintiff in the lawsuit that had convinced the City to abandon its at-large scheme. Voter registration efforts by Simon Salinas added nearly one thousand new voters in predominantly Latino precincts. This fact, combined with the competition among the Latino candidates in the election, meant that the traditional 15 percent turnout in the heavily Latino precincts of east Salinas more than doubled. For the first time in the City's history, the Latino precincts had a slightly higher turnout than the Anglo precincts and Simon Salinas became the City's first Latino council member. Indeed, throughout the Salinas Valley and the California Central Valley, cities with significant Latino populations now began to consider their legal position.[7]

Establishing the New Districts

Oscar Rios and Cruz Gomez regarded Watsonville's existing City Council as dominated by conservative real estate interests. They were particularly outraged that, while the appeal to *Gomez* was being heard, the Council had pushed through a redevelopment plan that could depopulate several downtown blocks with high Latino concentrations. Ironically, the first Latino member of Watsonville's city council, Tony

Campos, an affluent realtor, was elected at-large in 1987; but Gomez, Rios and other Latino activists regarded him as unrepresentative of the Latino community, terming him a "Tio Taco." Gomez accused Campos and the Council of conspiring with development interests to practice "a kind of segregation," and Gomez claimed that "a new middle-class upper-class is moving back into downtown." "It's a real critical period now," she said, "of whether we Latinos can even afford to live here. They are destroying our neighborhoods right across from city hall as a way to push us out."[8] In late April of 1989, the Watsonville City Council refused to postpone adoption of the new general plan prior to the implementation of districts.

Despite the divisiveness of the situation, the city's conservative mayor, Betty Murphy, met with Dolores Cruz Gomez to discuss an approach to laying out the districts. Following the Supreme Court ruling, the Watsonville City Council canceled the May 9 election and proceeded to develop districting plans. The City and the plaintiffs agreed to hire Rand demographer Peter Morrison, who had developed demographic data on behalf of the City and testified on behalf of at-large election systems in the 1987 federal court trial. The two sides reasoned that since he had already developed the data, he could move more quickly than a new consultant.

The demographer was instructed to draw a six-district plan (the mayor to be elected at-large) and a seven-district plan (the mayor to be elected by the council). The plaintiffs and their counsel, Joaquin Avila, made it clear, however, that they would contest an electoral arrangement that included an at-large mayor. When questioned as to why Salinas could retain a six district system with an at-large mayor, Mr. Avila replied that "the two cities can't be compared [since] Salinas negotiated a settlement out of court and was never proved by a court of law to have a Voting Rights violation."[9] At a meeting on May 23, the Council decided by a vote of 5-2 to accept a seven-district arrangement.

Three council members were appointed to meet with the Latino plaintiffs and their attorney to resolve differences between two seven-district plans—one submitted by Peter Morrison and the other submitted by MALDEF (originally developed during the 1987 federal court trial). The Morrison-drawn map had three Latino districts (78 percent, 76.3 percent, and 56 percent); three further districts with Latino populations in the 30 percent range (38.1 percent, 34.7 percent and 31.7 percent); and a final district that was 25.5 percent Latino. The MALDEF map had two Latino districts (78.9 percent and 80.4 percent);

two districts with Latino populations of 44 percent; two districts with Latino populations in the 30 percent range (37 percent and 31 percent); and a final district that was 26 percent Latino. Joaquin Avila had said in March, when it was decided to adopt a 7-district plan, that "At a minimum, he would want three districts established with a majority of the population being Latino."[10]

These plans were discussed by the committee at a meeting held on Tuesday, May 30; and, with only one small change, the MALDEF map was agreed upon as the plan to be presented to the Council for approval. It was also decided that all seven seats were to be elected at once, the successful candidates being required to draw lots for two- and four-year terms.[11]

Two weeks later, on June 13, the plan was adopted "without comment" and "unanimously."[12] The approved map appears as figure 1. The only remaining hurdle was a 30-day residency requirement for filing that the plaintiffs wished to see waived for the November election. The City Council, however, decided to keep the residency requirement, which was part of the City's Charter and which legally could only be amended by court order or a vote of the people. On Friday, August 4, 1989, U.S. District Judge, William Ingram, signed an agreement between the Watsonville City Council and the plaintiffs paving the way for a November 7 election.

Just a month before the election, the Loma Prieta earthquake, centered just outside Watsonville, produced enormous damage, particularly in the downtown and heavily Latino precincts. More than fifty-six downtown buildings were destroyed or damaged and an estimated 1,400 jobs were lost; citywide, there was more than $20 million in damage from the earthquake. The elections were, therefore, postponed to December. In Watsonville's first district elections, Tony Campos lost his bid for reelection and was replaced by an Anglo candidate. Oscar Rios was the only Latino candidate elected. By 1991, however, Latinos had won three seats on the City Council and Rios had become Watsonville's first Latino mayor. The City Council was now a different body from its predecessors. For example, the Council voted to support the workers' right to strike at the Sunshine Mushroom Plant and protested the move by Watsonville's Green Giant plant to Irapuato in Mexico, leaving 200 Latino immigrant workers unemployed.

Figure 1. Watsonville, California, Districts, 1989.

Watsonville, California Districts, 1989

(Provided by the City Clerk)

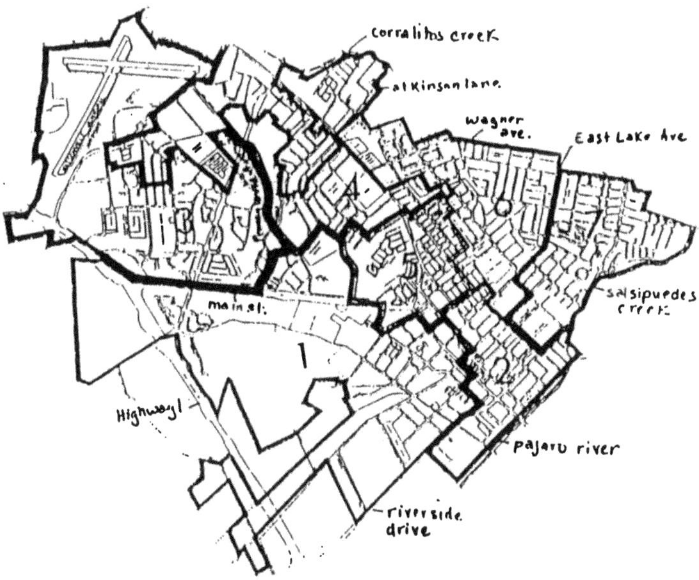

Redistricting Watsonville

After the 1990 census, Watsonville had to redistrict. This process highlighted, even sharpened, the continuing divisions between conservative and liberal, Anglo and Latino political forces. Anxious to avoid further litigation, the City hired Joaquin Avila, its nemesis in the *Gomez* case, as a consultant for drawing the new map and for preparing an analysis of registered voters. The City Council approved the formation of a 14-member citizen advisory committee to work with the consultant.

Between 1980 and 1990, Watsonville's total population had grown from 23,543 to 31,099; its Latino population had increased from 49 percent to 61 percent of the total. Avila's map identified significant growth in District 1, part of which was moved into District 2, while Districts 3 and 4 were adjusted to incorporate other parts of the old District 1.[13] The result was to increase the Latino population of District 1 from 75 percent to 86 percent. In Districts 2, 4 and 5, where Latinos were also in the majority, only slight changes were made.

Under the recommended plan, District 1 had a population of 4,446, of which 3,802, or 86 percent were Latino. District 2 had a population of 4,523, of which 3,931, or 87 percent were Latino. District 3 had a population of 4,452, of which 1,831, or 41 percent were Latino. District 4 had a population of 4,490, of which 2,909, or 65 percent were Latino. District 5 had a population of 4,409, of which 2,773 or 63 percent were Latino. District 6 had a population of 4,280, of which 2,113 or 49 percent were Latino. And District 7 had a population of 4,499, of which 1,568 or 35 percent were Latino.

In District 1, frozen food executive, Paul Milladin, had narrowly defeated Cruz Gomez in the 1989 election: the increase in the Latino population, assured by cutting from the district its newer subdivisions west of Main Street toward the shopping centers of Green Valley Road, was an obvious step to assist Gomez against Milladin. Another, even more dramatic step was the exclusion of Milladin from District 1 as first drawn. Milladin, the incumbent in District 1, was placed by Avila's map in District 2, where he would have to face the popular Oscar Rios.[14] A similar blow was struck at the conservative mayor, Betty Murphy, by including her with another Anglo incumbent, Betty Bobeda, in the same eastside district. Understandably, perhaps, accusations of ethnic gerrymandering were quickly made.[15] Initially,

Avila and the liberal majority on the Council declined to make any changes; and on Tuesday, May 16, the City Council voted 5 to 2 to accept the revised map. Ultimately, however, the Council voted on Tuesday, June 11, 1991, to implement a plan that would protect the incumbents. Avila moved lines to accommodate Milladin and Murphy. Only Oscar Rios and the most fervent of the Latino activists complained about the readjustments.[16] The redrawn map is shown as figure 2.

In November of 1991, four of the newly redrawn districts were up for election. Only four candidates filed—one for each district. Incumbents Vice Mayor Oscar Rios and Councilwoman Betty Bobeda faced no opposition in Districts 2 and 7; and Tony Campos (who had previously won at-large in 1987 only to lose under the new district system in 1989) and Al Alcala ran unopposed in Districts 1 and 6 respectively. They replaced retiring councilpersons Paul Milladin and Betty Murphy. After the 1991 election, Watsonville moved its election cycle to even-numbered years to coincide with the November General election. In November of 1994, Todd McFarren, Dennis Osmer and Betty Bobeda ran unopposed in Districts 4, 5 and 7, respectively, while Lowell Hurst defeated Jody Belgard Akimoto in District 3. In 1996, filed candidates include Al Alcala (District 1) and Tony Campos (District 6) running unopposed; and, Oscar Rios challenged by Larry Scroggins for District 2.

POMONA

In 1980, according to the Census, the City of Pomona's total population stood at 92,742 of whom 28,287 (30.5 percent) were Latino, 17,250 (18.6 percent) were black, and 43,318 (46.7 percent) were white. By 1984, when population was again calculated for Pomona, the City's total population had increased to 97,998, with little change in either Latino or black percentages: as of 1984, 49.5 percent of Pomona's population was calculated to be black or Latino.

In the century following its incorporation in 1888, only four Latinos had been elected to the Pomona City Council: the first in 1967; a second in 1973 and again in 1977; a third in 1987; and a fourth in 1989. No black had served on the City Council, although eleven individuals had run for office in fourteen campaigns.

Figure 2. Watsonville, California, Districts, 1991.

Watsonville, California Districts, 1991

(Rendered from a newspaper photo.)

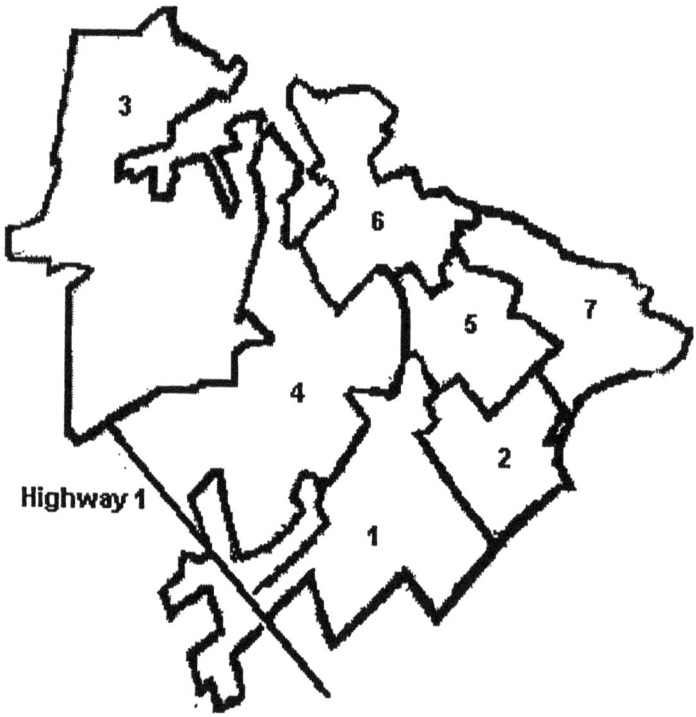

Pomona's 1911 Charter divided the City into four districts, and candidates for city council could compete only against other candidates residing in the same district; but, to be elected, they had to receive a majority of the votes in a city-wide election. Pomona's electoral system was a modified at-large system, with a "from district" requirement. If no candidate in a district election achieved a majority, the top two candidates competed in a run-off. Under the 1911 Charter arrangement, the mayor was elected in a city-wide election, could live in any district, and served for two years. Each of the four city council members served four-year staggered terms and, thus, the mayor and two city council members were elected every other year.

Romero v. The City of Pomona

Pomona's large minority population made it an attractive target for a challenge to its modified at-large electoral arrangements. In 1987, Dr. Gloria J. Romero, Willie E. White, Joseph Lee Duncan, Tomas Ursua, and Harold Webb, brought suit claiming that the City's electoral arrangements had disenfranchised them and other Latino and African American residents. The case, *Romero v. The City of Pomona*, centered on their argument that the ability of black and Latino voters to elect candidates of their choosing had been diluted.

Just after the plaintiffs had made their argument in district court, the U.S. Supreme Court handed down its *Thornburg v. Gingles* decision. The district court, granting the City's motion for dismissal, applied the *Thornburg* tests to find that "plaintiffs failed to establish any of the three threshold requirements for proving a violation of Section 2 of the Voting Rights Act: (1) geographical compactness; (2) minority group cohesion; and (3) bloc voting by the majority."[17] The district court further held that, "Plaintiffs failed to prove that the black and Hispanic voters of Pomona comprised a politically cohesive group."[18] Indeed, exit polls conducted in the City during the March 1985 City Council primary had revealed that "a majority of black voters supported the white opponents of the Hispanic candidate for City Council District 3, while a majority of Hispanic voters supported the white opponents . . . of the black candidate for City Council District 2."[19] The Court further determined that none of the seven factors that accompanied the 1982 Section 2 amendment in the U.S. Senate had been used "to discriminate against Hispanic or black voters."[20] In fact, the Court found that the "overall success rate of Hispanic candidates [in

Pomona council races] for the period 1965-1985 was 33% compared to a success rate of only 27.7% for white candidates."[21]

The plaintiffs appealed on the grounds that *Thornburg* had changed the rules for proving a vote dilution claim under Section 2. Their appeal contained four specific arguments: (1) they should be allowed to introduce further evidence in light of the *Thornburg* ruling; (2) the district court "misapplied" the geographical compactness test; (3) the district court should not have engaged in "verbatim" and "wholesale" adoption of defendants' proposed findings of fact; and (4) the district court erred in refusing to grant them class certification.[22]

The appeals court, however, agreed with the district court's determination that "*Thornburg* did not announce such a fundamental, unanticipated or sweeping change in the law as to warrant reopening plaintiff's case."[23] According to the opinion of the appeals court, Thornburg "merely explained which of the Senate factors were most relevant in proving a Section 2 violation."[24] As to the plaintiffs' dispute that the district court misapplied *Thornburg's* geographical compactness test, the court held that *Thornburg* "repeatedly makes reference to effective voting majorities, rather than raw population totals as the touchstone for determining geographical compactness."[25] In reference to the third argument, the appeals court, having agreed with the district court's findings of a lack of geographic compactness and cohesion, found it unnecessary to address the purported lack of detailed findings concerning the Senate factors. Finally, the appeals court stated that the district court had "denied class certification because it found that black and Hispanic voters in Pomona lacked commonality of interests, a showing required under Federal Rule of Civil Procedure 23 (a)(2)," and that because they affirmed "the district court's dismissal of plaintiffs' case on the merits, the class certification issue is moot."[26]

A Council-Inspired Districting

The City spent a million dollars on its successful defense in the *Romero* case. Yet the political forces that had inspired the litigation now turned for recourse to City Council politics. One pressure point was a maverick Anglo councilmember, Clay Bryant. Ironically, in an unsuccessful effort to avoid recall, Bryant became an advocate of districts. Joining him in constituting a majority on the Council in favor of districts were two Latino Councilmembers, Nell Soto and Tomas

Ursua (both elected after the initial filing of the lawsuit). Thus, in February of 1990, the Council voted 3 to 1[27] to place the issue on the June 5th ballot, along with the recall to oust Councilman Clay Bryant.[28]

The City now retained a consultant—this writer—to furnish professional services associated with preparing council districts. The Council had decided, after advice from the office of the Attorney General of California, that rough plans or concepts would have to appear on the ballot to enable the voters to understand the likely general location of the districts, in the event that a district scheme would be adopted. The consultant was instructed to devise two concepts, A and B, for the creation of six single-member districts, and two concepts, A and B, for the creation of seven single-member districts.

The process of developing the four conceptual districts was dominated by two incumbent members of the Council. Other members, the Mayor, and senior city staff played only minor roles. Although the consultant met with each council member at least once, Nell Soto and Tomas Ursua made the greatest claim on the consultant's time and attention. The interests of these two Latino councilmembers diverged sharply on the question of how to distribute Latino voters between their districts, especially in the downtown area. Moreover, Soto, who had a long-standing political alliance with Willie White, was anxious to assist the election of an African American in the area to the north and west of her own home base, that is just south of Interstate 10 and west of Garey Avenue. Ursua, by contrast, was more interested in the creation of a third Latino district, which required creating a district to the east of his base or, more specifically, east of Garey Avenue and south of the Union Pacific Railroad tracks.

The two Anglo councilmembers and the Mayor appeared barely interested in the process. Mayor Donna Smith had her eye on a possible run for the state legislature or Congress. Councilman Nymeyer was more interested in his campaign for State Assembly against Jim Brulte than in the redistricting. Councilman Bryant was busy trying to fend off a potential recall.

Thus, four alternative concepts were reviewed by the City Council in a public hearing in March prior to the placement of three measures—M, N and O—on the June ballot. Concepts A and B for illustration of Measure O (see figures 3 and 4 and tables 1 and 2) both provided for six single-member districts.[29]

The districts for Concept A can be summarized as follows:

1. *A North East District*, with a total population of 21,291, a 26.0 percent Latino population (10.3 percent voting age), and a 29.9 percent African American population. Geographically, this district encompasses the area north of the Santa Fe railroad tracks, the area east of Orange Grove Avenue above the 10 Freeway and east of San Antonio Avenue below the 10 Freeway. The southern boundary is Lincoln Avenue.
2. *A South East District*, with a total population of 22,824, a 45.5 percent Latino population (17.8 percent voting age), and a 10.5 percent African American population. Geographically, this district is bounded on the north by Lincoln Avenue, on the west by San Antonio Avenue to Phillips Boulevard and then Towne Avenue to the 60 Freeway and the 71 Expressway.
3. *A South Central District*, with a total population of 22,760, a 65.4 percent Latino population (24.7 percent voting age), and a 15.8 percent African American population. Geographically, this district encompasses the area east of the 71 Expressway, south of downtown and west of San Antonio Avenue to Phillips Boulevard and then west of Towne Avenue to the 60 Freeway.
4. *A Phillips Ranch/Westmont District*, with a total population of 21,094, a 17.2 percent Latino population (6.6 percent voting age), and a 7.6 percent African American population. Geographically, this district encompasses the Phillips Ranch, Chino Hills and Westmont areas along with the trailer parks on Valley Boulevard south of Temple Avenue.
5. *A West Central District*, with a total population of 22,310, a Latino population of 47.1 percent (17.9 percent voting age), and an 18.0 percent African American population. Geographically, this district is bounded on the north by the 10 Freeway, on the east by White Avenue and on the South by 9th Street west to Dudley Avenue and by Mission Boulevard to the 57 Freeway.
6. *A Lincoln Park/Ganesha District*, with a total population of 20,741, a Latino population of 34.6 percent (12.6 percent voting age), and a 15.9 percent African American population. Geographically, this district includes the Fairgrounds, Mountain Meadows, Val Vista area and Ganesha Hills north of the 10 Freeway, and the area between White Avenue and San Antonio Avenue (including downtown) south of the 10 Freeway.

Figure 3. Pomona, California, Six District Plan, Concept A

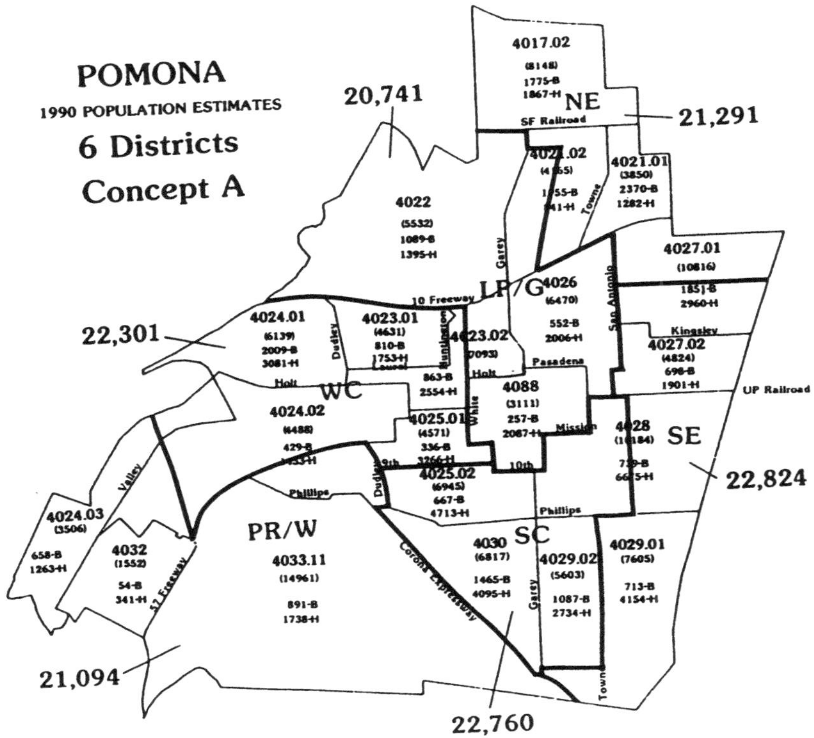

Table 1. Pomona, California, Six District Plan, Concept A

District	Total Population	Deviation from Ideal	Latino 18+ Population	Latino Population	African American Population
NE	21,291	544	2,188	5,543	6,357
(North East)		-2.5%	10.3%	26.0%	29.9%
SE	22,824	989	4,052	10,380	2,398
(South East)		+4.5%	17.8%	45.5%	10.5%
SC	22,760	925	5,613	14,879	3,588
(South Central)		+4.2%	24.7%	65.4%	15.8%
P/W	21,094	741	1,385	3,638	1,598
(Phillips Ranch/ Westmont)		-3.4%	6.6%	17.2%	7.6%
WC	22,301	466	3,983	10,514	4,021
(West Central)		+2.1%	17.9%	47.1%	18.0%
LP/G	20,741	1,094	2,618	7,185	3,306
(Lincoln Park/ Ganesha)		-5.0%	12.6%	34.6%	15.9%
TOTALS	131,011		19,839	52,139	21,268
Ideal District:	21,835				

The Districts for Concept B can be summarized as follows:

1. *A North District*, with a total population of 21,695, a 24.8 percent Latino population (9.3 percent voting age), and a 33.1 percent African American population. Geographically, this district encompasses all the area north of the 10 Freeway.
2. *An East Central District*, with a total population of 22,110, a 31.1 percent Latino population (11.7 percent voting age), and a 14.0 percent African American population. Geographically, this district includes the area south of the 10 Freeway, east of Garey Avenue to Pasadena Avenue and east of Towne Avenue to the Union Pacific Railroad tracks.
3. *A South East District*, with a total population of 23,392, a 58.0 percent Latino population (22.6 percent voting age), and a 10.9 percent African American population. Geographically, this district includes the area south of the Union Pacific Railroad tracks, and the area southeast of downtown and east of Garey Avenue from 10th Street to the southern city boundary.
4. *A South Central District*, with a total population of 21,444, a 66.0 percent Latino population (24.7 percent voting age), and a 12.7 percent African American population. Geographically, this district includes downtown from Towne Avenue to White Avenue and south of Holt Boulevard and Pasadena Avenue, and that area south of Mission Boulevard between Dudley Avenue and the 71 Expressway on the west and Garey Avenue on the east.
5. *A Phillips Ranch/Westmont District*, with a total population of 21,258, a Latino population of 17.2 percent (6.5 percent voting age), and a 7.3 percent African American population. Geographically, this district is bounded on the east by Dudley Avenue and the Corona Expressway and on the north by Mission and Valley Boulevards to Temple Avenue. It includes Phillips Ranch, Chino Hills, Westmont and the trailer parks along Valley Boulevard south of Temple Avenue.
6. *A West Central District*, with a total population of 21,112, a Latino population of 40.2 percent (15.4 percent voting age), and a 19.7 percent African American population. Geographically, this district includes the area south of the 10 Freeway, west of Garey Avenue and north of Mission and Valley Boulevards to Temple Avenue.

Figure 4. Pomona, California, Six District Plan, Concept B

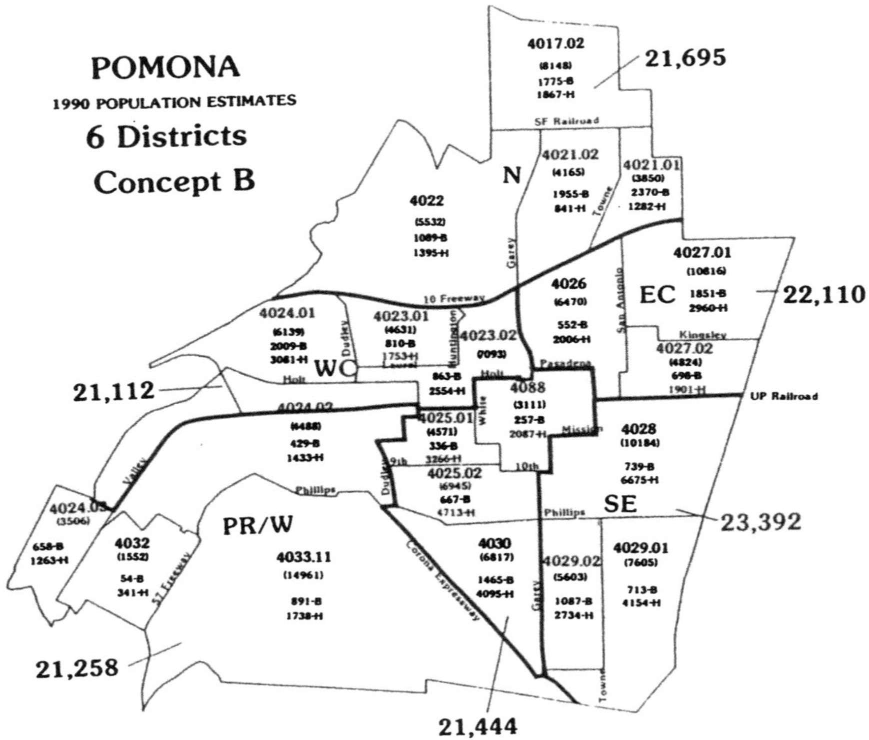

Table 2. Pomona, California, Six District Plan, Concept B

District	Total Population	Deviation from Ideal	Latino 18+ Population	Latino Population	African American Population
N	21,695	140	2,022	5,385	7,189
(North)		-0.6%	9.3%	24.8%	33.1%
EC	22,110	275	2,587	6,867	3,101
(East Central)		+1.3%	11.7%	31.1%	14.0%
SE	23,392	1,557	5,295	13,563	2,539
(South East)		+7.1%	22.6%	58.0%	10.9%
SC	21,444	391	5,296	14,161	2,725
(South Central)		-1.8%	24.7%	66.0%	12.7%
P/W	21,258	577	1,386	3,666	1,560
(Phillips Ranch/		-2.6%	6.5%	17.2%	7.3%
Westmont)					
WC	21,112	723	3,253	8,497	4,154
(West Central)		-3.3%	15.4%	40.2%	19.7%
TOTALS	131,011		19,839	52,139	21,268
Ideal District:	21,835				

These districts appeared in map form on the June 1990 Primary ballot. The first proposed charter amendment, Measure M, asked voters if they wanted district elections: 6,650 voters, or 55.9 percent of the ballots, supported this measure; while 5,245 voters, or 44.1 percent of the ballots voted against it. Thus, voters changed the process of electing council members from a scheme of four council districts, each represented by candidates elected in citywide elections, to a single-member district system, with candidates residing in and elected by districts. Two other measures, Measure N and Measure O, along with their illustrative maps, offered the voters a choice between single-member districting schemes. Measure N proposed a 7-member council elected by districts, with the mayor elected from among the council members: N attracted 3,070 voters or 28 percent of the ballots and was opposed by 8,235 or 72.8 percent. Measure O enlarged the council to six members, with the mayor elected citywide: O attracted 6,944 supporting votes or 60.8 percent, while 4,472 voters or 39.2 percent voted against it.

The Districting Process

With the adoption of Measures M and O as amendments to the City's Charter, six single-member districts now had to be completed. The City contracted with the same consultant to assist in deciding which of the six single-member district concepts, A or B, to choose. The Council determined that choosing, amending and putting the chosen concept into final plan format, would be the result of a full public process.

The consultant now met with each member of the Council[30] and with senior members of the city staff, to obtain their insights on a choice between the two concepts and the required adjustments. More important than these meetings with officials, however, were the public meetings mandated by the Council that took place in different parts of the City and that were attended by citizens and a variety of group leaders. Further emphasizing the openness of this process, the City authorized the consultant to produce "citizen kits" for the general public: these kits included maps of the two alternative concepts, tract and block maps, tract populations, a school division overlay and statistics, a precinct boundary overlay, a current district overlay, registration statistics, basic guidelines on adjustments and line-drawing, and instructions on how to communicate with the consultant. A 72-hour turn-around analysis of proposals submitted by council members and members of the public was guaranteed by the consultant.[31]

The public meetings in different parts of the City became arenas for many different kinds of citizen politics, often involving prospective candidates for council. Thus, one citizen group was headed by Robert Jackson, an Anglo school teacher, who was anxious to run in a district just west of Councilwoman Soto's home. Jackson's aim, therefore, was to minimize the Latino percentage in his area so as to avoid giving an advantage to his likely incumbent opponent. Favian Nunez, the staff head of "One Stop," an immigration support center, began as a member of Robert Jackson's group, but later diverged and submitted his own plan that was clearly intended to advantage Latino elected interests.[32] Similarly, another prospective candidate, Willie White, an African American and a plaintiff in the *Romero* case, participated in the meetings with the purpose of protecting the concentration of African Americans in the northern portion of the City, where he hoped to run as a candidate. The meetings brought to the fore the tension between Latino and African American interests. They also illustrated splits in the Latino community, especially between the established Latino groups, represented principally by Nell Soto, and the newcomer Latino groups, led by Tomas Ursua, another *Romero* plaintiff, and Favian Nunez, who were intent on breaking into the system and establishing a larger role for themselves.

In its public hearings, the City Council (with the advice of the consultant) had emphasized the importance of meeting the principal constitutional criteria of population equality and minority representation, while also satisfying other "good government" criteria. Of these, "community identity" was the most important. The Council instructed the consultant to "Respect, and where possible, to build and support the sense of local community" in developing districts. Compactness and contiguity were also cited with an instruction to the consultant that, "Ease of voter access to all parts of a district is desirable, as also is the requirement that all parts of a district be territorially linked." Another criterion was recognition of natural and manmade features: "Recognizable features," read the Council instructions, "particularly those that have assisted the formation of community identity and helped shaped the social, political and economic life of the City, should be given some degree of recognition in the development of districts." Administrative units were also cited as a factor in the districting process: the Council instructions noted that,

"Census tract and precinct boundaries are examples of administrative units which should be given respect in developing new districts; thus, some cosmetic irregularities in district lines should be accepted in order to preserve existing tracts and precincts." Finally, because the Census data were not due until 1991 and, therefore, would not be available for the districting process, population growth had to come into account: "If the new districts are weighted to reflect likely growth patterns, they may need less adjustment after the full data from the 1990 U.S. Census become available."

With these criteria as guides, the consultant determined to use a "Units of Representation" or UR approach.[33] That is, the consultant employed public comment and demographic research to identify "community units" that, in turn, were aggregated into units of representation or URs. The URs were basic building blocks in the districting process to assure that districts did not discriminate against minority populations, but enhanced community identity, permitted ease of voter access, recognized all natural and man-made boundaries, and gave appropriate respect to existing administrative or jurisdictional lines.

The Choice Between Concepts A and B

To most citizens who attended the public meetings, the principal distinction between Concept A and Concept B was that the latter provided for a stronger African American district (i.e., the north District with its 33.1 percent population of African Americans) and it was to Concept B that most of the citizen comments were directed. A representative from the business community, for example, urged the use of Concept B, but with a modification that would divide the business district among three of the councilmembers so that each would be concerned with the interests of the downtown area.[34] Favian Nunez also submitted a plan to modify Concept B with the aim of enhancing Latino representation in two of its districts.[35] The citizens' group headed by Robert Jackson, who had already indicated a hope to run in the new districts, supported Concept B, but with modifications intended to advantage his own electoral chances by diluting his district's Latino population.[36]

In general, the consultant sought to maintain the major themes of Concept B, while accepting proposed citizen modifications that tended to enhance community of interest and ease of communication within the districts. The principal modifications to Concept B in the consultant's final proposal were: division of census tract 4088 (the downtown area) on an east-west line (at the Pomona Mall to Eleanor and north to the railroad tracks) and on a north-south line (along Garey Avenue from Holt Boulevard to the Pomona Mall); inclusion of the resulting northeast section of census tract 4088 in the East Central District, of the resulting northwest section in the West Central District and of the balance of the tract south of the Pomona Mall in the South Central District; the division of census tract 4028 along the eastern and southern boundary of precinct 66 and the inclusion of nearly all of precinct 66 in the South Central District; inclusion of all of precinct 28 in the West Central District; inclusion of all of Precinct 33 in the South Central District; and removal of the dividing line between the West Central District and the Phillips Ranch/Westmont District from the Southern Pacific Railroad tracks to the Union Pacific Railroad tracks and the extension of this line from the 71 Expressway to Temple Avenue. The results of these emendations to Concept B were to give additional Latino voters to the West-Central district (still only 42.7 percent Latino) and to divide the downtown area among three councilmembers. The "Consultant's Recommended Plan," which was adopted by the Council on September 17, 1990, can be seen as figure 5, the accompanying data table as table 3.

In the first election following the implementation of districts, Nell Soto faced opposition from Bob Jackson and two other candidates (one of whom was Latino) for the 1st District seat (known during the districting process as the "West Central" district). Jackson edged out Soto by six votes in the primary but was defeated by her in the run-off by 59 votes. In the same election, African American Willie White overwhelmingly won the 6th District (known during the districting process as the "North" district) in the primary with 1158 votes, defeating two Latino candidates (Cortez with 475 votes and Quintero with 59 votes) and one Anglo candidate who received 612 votes. In a one-on-one race in the 1995 election, Soto defeated Jackson in the primary, 705 votes to 487 votes, solidly retaining her seat.

Figure 5. Pomona, California, Consultant's Recommended Plan

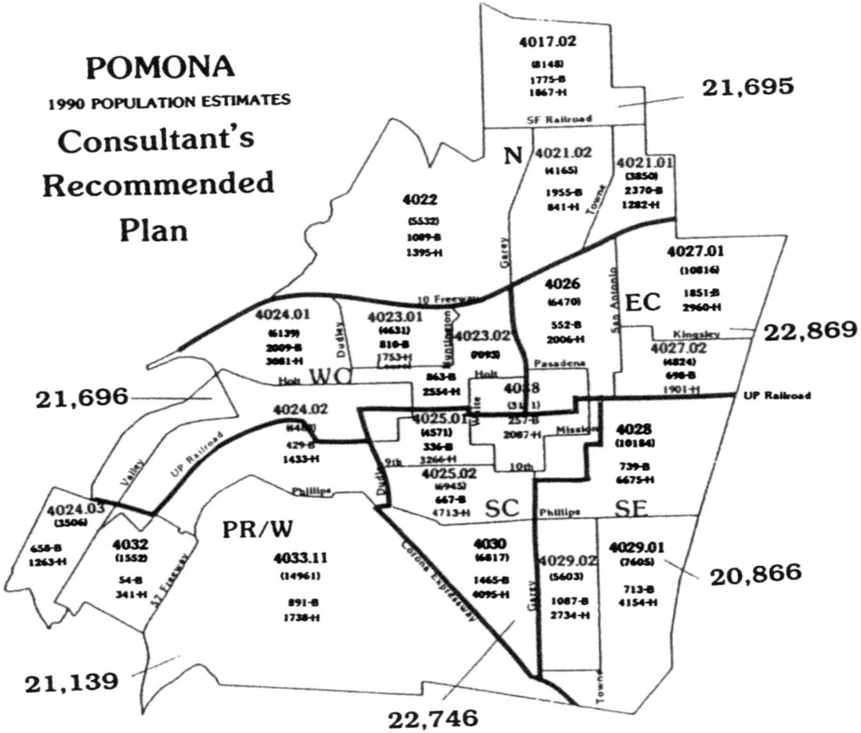

Table 3. Pomona, California, Consultant's Recommended Plan

District	Total Population	Deviation from Ideal	Latino 18+ Population	Latino Population	African American Population
N	21,695	140	2,022	5,385	7,189
(North)		-0.6%	9.3%	24.8%	33.1%
EC	22,869	1,034	2,796	7,389	3,165
(East Central)		+4.7%	12.2%	32.3%	13.8%
SE	20,866	969	4,627	11,908	2,356
(South East)		-4.4%	22.2%	57.1%	11.3%
SC	22,746	911	5,601	14,915	2,725
(South Central)		+4.2%	24.6%	65.6%	12.4%
P/W	21,139	696	1,213	3,272	1,344
(Phillips Ranch/ Westmont)		-3.2%	5.7%	15.5%	6.4%
WC	21,696	139	3,580	9,270	4,391
(West Central)		-0.6%	16.5%	42.7%	20.2%
TOTALS	131,011		19,839	52,139	21,268

Ideal District: 21,835

Watsonville and Pomona Compared

Watsonville paid 1.7 million dollars to lose its bid to maintain at-large electoral arrangements,[37] while Pomona paid a little less[38] and won the right to continue its at-large system; but, because of a change in council politics, Pomona then voted to establish districts after all.

Watsonville had districts enforced by the court and drawn by the attorney who had brought suit against the City. In Pomona, districts were voted in by the people and drawn in an open public process with input from groups of many different kinds. In Watsonville, rancor and bitterness affected city politics for many years after *Gomez*; but, in Pomona, districts seem to have reduced the tensions that had troubled the City Council before *Romero*. The contrast between the two cities is so great, of course, that many factors may have influenced the ways in which districts were implemented and accepted. From the start, Pomona seemed better suited to a district system than Watsonville. In Pomona, the size of the population, and the difficulty and costs of campaigning city-wide, were cited by many as justifications for the move from at-large. The presence in Pomona of a sizable African American minority, with interests and problems that seemed to set it apart from both the Anglo and Latino communities, was also a justification for districts to some residents. Moreover, Pomona was large enough and so long- established that its neighborhoods possessed their own strong sense of identity and saw districts as a means of preserving and enhancing them. Yet, it is hard to resist the conclusion that the difference in origin of the two systems—the one imposed from outside, the other voluntarily voted in—is an important reason for the differences in their results.

It is doubtful, also, whether Watsonville has fulfilled the expectations of Joaquin Avila and the other Latino activists who sued the City. Betty Bobeda, the target of the radical Latino activists in the wake of their legal victory, became the mayor, a result that may have been unlikely if an at-large mayoral arrangement had been implemented. Tony Campos, the realtor whose political demise was another aim of the activists in the era after the court decision, is still on the Council; and there are only two other Latinos (Oscar Rios and Al Alcala) on the seven-member body. Thus, Watsonville's population, with its huge and rapidly growing Latino majority, is still represented and likely will continue to be represented, at least until November 1998, by an Anglo majority city council.

Figure 6. Watsonville 1989 and 1991 Plans Compared.

Watsonville, California Districts, 1989

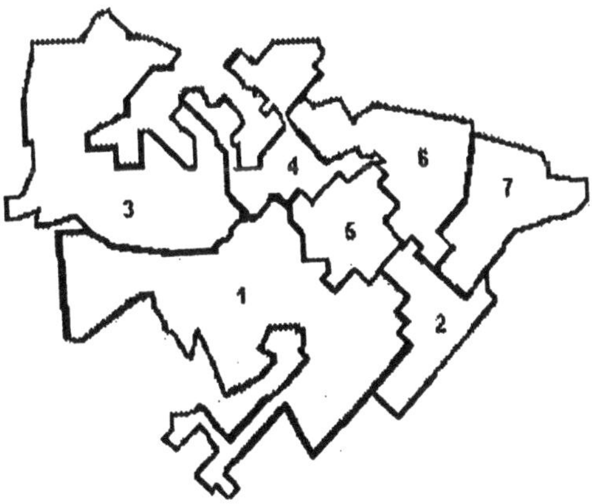

Watsonville, California Districts, 1991

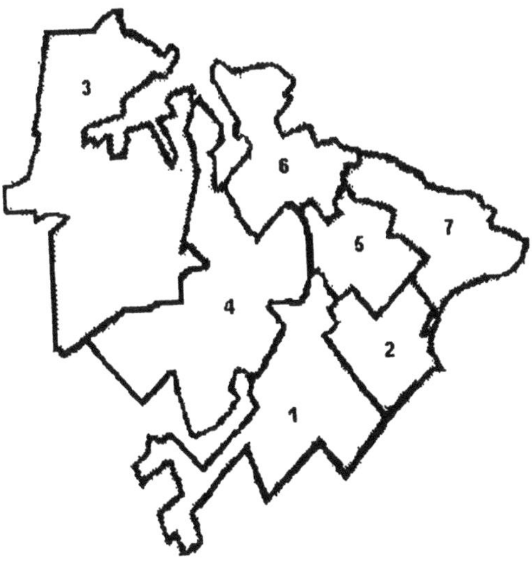

Figure 7. Watsonville and Pomona Plans Compared.

Pomona, California Districts, 1990

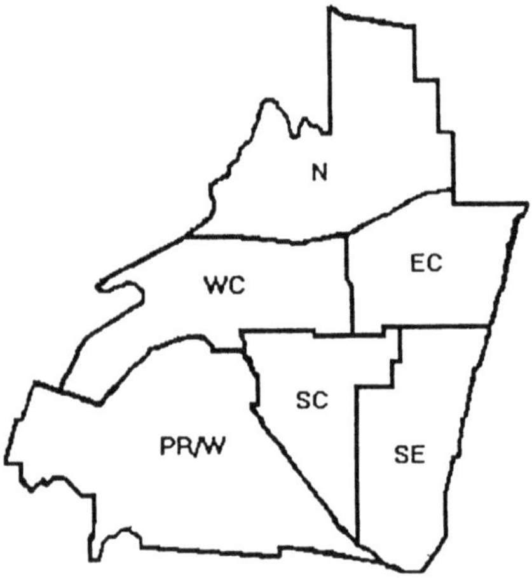

Watsonville, California Districts, 1991

Meanwhile, Pomona, with a smaller percentage of Latinos than Watsonville, has a Latino Mayor (Eddie Cortez) elected at large, and three other Latinos on its seven-member Council. The district that was drawn to incorporate the black "ghetto" is still represented by an African American (Willie White); and the three districts that were drawn around Latino neighborhoods are still represented by Latinos (Nell Soto, Christina Carrizosa, and Marco Robles). If ethnic representation is the test, then, Pomona seems ahead of Watsonville.

Retaining an at-large mayor when moving to a district system seems to assist the transition by allowing citizens to vote for two members of their representative body. Some citizens resent going from voting on all of their councilmembers to choosing just one. Watsonville's former Mayor, Betty Murphy, expressed citizens' frustration over this issue saying, "I sure have heard a lot of questions . . . . And I'm still hearing from people who can't understand why they can't vote for mayor."[39]

A final point can be made by comparing the district maps for Pomona and Watsonville. The initial MALDEF-drawn Watsonville districts have such irregular lines that the term gerrymander seems appropriate. The Santa Cruz Sentinel stated:

> And confusion stems from the configuration of the seven electoral districts. None of the districts is an easily defined block of streets.
>
> For example, District 1, which is generally described as the "industrial westside," takes in new housing at Green Valley Road and Main Street, as well as several blocks along Pennsylvania Drive north of Main Street.
>
> District 4 is nearly impossible to define. The district is U-shaped, with part of it jutting up Pennsylvania Drive (only the north side of the street) and part of it running down Freedom Boulevard.[40]

But a comparison of the MALDEF plan with Joaquin Avila's 1991 redistricting plan (see figure 6) reveals an even greater reach, at the expense of even more extreme contortions, to elect selected Latino candidates.[41]

By way of comparison, the Pomona districts, while preserving the core of the communities they represent, whether Latino, African American or Anglo, follow major thoroughfares to the extent possible, so that the districts are easily recognized and defined. (See comparison of Avila Plan and Pomona Plan at figure 7.) Straight lines and compact shapes result in districts that cause much less confusion to voters, particularly new voters who may find it difficult to understand the new system. Such districts that retain the core of the communities that they serve enhance political organization far more effectively than a few more percentage points of minority population.

NOTES

1. *Gomez v. City of Watsonville*, 863 F.2d 1407 (9th Cir. 1988), *cert. denied* 489 U.S. 1080 (1989).

2. *Romero v. City of Pomona*, Civ. Act. No. CV 85-3359 JMI (6x) (1989).

3. *Gomez vs. City of Watsonville*, 663 F.2d 1407 (9th Cir. 1988).

4. Peter Chacon, "Watsonville: A Beginning for Latino Aspirations," *Los Angeles Times*, August 31, 1988.

5. In the preceding decade in Texas, nearly 100 cities either had been ordered or had agreed to switch from at-large to single-member district systems as a result of lawsuits brought under the U.S. Voting Rights Act; and, indeed, significantly greater numbers of minorities, particularly Hispanics, then won seats on city councils.

6. Unlike Watsonville, whose legal costs came out of an insurance policy, Salinas was uninsured.

7. In June of 1989 a U.S. district court judge, Edward Garcia, threw out a challenge to Stockton's newly adopted districting system. Stockton had traditionally elected council members from nine districts; but in 1985 voters changed the system to select two candidates each from six districts who later would appear with the Mayor on a city-wide ballot. At the time of the change, under the old nine-district system, council members for the city of 190,000 residents had included one Hispanic and three African Americans. A MALDEF-supported challenge claimed that the new system diluted the voting rights of minorities.

8. "Watsonville Loss on Election Issue Could be Victory for State Latinos," *Los Angeles Times*, May 1, 1989.

9. "Watsonville Throws in the Towel," *Santa Cruz Sentinel*, May 24, 1989.

10. "Watsonville Election Compromise," *Santa Cruz Sentinel*, March 29, 1989.

11. The public was invited to be present at the committee meeting but was not allowed to comment.

12. "Election Districts Approved," *Santa Cruz Sentinel*, June 14, 1989.

13. Hispanics constituted 89 percent of the population of old District 2 and 61 percent of its registered voters.

14. Milladin, who lives on East Lake Avenue, the boundary between Districts 1 and 2, found himself excluded from District 1 because he lived on the south side of the block. Avila claimed to have been unaware of Milladin's address.

15. See "New District Map Under Fire," *Register Pajaronian*, June 5, 1991.

16. See "No Challenge Planned to Latest District Map," *Register Pajaronian*, June 14, 1991.

17. *Romero*, 10054.

18. *Romero*, 10054.

19. *Romero*, 665 F Supp. at 858.

20. *Romero*, 665 F. Supp. at 868.

21. *Romero*, 665 F. Supp. at 860-61.

22. *Romero*, 10055.

23. *Romero*, 10058.

24. *Romero*, 10058-9.

25. *Romero*, 10063.

26. *Romero*, 10067.

27. Mayor Donna Smith dissented and Councilman Mark Nymeyer was absent.

28. "Pomona Hires Firm to Devise Election Plan," *Progress Bulletin*, February 21, 1990.

29. Concepts A and B for Measure N are not discussed here, since Measure N failed; but, in general, they conformed to the same approach and aimed to achieve similar results as Concepts A and B for Measure O.

30. Clay Bryant had been removed immediately after being recalled and was replaced by Boyd Bradencamp, who had been a member of the City planning commission.

31. See Bill Boyarsky, "Redrawing Districts in Public," *Los Angeles Times*, July 27, 1990.

32. Perhaps including a district for Nunez himself.

33. The UR or Units of Representation approach was developed by Leroy Hardy, a professor at California State University, Long Beach and Senior Research Associate at the Rose Institute, Claremont McKenna College. It gave a name and structure—the development of actual "community units"—to the "good government" concept of preserving communities of interest in the districting process.

34. See *The Districting Process in Pomona: A Report to the City Council*, September 12, 1990, The Rose Institute of State and Local Government, 22.

35. The Nunez modification of Concept B was designed to: include the area south of Val Vista Street and north of the 10 Freeway in the West Central District; include the area south of the 10 Freeway, north of San Bernardino Avenue and west of Mountain Avenue in the north district; divide census tract 4088 at Garey Avenue to the railroad tracks; include the portion of the Westmont area east of the 71 Expressway in the South Central District; and divide census tract 4024.03 at the 57 Freeway rather than at Temple Avenue. See *The Districting Process in Pomona*, 22.

36. The Jackson modifications provided that: Garey Avenue should be followed from the I-10 Freeway to the 60 Freeway; voter precincts should be maintained intact; and the Phillips Ranch District should include all territories west of the 71 Expressway, south of Pomona Boulevard and west of Temple Avenue. See *The Districting Process in Pomona*, 21.

37. In fact, Watsonville spent only $2,400 out of its city treasury on legal charges; the remainder of the total of 1.7 million was covered by a policy with the Republic Insurance Group.

38. Approximately 1.2 million from the city treasury.

39. Jamie Marks, "Watsonville plans a campaign to educate confused city voters," *Santa Cruz Sentinel*, September 24, 1989.

40. Ibid.

41. Concern over the failure of the MALDEF lines to elect a majority of Hispanics to the Council most likely inspired these lines.

CHAPTER 4

Dinuba and Its Aftermath

THE DINUBA CASES

California's Central Valley extends from Bakersfield in the south to Sacramento in the north. Between Interstate 5 and Highway 99, the two main transporation corridors of this vast agricultural area, and between Highway 99 and the foothills of the Sierra Nevada are located scores of cities. All of the these cities experienced dramatic growth between 1970 and 1990: Fresno, the largest, grew from 165,972 to 354,202 and Kerman, one of the smallest, grew from 2,667 to 5,448. Latinos represented a significant portion of this growth and, therefore, made the area ripe for districting challenges. This chapter and the next two chapters focus on a number of jurisdictions in the Central Valley, the largest of which is just over 30,000 persons. Redistricting fights can be extremely expensive and labor intensive. State legislatures have the resources to deal with such battles; but small, local jurisdictions do not. Studies at the state level tend to overlook this fact.

The 1990 census reported Dinuba's population as 12,743, of which 60 percent were Latino—an increase of 12.3 percent over the 1980 census. The City had elected its representatives on an at-large basis ever since its incorporation in 1906. Over the years, several Latinos had served on the Dinuba City Council, including Frank Gomez, who had four times been elected to the Council and who twice had served as mayor. In 1992, however, there was only one Latino on the Dinuba City Council. Voting rights attorney Joaquin Avila targeted Dinuba as the pre-eminent Central Valley site for a challenge to the use of an at-large electoral system. At about the same time, Avila filed voting rights suits against the Alta Hospital District in Dinuba, the Dinuba Elementary and High School Districts, and the Cutler-Orosi Unified School District (also in the Dinuba area).[1] Three Dinuba residents, Enrique Reyes, Jr., Noe Elizondo, and Teresa Reyes filed suit on April 5, 1991,[2] asking that the City's electoral system be declared violative of the protections of the Federal Voting Rights Act and replaced with single-member districts.

In May of 1992, in an effort to compromise the issue and save costs of litigation, the Dinuba City Council adopted a two-district system combined with a three-member at-large arrangement: the two districts were drawn to be overwhelmingly Latino in voter registration. The City's representative in the negotiations, John McDermott, a Los Angeles-based attorney and voting rights specialist, argued that the plan was equitable because it would practically assure the election of two Latinos to the Council; and, noting that Latinos constituted only 40 percent of the City's registered voters, he argued that two Latino members on the five-member city council would be reasonably proportional. Avila rejected the City's proffered compromise, however, and asked a Federal District Court in Fresno to issue an injunction to prevent the plan from being used for the 1992 elections.

In August of 1992, Federal District Judge Robert Coyle refused to issue the injunction requested by Avila, saying that no irreparable harm would result from the City's plan and that the two-district system represented at least a step toward improved representation. Elections, therefore, went forward in the three-two arrangement. The election held in the district scheduled for the 1992 contest resulted in the election of Rachel Morales, a strong advocate of the district system.

As the litigation in *Reyes* continued, Judge Coyle issued new rulings indicating that the City's new electoral arrangements might be thrown out. There was also a challenge by the plaintiffs to the failure of the City to submit its new plan for approval by voters. Moreover, in November of 1992, the Dinuba-based Alta Hospital District decided to settle, handed over $200,000 in legal fees to Avila, and agreed to hold single-member district elections in 1994. At about the same time, the Dinuba school districts also settled, handing over $100,000 in fees to Avila and agreeing on single-member district elections for their governing boards. Thus, at its April 13, 1993 meeting, the Dinuba City Council voted to abandon its three-two system and to establish five single-member districts and scheduled a city-wide vote in November of 1993 to approve the new plan.[3]

Finally, in mid-May of 1993, Avila and the City agreed to establish five districts, each with a population of around 2,500 persons, three of which were two-thirds or more Latino. The Latino percentages were as follows: District 1, 79.7 percent; District 2, 70.9 percent; and District 3, 62.6 percent. Districts 1 and 2 had substantial majorities of Latino registered voters; but in District 3, only 45 percent of the registered voters were Latino. District 1 was basically formed from the southeastern portions of Dinuba; District 2 comprised the southwestern portions; and District 3 combined eastern portions of the City south of El Monte and north of Magnolia. Districts 4 and 5 concentrated the Anglo vote in the area north of El Monte Way: in District 4, the non-Latino voting age population was 55.9 percent; and in District 5 it was 77.9 percent. The incumbent Council members, John de la Montanya, Ray Millard, and Mayor Ray Fudge would serve until November of 1994, when their terms would normally expire.

The City, which had previously offered $200,000 in legal fees to Avila, now offered a settlement at the $300,000 level. The general expectation was that, although there might be some continued dispute over the exact size of the settlement, Dinuba's voting rights travails were over.[4] As it turned out, however, Avila submitted a bill more than twice what the City had, in the worst case, expected. He demanded fees of $817,653; but he offered the City a five percent discount to $739,767. Since the official population of the City of Dinuba had climbed to 13,935, the bill would cost every man, woman and child in the City $58.68. The bill far exceeded the annual cost of Dinuba's Fire Department. Thus, the City rejected Avila's claim on August 24, 1993.[5]

The contest in Dinuba quickly reverberated through other Central Valley communities. In August of 1992, *The Fresno Bee* reported:

> Elected officials in the San Joaquin Valley don't openly admit being intimidated by voting-rights lawyer Joaquin Avila, but his name and their recession-ravaged budgets are often mentioned in the same breath. . . . In the last two months, the Milpitas lawyer has reached fee settlement agreements totaling $300,000 in Dinuba and forced the town's public entities to abandon at-large elections in favor of voting in geographical districts.
>
> He will receive $200,000 from the Alta District Hospital and $100,000 from Dinuba Public Schools. The city has changed to district elections as well, but Avila is still disputing the new system in federal court.[6]

In some cases, the threat of suit was sufficient to persuade jurisdictions to make the move from at-large to single-member districts. Thus, *The Fresno Bee* reported:

> Sanger with a Hispanic population totaling 72.9 percent, changed to district elections last year without hearing from Avila.
>
> Gina Holguin, Sanger City Council member, said, "For me, I knew it was a matter of time. I knew we might have this guy come to our community, and the city would wind up paying a bundle" . . . after Sanger and Dinuba changed in the last year, Visalia began putting together a task force to study election by geographical representation.
>
> Fabrizio, Dinuba Public Schools superintendent, said he would advise other public agencies to take a look at the issues. "No one ever approached our board," he said. "The lawsuit was filed out of the clear blue sky. I would tell people in other cities to take a close look at the issues, because you might hear from him."[7]

OTHER CENTRAL VALLEY CITIES

The shadow of the Dinuba cases and the threat posed by Joaquin Avila and a Latino activist named Ben Benevides, caught the attention of the Mayor of Visalia, Peter Carey. In October of 1992, Carey, with the reluctant support of other members of the Council, appointed a task force to study election districts for the City of Visalia. The 1990 Census had reported Visalia's population as 75,636, with 19,005 or 25.13 percent Latino persons. Mayor Carey and the city manager and staff thought that they could lose an expensive Dinuba-style lawsuit.[8] In May of 1993 the Task Force, more than half of whose members were Latino,[9] reported in favor of districts. Testimony before the Task Force had emphasized that Visalia had never elected a Latino councilmember; that people elected to the Council almost always lived in neighborhoods with less than 30 percent Latino population; and that voter turnout, which was 32 percent city-wide in 1991, was only 17.5 percent in north Visalia, where most Latinos lived.[10]

Despite the unanimous report of the Task Force, Visalians balked at districts. The first sign of trouble came on the City Council, whose members split over their support for Measure C, the initiative that would allow voters to elect by district. The Mayor continued to support the proposition and was joined by one of his colleagues; but two opposed it vigorously and another was undecided.[11] The measure appeared to have support in the Latino community, but little campaigning was done for it.[12] Leaders of Visalia's Latino community said that they were loathe to campaign for districts because they said they feared racial polarization.[13] On November 3, 1993, Visalia voters rejected the measure by a substantial margin.[14] Voting rights activists promised litigation; but the decisive rejection at the polls, and the Latino community's failure to participate, seemed to have demoralized the pro-district forces. There was also a sentiment, expressed by both Anglo and Latino residents, that the whole process had been damaging to community relationships.

Two other Central Valley cities, Lemoore and Reedley, on the advice of their attorney, conducted demographic studies using this writer as consultant. Both cities opted not to move to districts. The Lemoore study revealed that Latino voting age citizens made up only 13.35 percent of Lemoore's total population; and test districts did not yield a majority-minority district or even a credible (35 to 49 percent) "influence" district. Reedley, however, had a Latino population of 9,196 or 58.24 percent Latino in a city of 15,791 persons, and the consultant was able to create three majority-minority districts. Nevertheless, the process was tabled in January of 1995.[15]

OTHER CENTRAL VALLEY HOSPITAL DISTRICTS

Tulare District Hospital, located in Tulare County just south of Fresno County, held discussions with this writer as early as the spring of 1992. In August of 1992, the consultant was asked to conduct a demographic study and prepare model districts. It was determined that the Hospital District had a total population of 53,473 persons, of whom 18,663 (34.9 percent) were Latino. It was also determined that, except for a small area in city of Tulare, the Latino population was mostly located in the rural areas of the district.

A full public process ensued: notices were placed in the newspapers and presentations were made to the Board and various community groups. In March of 1993, two districting plans were presented to the Board: one was a two-district (or "zone") plan (two members to be elected from one district and three members from another)[16] and the other was a five-district (or "zone") plan. The five-district plan had one district (located in the city of Tulare) with a majority of Latino persons (53.89 percent), but the district had only 49.92 percent voting age Latino population, and would likely drop several more percentage points if citizenship were to be factored in. A second district (mostly created from rural areas) was 47.36 percent total Latino, but dropped to 40.84 percent voting age Latino. The remaining three districts were 25.65 percent, 22.39 percent and 25.20 percent total Latino.

The same month that these plans went to the Board, the Hospital District decided to put the process on hold. Board members had been observing the City of Tulare and the Tulare school districts wrestling with the same issue and decided to monitor the deliberations of those jurisdictions prior to making a final decision themselves.

While the process was on hold, *Shaw v. Reno* was decided and the consultant was asked to provide advice to the District regarding the ruling. She commented as follows:

> 1. *Shaw* does not constitute a definitive ruling in any technical sense: that is, it is impossible to derive from the opinion any clear direction as to the actual drawing of district lines. . . .
> 2. The *Shaw* case is about gerrymandering: that is, it concerns the distortion of district boundaries in a jurisdiction already possessed of districts. The case does not involve the issue of moving from an at-large electoral arrangement to single-member districts.
> 3. There is nothing in *Shaw*, so far as I can see, that is likely to deter the U.S. Department of Justice from its past course concerning the effort to establish districts in at-large jurisdictions with substantial minority populations. . . .
>
> I think [these points] warn against the view that *Shaw* has somehow re-configured the whole issue of movement from at-large arrangements.[17]

In January of 1994, the city of Tulare and the two Tulare school districts formed a 21-member advisory panel, the District Elections Advisory Committee, to study the move to districts and to make recommendations. The final determination of the Advisory Committee was that the voters should decide the issue. By June of 1994, the city of Tulare had voted to place a charter amendment on the November ballot to move to five single-member districts; and, the two school districts voted to place advisory measures on the same ballot. At its June meeting, the Hospital District voted to place an advisory measure on the ballot as well. Joe Adair, the Board President said, "I think the whole community is moving in some kind of direction. Perhaps this will give us the direction."[18]

The day before the election, very little enthusiasm had been generated for districts. According to the *Tulare Advance-Register*, "No public officials have come out in favor of district elections—with the exception of Nettie Washington. Many say they oppose district voting."[19] The turnout was low and the measures were all defeated convincingly.

A second hospital district, Coalinga Regional Medical Center in Fresno County, had a total population of 14,675, 8,483 or 57.81 percent of whom were Latino. The Center also conducted an open process and invited full public participation. A demographic report was developed and test and draft plans were created and studied. The Medical Center has two main population centers: Coalinga with a total population of 8,212 and a Latino population of 2,593 or 31.58 percent; and Huron, with a total population 4,766 and a Latino population of 4,597 (96.45 percent). The intervening territory is rural and sparsely populated. The Board members typically are non-Latino and come from the Coalinga area.

A pre-final draft plan, presented to the Board on December 15, 1993, was approved and was to be scheduled for public hearings. The plan created five districts or "zones:" three with Latino populations of 24.38 percent, 32.63 percent and 42.82 percent, centered in the Coalinga area; and two, with Latino populations of 95.37 percent and 95.42 percent, centered in the Huron area. The first scheduled public hearing was postponed due to fog; it was never rescheduled. In early 1994, under the leadership of a new Center Director, the process was put on hold. This writer, the technical consultant for the process, recently has been put on notice that due to pressure from Latino activists, the process, which has been "on hold" for more than two and a half years, may soon be revived.

OTHER CENTRAL VALLEY SCHOOL DISTRICTS

Included here are three school districts that moved from at-large to single-member-district systems primarily as a result of concern over the Dinuba cases and the financial implications of potential lawsuits.

Sanger Unified School District

The City of Sanger, the commercial and market center for the surrounding agricultural area, lies only 20 miles from Dinuba. According to the 1990 Census, Sanger's population stood at 16,839, of which 72.9 percent were Latino. The City's at-large electoral arrangements had nevertheless resulted in the election of two Latino council members, Gina Holguin and Elliot Martinez. The Latino's complained, however, that none of the councilmembers lived east of the Southern Pacific Railroad tracks, where much of Sanger's Latino population lived and where its barrio was located. In the wake of the Dinuba litigation, Sanger's Council focused on the threat of a voting rights challenge and placed two districting measures on the November 1991 ballot. Measure F provided for election "from district:" that is, councilmembers would necessarily reside in (be from) one of five new districts, but they would be elected at-large. Measure G provided "by district" elections, that is councilmembers would have to reside and be elected in district boundaries. Mayor Kevin Kennedy, explaining the decision to place the measures on the ballot, said: "Potential litigation by the Mexican-American Political Association spurred our interest to change."[20] Both measures provided for the same city councilmanic boundaries. The measures were placed on the ballot by the mayor, Martinez, Holguin and another councilmember, Bruce Farmer. Under both measures, the east side of town won two complete districts.

The City's response to the threat of Dinuba-style litigation caused an even wider stir. The Sanger Unified School District, half of whose population was located in the City of Sanger, had neither districts nor Latino trustees.[21] Joaquin Avila, who was representing the Mexican American Political Association (MAPA) in the area, had publicly stated that he was collecting data and that he was prepared to file the same sort of suit that he had launched against the various Dinuba jurisdictions. Although the trustees and school administrators went to great lengths to deny that Avila was the stimulus to their action, they voted to move from at-large to single-member district elections in April of 1992.[22] Among the facts that gave the Board and its legal advisors[23] a sense of great vulnerability was that only three Latinos had served on the school district board in twenty-seven years, and the last had served in 1987. The District was 55 percent Latino and there had been complaints of discrimination in several schools.

The MAPA chapter in the Sanger area was headed by Margaret Alvarez, President, and Alonso Gomez, Vice-president. Ben Benavides, Gregory Perez, Robert Quiroz (who functioned as technical assistant to Perez), Joaquin Avila and other activists in the Latino community vowed to monitor the districting process in the Sanger Unified School District with the closest possible attention.

The writer, serving as the principal demographer and technician for the school district, developed an initial plan with seven trustee areas or districts. Each district had a deviation of less than 1 percent from the population ideal, and there were four strong Latino districts, with populations of more than 70 percent, in the plan. In revised draft plan A (the plan finally adopted by the Board in May of 1993), Area 4 had a total Latino population of 77.70 percent and a Latino 18-plus population of 73.13 percent; Area 5 had a total Latino population of 79.97 percent and a Latino 18-plus population of 76.18 percent; Area 6 had a Latino population of 77.77 percent and a Latino 18-plus population of 74.00 percent; and Area 7 had a Latino population of 72.94 percent and a Latino 18-plus population of 67.78 percent. The plan and accompanying data sheet appear as figures 8 and 9 and table 4.

Another plan that divided the city area horizontally rather than vertically also provided for four strong Latino districts, each with 70 percent or more Latino population. Revised Draft Plan B's Area 4 had 76.36 percent total Latino population and 72.0 percent Latino 18-plus; Area 5 had 81.31 percent total Latino population and 78.18 percent Latino 18-plus; Area 6 had total Latino population of 69.83 percent and 64.66 percent Latino 18-plus; and Area 7 had a total Latino population of 78.65 and 74.01 percent Latino 18-plus. Population deviations were slightly greater than in Revised Draft Plan A: one of Plan B's areas had a 1.16 percent deviation from the ideal. Revised Draft Plan B appears as figures 10 and 11 and table 5.

Either of these plans seemed to the Sanger Unified School District officials and their consultant to provide for effective representation of Latinos on the Board. On April 9, of 1993, however, Gregory Perez submitted proposals that diverged sharply from those made by the Sanger Unified School District consultant.[24] The essential difference between the Perez plan and that of the Sanger Unified School District consultant is that the Perez Plan aimed to make *five* "Latino opportunity districts." The Latino voting age population (VAP) or Latino 18-plus population of the Sanger Unified School District was less than one-half[25] of the total population. Clearly, the aim of creating five districts

Figure 8. Sanger Unified School District, Revised Draft Plan A

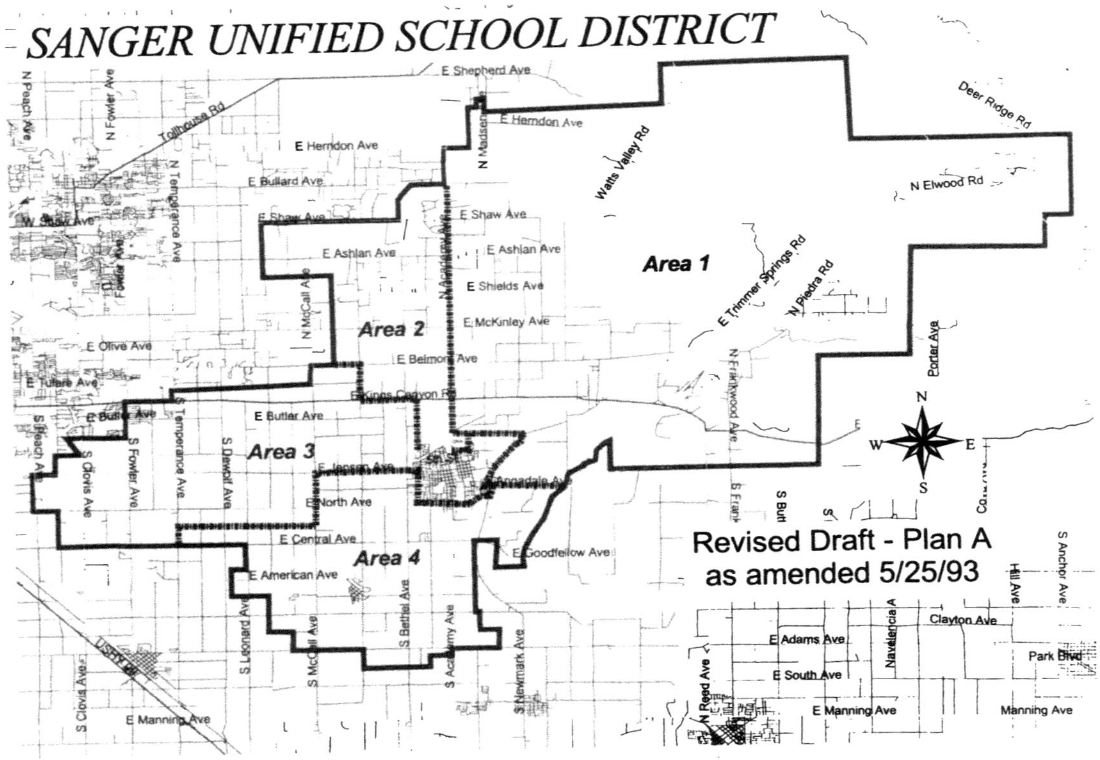

Figure 9. Revised Draft Plan A (Inset map)

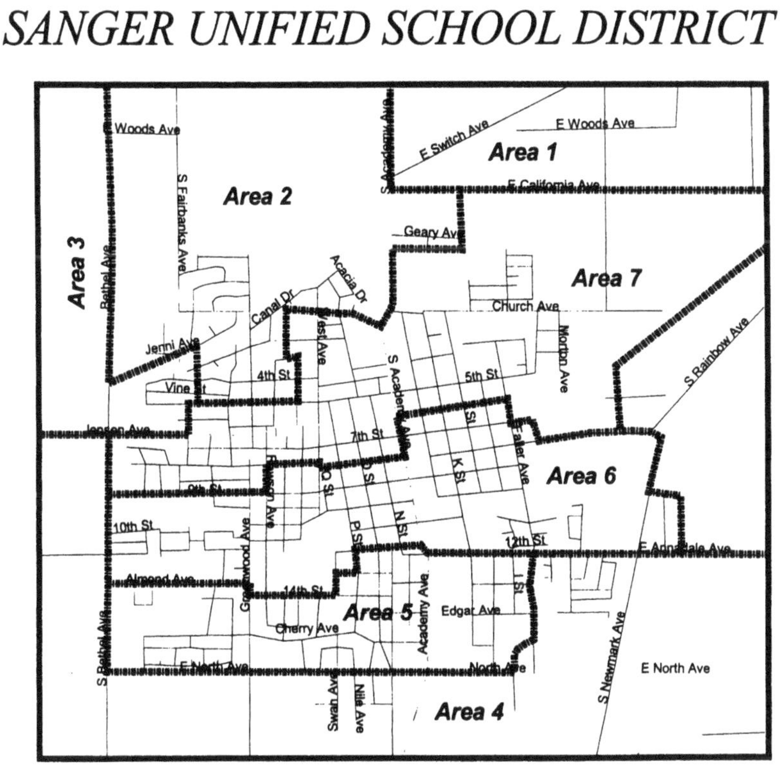

Table 4. Sanger Unified School District, Revised Draft Plan A (as amended 5-25-93)

	Area 1	%	Area 2	%	Area 3	%	Area 4	%	Area 5	%	Area 6	%	Area 7	%	SUSD	SUSD %
Persons	4489		4484		4498		4427		4483		4435		4442		31258	
Hispanic	923	20.56	1216	27.12	1299	28.88	3440	77.70	3585	79.97	3449	77.77	3240	72.94	17152	54.87
NH White	3391	75.54	3012	67.17	2768	61.54	787	17.78	756	16.86	886	19.98	1085	24.43	12685	40.58
NH Black	12	0.27	27	0.60	75	1.67	2	0.05	1	0.02	2	0.05	1	0.02	120	0.38
NH Amer. Ind.	55	1.23	31	0.69	12	0.27	13	0.29	9	0.20	5	0.11	27	0.61	152	0.49
NH Asian	107	2.38	194	4.33	336	7.47	171	3.86	105	2.34	84	1.89	76	1.71	1073	3.43
NH Other	1	0.02	8	0.18	8	0.18	14	0.32	27	0.60	9	0.20	13	0.29	80	0.26
Total 18+	3262		3071		3450		2981		2876		2915		2877		21432	
18+ Hispanic	572	17.54	741	24.13	859	24.90	2180	73.13	2191	76.18	2157	74.00	1950	67.78	10650	49.69
NH 18+ White	2562	78.54	2165	70.50	2258	65.45	636	21.34	581	20.20	692	23.74	840	29.20	9734	45.42
NH 18+ Black	9	0.28	17	0.55	50	1.45	2	0.07	1	0.03	2	0.07	1	0.03	82	0.38
NH 18+ Amer. Ind.	34	1.04	17	0.55	11	0.32	6	0.20	5	0.17	4	0.14	22	0.76	99	0.46
NH 18+ Asian	84	2.58	125	4.07	266	7.71	147	4.93	82	2.85	52	1.78	55	1.91	811	3.78
NH 18+ Other	1	0.03	6	0.20	6	0.17	10	0.34	16	0.56	8	0.27	9	0.31	56	0.26

"NH" = "Not of Hispanic Origin"

Area Deviations (Ideal Area: 4465)

	Area 1	Area 2	Area 3	Area 4	Area 5	Area 6	Area 7
Population	4489	4484	4498	4427	4483	4435	4442
Deviation	24	19	33	-38	18	-30	-23
	0.54%	0.43%	0.74%	-0.85%	0.40%	-0.67%	-0.52%

Figure 10. Sanger Unified School District, Revised Draft Plan B

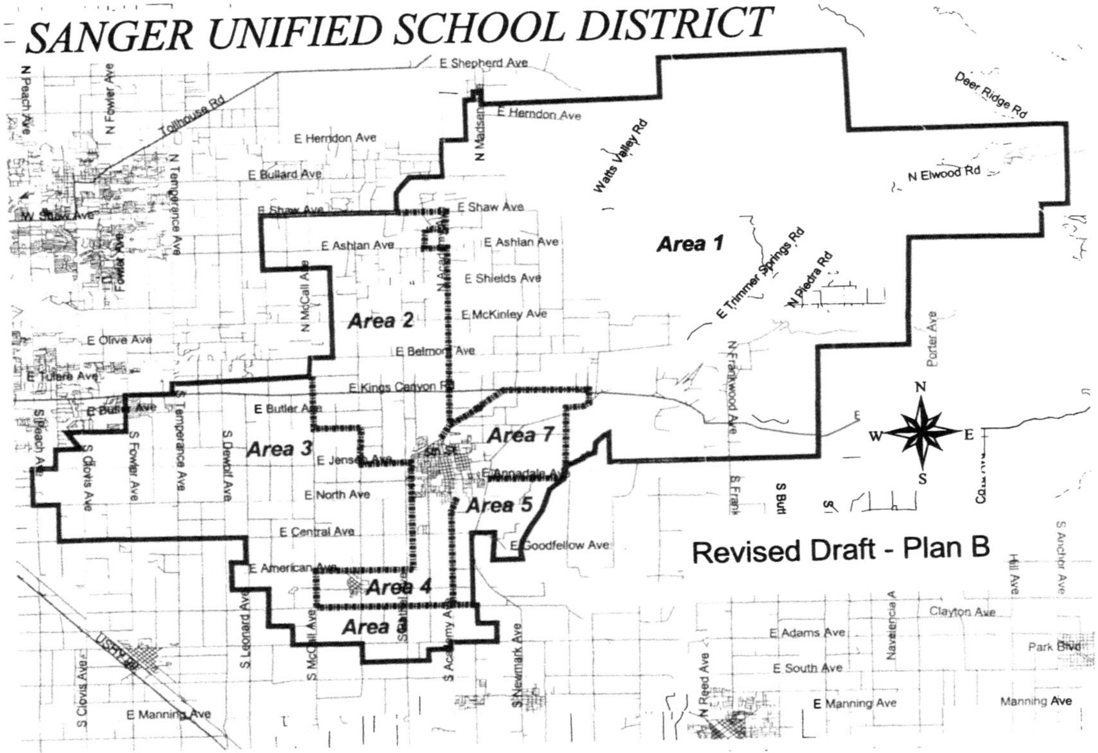

Figure 11. Revised Draft Plan B (Inset map)

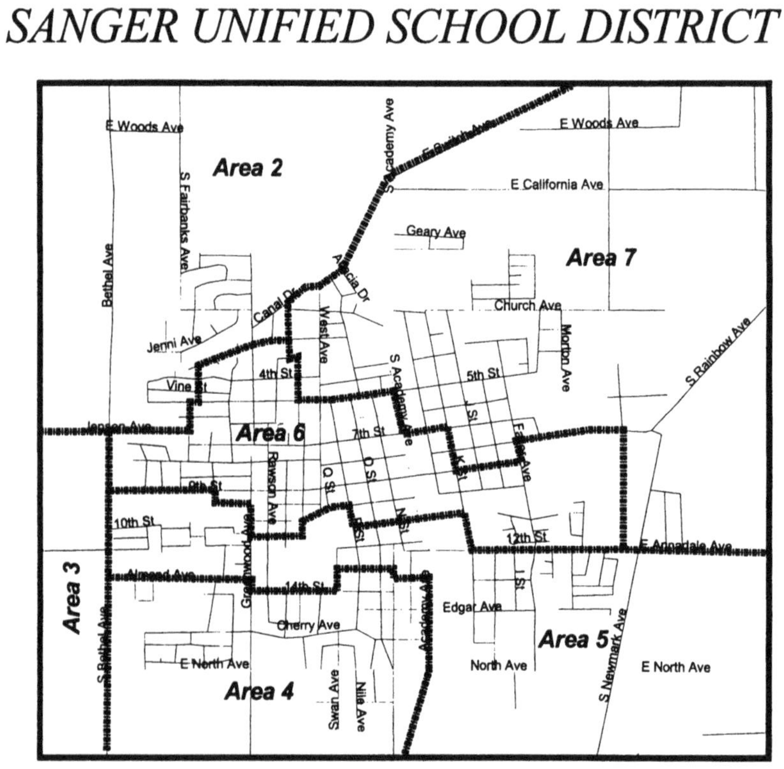

Table 5. Sanger Unified School District, Revised Draft Plan B

	Area 1	%	Area 2	%	Area 3	%	Area 4	%	Area 5	%	Area 6	%	Area 7	%	SUSD	SUSD %
Persons	4447		4480		4517		4437		4446		4468		4463		31258	
Hispanic	733	16.48	1235	27.57	1551	34.34	3388	76.36	3615	81.31	3120	69.83	3510	78.65	17152	54.87
NH White	3536	79.51	2947	65.78	2527	55.94	879	19.81	709	15.95	1235	27.64	852	19.09	12685	40.58
NH Black	14	0.31	28	0.63	72	1.59	1	0.02	4	0.09	1	0.02	0	0.00	120	0.38
NH Amer. Ind.	59	1.33	30	0.67	20	0.44	5	0.11	6	0.13	17	0.38	15	0.34	152	0.49
NH Asian	105	2.36	233	5.20	341	7.55	146	3.29	90	2.02	84	1.88	74	1.66	1073	3.43
NH Other	4	0.09	7	0.16	6	0.13	18	0.41	22	0.49	11	0.25	12	0.27	80	0.26
Total 18+	3234		3143		3390		2936		2851		3050		2828		21432	
18+ Hispanic	459	14.19	785	24.98	998	29.44	2114	72.00	2229	78.18	1972	64.66	2093	74.01	10650	49.69
NH 18+ White	2651	81.97	2150	68.41	2057	60.68	683	23.26	540	18.94	994	32.59	659	23.30	9734	45.42
NH 18+ Black	10	0.31	19	0.60	47	1.39	1	0.03	4	0.14	1	0.03	0	0.00	82	0.38
NH 18+ Amer. Ind.	38	1.18	16	0.51	12	0.35	4	0.14	3	0.11	15	0.49	11	0.39	99	0.46
NH 18+ Asian	73	2.26	168	5.35	271	7.99	121	4.12	63	2.21	58	1.90	57	2.02	811	3.78
NH 18+ Other	3	0.09	5	0.16	5	0.15	13	0.44	12	0.42	10	0.33	8	0.28	56	0.26

"NH" = "Not of Hispanic Origin"

Area Deviations (Ideal Area: 4465)

	Area 1	Area 2	Area 3	Area 4	Area 5	Area 6	Area 7
Population	4447	4480	4517	4437	4446	4468	4463
Deviation	-18	15	52	-28	-19	3	-2
	-0.40%	0.34%	1.16%	-0.63%	-0.43%	0.07%	-0.04%

with Latino voting majorities was impractical. The trustee areas created by Mr. Perez had total Latino populations of 66 percent (Area 4), 66 percent (Area 2), 65 percent (Area 5), 73 percent (Area 6) and 70 percent (Area 7). The districts had population deviations of as much as 2.6 percent; and the boundary lines were quite irregular, reflecting Mr. Perez's effort to capture even partial blocks where Latino residents were concentrated.

As a result of an exchange with the consultant regarding the deficiencies of the first plan, Gregory Perez and Robert Quiroz submitted an alternative, Perez Plan 2. Rather less ambitiously, this plan achieved four "majority-minority" Latino districts and one influence district: Area 1 had 72 percent Latino population; Area 2, 81 percent; Area 3, 73 percent; Area 4, 82 percent; and Area 5, 47 percent. Although deviations were reduced, boundary line irregularities were even greater. The plan appears as figures 12 and 13 and tables 6 and 7.

Another group of Latinos now entered the process.[26] Headed by Tanis Ybarra, a local businessman, and with support from Roy Mendoza and Alonso Gomez of MAPA, this group's aim was "to maintain the Del Rey area ... as an area in and of itself without combining it with the City of Sanger."[27] Ybarra noted in his letter: "It seems that by leaving them as they are, we would at least begin to address the issue of community interest."[28] Mr. Ybarra also wished to "look at the possibility of having four districts within the City of Sanger boundaries instead of the proposed five."[29] This writer noted, by way of response, that the Del Rey area had insufficient population to form a single- member trustee area.[30] Given equal population requirements, it would be unconstitutional to locate only four trustee districts in the City of Sanger. Next, Ybarra and his colleagues developed an alternative (see map and data for Ybarra District Plan at figure 14 and table 8) that provided for only four Latino majority districts, one of which seemed to have a bare majority of eligible Latino voters: this was Area 4, with a total Latino population of 67 percent, a Latino 18-plus population of only 61 percent, and a Latino citizen population of approximately 55 percent.

The consultant recommended against accepting either of the Latino-drawn plans, for each seemed vulnerable on both constitutional and political grounds. The consultant's own plan seemed, on the basis both of statistics and knowledge of Sanger's Latino political organization, to offer a surer route to representation on the District's board. The consultant found it difficult to repress the suspicion that

Figure 12. Sanger Unified School District, Perez Plan

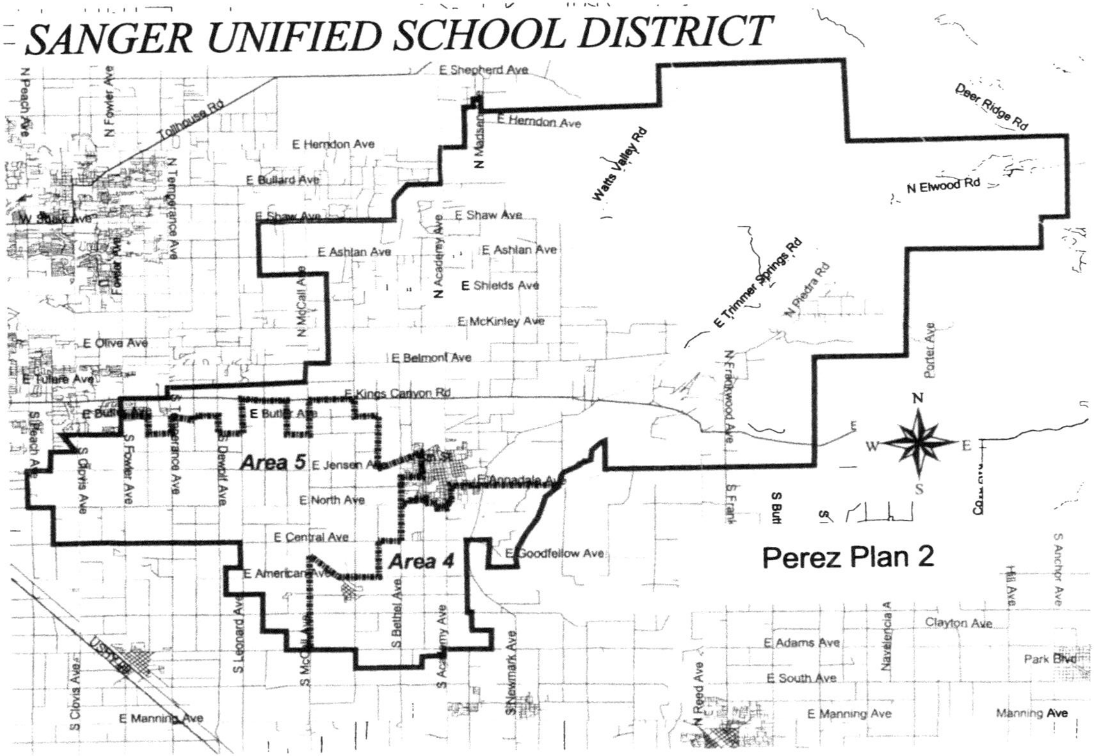

Figure 13. Sanger USD Perez Plan (Inset Map)

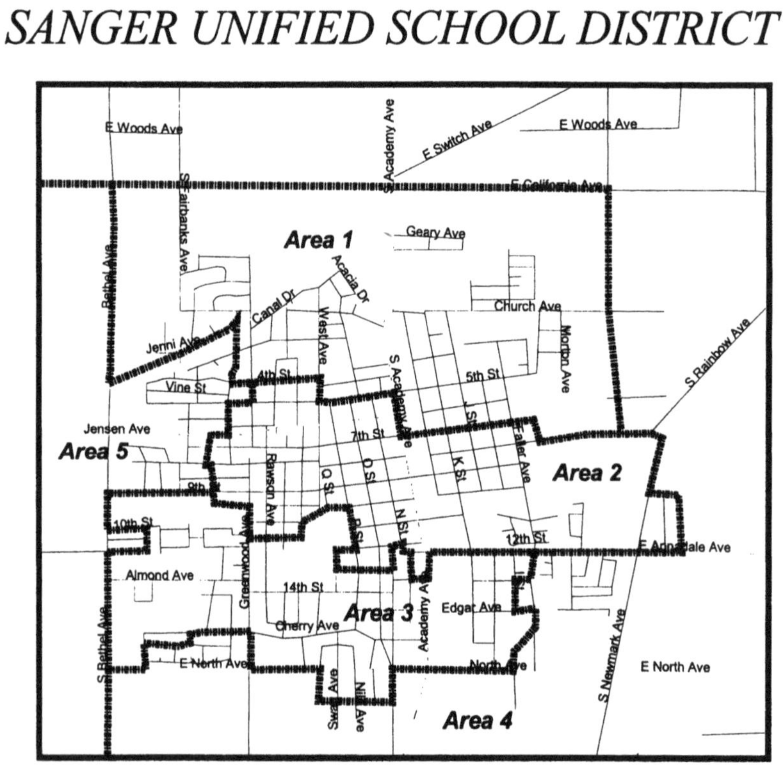

Table 6. Sanger Unified School District: Perez Plan—Consultant's Analysis

	Area 1	%	Area 2	%	Area 3	%	Area 4	%	Area 5	%	Area 6	%	Area 7	%	SUSD	SUSD %
Persons	4392		4436		4427		4385		4467						22107	
Hispanic	3169	72.15	3590	80.93	3252	73.46	3584	81.73	2118	47.41					15713	71.08
NH White	1090	24.82	781	17.61	1023	23.11	640	14.60	1978	44.28					5512	24.93
NH Black	7	0.16	0	0.00	3	0.07	2	0.05	52	1.16					64	0.29
NH Amer. Ind.	20	0.46	14	0.32	10	0.23	2	0.05	19	0.43					65	0.29
NH Asian	94	2.14	40	0.90	111	2.51	144	3.28	290	6.49					679	3.07
NH Other	12	0.27	11	0.25	28	0.63	13	0.30	10	0.22					74	0.33
Total 18+	2771		2932		2924		2877		3195						14699	
18+ Hispanic	1884	67.99	2249	76.71	2024	69.22	2250	78.21	1350	42.25					9757	66.38
NH 18+ White	789	28.47	635	21.66	795	27.19	491	17.07	1562	48.89					4272	29.06
NH 18+ Black	3	0.11	0	0.00	3	0.10	2	0.07	35	1.10					43	0.29
NH 18+ Amer. Ind.	12	0.43	12	0.41	6	0.21	2	0.07	12	0.38					44	0.30
NH 18+ Asian	75	2.71	26	0.89	79	2.70	123	4.28	228	7.14					531	3.61
NH 18+ Other	8	0.29	10	0.34	17	0.58	9	0.31	8	0.25					52	0.35

"NH" = "Not of Hispanic Origin"

Area Deviations (Ideal Area: 4465)

	Area 1	Area 2	Area 3	Area 4	Area 5	Area 6	Area 7
Population	4392	4436	4427	4385	4467		
Deviation	-73	-29	-38	-80	2		
	-1.63%	-0.65%	-0.85%	-1.79%	0.04%		

Table 7. Perez Data as Presented by Perez. Sanger Unified School District, April 19, 1993, Total Population Summary Table (plan 2)

	Total	Hispanic	White	Black	Amindian	asianp
0						
Sum	9115	1487	7071	59	88	403
1						
Sum	4392	3169	1090	7	20	94
2						
Sum	4419	3573	781	0	14	40
3						
Sum	4427	3252	1023	3	10	111
4						
Sum	4444	3613	662	2	2	151
5						
Sum	4462	2112	1978	52	20	290
Totals:						
Sum	31259	17206	12605	123	154	1089

Figure 14. Singer Unified School District, Ybarra Plan

SANGER UNIFIED SCHOOL DISTRICT

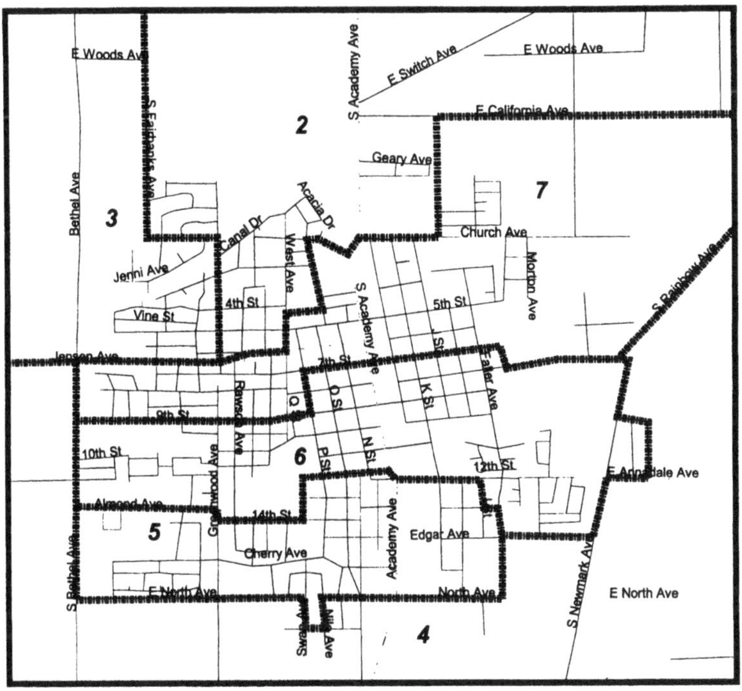

Table 8. Sanger Unified School District, Ybarra District Plan—Consultant's Analysis

	Area 1	%	Area 2	%	Area 3	%	Area 4	%	Area 5	%	Area 6	%	Area 7	%	SUSD	susd %
Persons	4814		4336		4246		4464		4481		4496		4421		31258	
Hispanic	1187	24.66	1076	24.82	1338	31.51	2971	66.55	3582	79.94	3566	79.31	3432	77.63	17152	54.87
NH White	3452	71.71	3009	69.40	2588	60.95	1181	26.46	763	17.03	811	18.04	881	19.93	12685	40.58
NH Black	13	0.27	26	0.60	30	0.71	48	1.08	1	0.02	2	0.04	0	0.00	120	0.38
NH Amer. Ind.	55	1.14	30	0.69	13	0.31	15	0.34	9	0.20	5	0.11	25	0.57	152	0.49
NH Asian	105	2.18	187	4.31	269	6.34	248	5.56	92	2.05	100	2.22	72	1.63	1073	3.43
NH Other	2	0.04	12	0.28	8	0.19	1	0.02	34	0.76	12	0.27	11	0.25	80	0.26
Total 18+	3500		2994		3221		3052		2878		2954		2833		21432	
18+ Hispanic	755	21.57	667	22.28	885	27.48	1848	60.55	2190	76.09	2253	76.27	2052	72.43	10650	49.69
NH 18+ White	2617	74.77	2161	72.18	2092	64.95	954	31.26	588	20.43	622	21.06	700	24.71	9734	45.42
NH 18+ Black	10	0.29	16	0.53	21	0.65	32	1.05	1	0.03	2	0.07	0	0.00	82	0.38
NH 18+ Amer. Ind.	34	0.97	17	0.57	10	0.31	8	0.26	5	0.17	4	0.14	21	0.74	99	0.46
NH 18+ Asian	82	2.34	123	4.11	207	6.43	209	6.85	72	2.50	65	2.20	53	1.87	811	3.78
NH 18+ Other	2	0.06	10	0.33	6	0.19	1	0.03	22	0.76	8	0.27	7	0.25	56	0.26

"NH" = "Not of Hispanic Origin"

Area Deviations (Ideal Area: 4465)

	Area 1	Area 2	Area 3	Area 4	Area 5	Area 6	Area 7
Population	4814	4336	4246	4464	4481	4496	4421
Deviation	349	-129	-219	-1	16	31	-44
	7.82%	-2.89%	-4.90%	-0.02%	0.36%	0.69%	-0.99%

both Perez plans—even perhaps the Ybarra revised alternative—were designed around the needs of particular political candidates rather than the more general aim of advantaging the Latino community.

Were the Latino opportunity districts of the Perez and Ybarra plans more likely to elect Latino representatives than the consultant's plan? On the grounds both of statistical analysis and a review of previous Latino political organization, it seemed most unlikely. Perhaps the needs of particular candidates would have been better served by these plans; but it was the judgment of the school district and the consultant that a districting plan should not revolve around the ambitions of individuals when the interests of the entire community were so clearly at stake.

The results of the first election following the adoption of districts provided some surprises. The nearly 77.77 percent Latino Trustee Area 6 elected an Anglo (Brent D. Hopper) over a Latina (Dalia C. Ontiveros), 58.2 to 41.7 percent. Trustee Area 7, with a Latino population of 72.94 percent elected Latino Eutimio Chapa over incumbent trustee, Bill Collins, 58.0 to 41.9 percent. In predominantly Anglo Area 2, incumbent Bill Daily was unseated by Kathy Keiser, 67.5 to 32.4 percent.

Kings Canyon Unified School District

Just five miles from Dinuba and sharing a common boundary with both Cutler-Orosi School District and Sanger Unified School District, Kings Canyon Unified School District was reported by the 1990 census to have a population of 31,744, of whom 53.1 percent were Latino and 47.64 percent were Latino 18-plus or voting age. Again, the names of Ben Benavides, Gregory Perez and Joaquin Avila were much mentioned at the meeting of the Kings Canyon board, which included only one appointed Latino representative.

The district elected at-large, but with candidates nominated from seven areas. In terms of the 1990 census, several of these areas were widely divergent from the ideal district or "trustee area" population of 4,535.[31] The lines had been drawn with a focus on elementary schools. Two of the existing areas had majority Latino populations: Area 2 with a total Latino population of 60.40 percent (55.73 percent Latino 18-plus) and Area 5 with 81.67 percent Latino population (76.16 percent Latino 18-plus).

Figure 15. Kings Canyon Unified School District, Final Plan

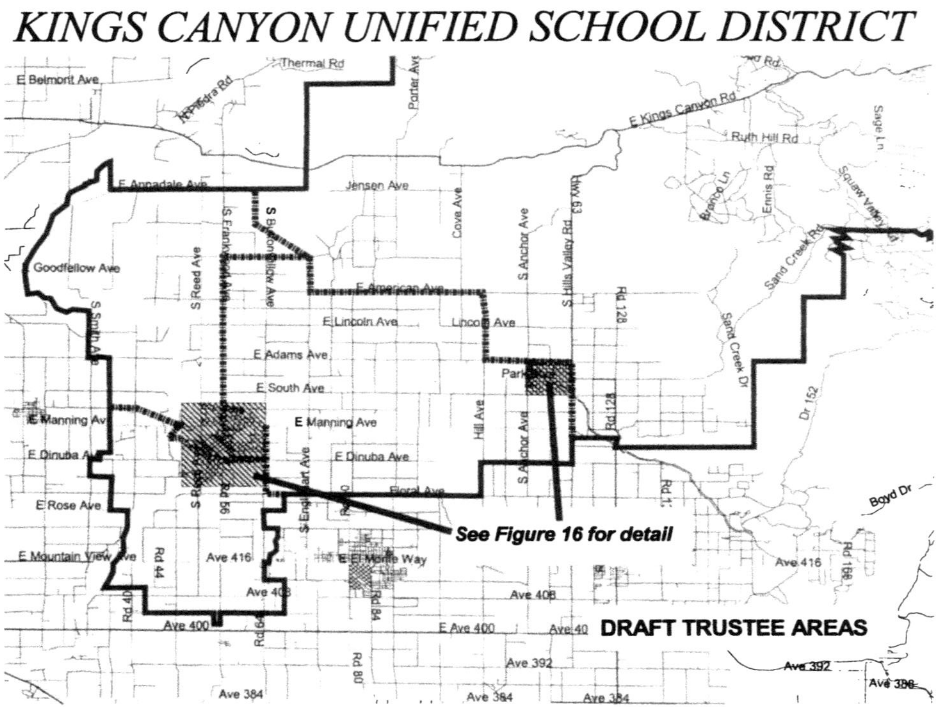

Figure 16. Kings Canyon Unified School District, Inset Map, Final Plan

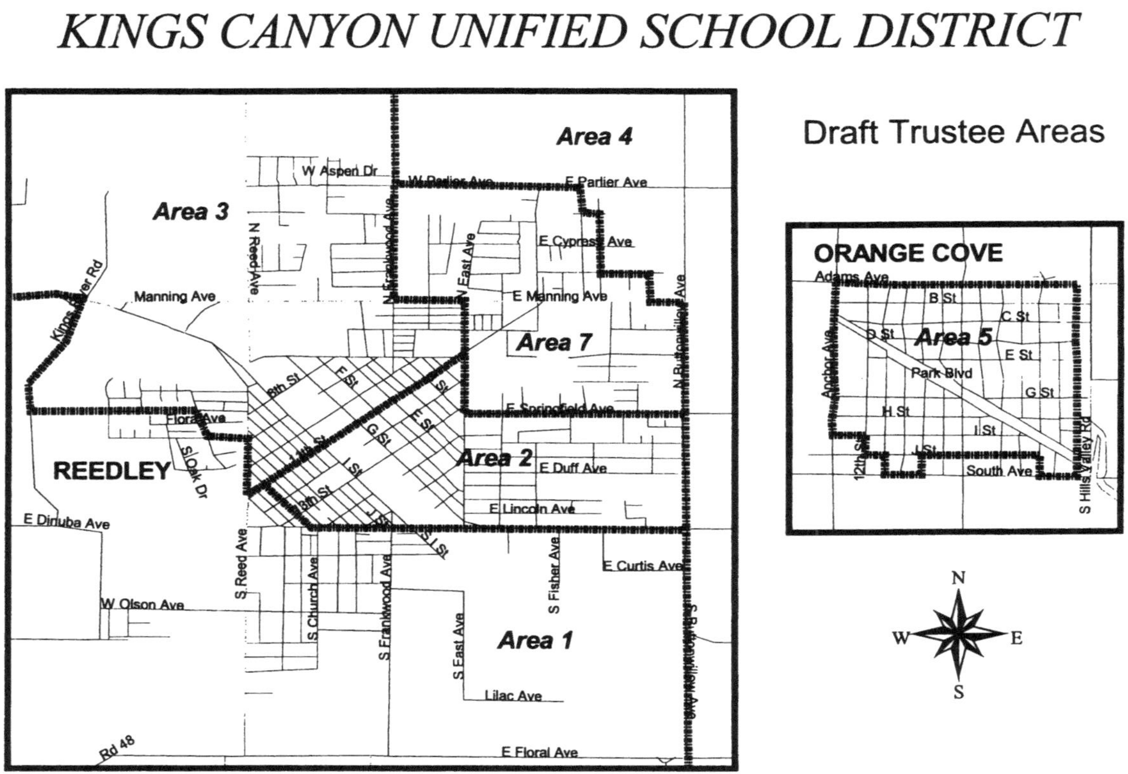

Table 9. Kings County Unified School District Plan

	Area 1	%	Area 2	%	Area 3	%	Area 4	%	Area 5	%	Area 6	%	Area 7	%	KCUSD	%
Persons	4569		4554		4493		4466		4585		4583		4494		31744	
Hispanic	1329	29.09	3484	76.50	1720	38.28	2346	52.53	3948	86.11	799	17.43	3233	71.94	16859	53.11
NH White	2913	63.76	825	18.12	2405	53.53	1876	42.01	485	10.58	3590	78.33	1033	22.99	13097	41.26
NH Black	4	0.09	9	0.20	26	0.58	0	0.00	0	0.00	69	1.51	8	0.18	116	0.37
NH Amer. Ind.	9	0.20	12	0.26	30	0.67	19	0.43	40	0.87	71	1.55	27	0.60	208	0.66
NH Asian	313	6.85	218	4.79	300	6.68	215	4.81	80	1.74	40	0.87	210	4.67	1376	4.33
NH Other	4	0.09	6	0.13	12	0.27	10	0.22	32	0.70	13	0.28	13	0.29	90	0.28
Total 18+	3363		3051		3244		3018		2881		3340		2944		21841	
18+ Hispanic	783	23.28	2176	71.32	1113	34.31	1419	47.02	2362	81.99	462	13.83	2091	71.03	10406	47.64
NH 18+ White	2296	68.27	691	22.65	1840	56.72	1394	46.19	407	14.13	2733	81.83	678	23.03	10039	45.96
NH 18+ Black	2	0.06	6	0.20	21	0.65	0	0.00	0	0.00	51	1.53	6	0.20	86	0.39
NH 18+ Amer. Ind.	9	0.27	11	0.36	19	0.59	9	0.30	26	0.90	55	1.65	13	0.44	142	0.65
NH 18+ Asian	271	8.06	162	5.31	242	7.46	189	6.26	67	2.33	34	1.02	149	5.06	1114	5.10
NH 18+ Other	2	0.06	5	0.16	9	0.28	7	0.23	19	0.66	5	0.15	7	0.24	54	0.25

"NH" = "Not of Hispanic Origin"

Area Deviations (Ideal Area: 4535)

	Area 1	Area 2	Area 3	Area 4	Area 5	Area 6	Area 7
Population	4569	4554	4493	4466	4585	4583	4494
Deviation	34	19	-42	-69	50	48	-41
	0.75%	0.42%	-0.93%	-1.52%	1.10%	1.06%	-0.90%

This writer was engaged as the technical consultant to the Kings Canyon Unified School District and developed a plan for seven single-member districts, each with deviations of less than 2 percent and providing for three strong Latino districts: Area 2 with 76.50 percent total Latino population (71.32 percent Latino 18-plus); Area 5 with a 86.11 percent total Latino population (81.99 percent Latino 18-plus); and Area 7 with 71.94 percent total Latino population (71.03 percent Latino 18-plus). The boundary lines of the plan were quite clean and accorded with both the natural and man-made geography of the area. The plan and data appear as figures 15 and 16 and table 9.

The plan went through with little controversy, in large part because it was widely recognized that District 5 would advantage a leading representative of the Latino community in Orange Cove. Both the Anglo and Latino members of the board greeted the plan with enthusiasm. The plan was adopted and approved by the Committee for School District Reorganization in May of 1993, in time to be used in the November elections. In those elections the only contested areas were Trustee Areas 3 and 4. As expected Trustee Area 3 elected a non-Latino. Trustee Area 4, a transitional area between Orange Cove and Reedley that was 52.53 percent Latino and to which Latino Jim Figueroa had been appointed just prior to approval of the district system, failed to elect him. It elected, instead, Anglo Craig Jacobson with 60.8 percent of the vote.

Kerman Unified School District

Another Fresno County school district, Kerman Unified, lay athwart the road from Dinuba. The 1990 census had reported that, of its 11,792 persons, 53.91 percent were Latino. The census also showed extensive growth in the Latino areas of the district, resulting in deviations from an ideal area population (2,358 persons) of nearly 100 percent.[32] The existing area breakdown provided for only two Latino majority districts, Area 4 with 56.69 percent total Latino population (51.87 Latino 18-plus population) and Area 5 with 68.68 percent Latino total population (64.67 percent Latino 18-plus population). The other three districts ranged from 45.02 percent total Latino through 45.62 percent, to 47.66 percent. Only one Latino had been elected to the district in its history.[33]

The threat of Dinuba-style litigation persuaded the district superintendent, John B. Burns[34] to move toward a single-member district arrangement. Their first step was to ask the Latino community to constitute an advisory committee.

The twelve member, all-Latino advisory committee met with this writer in the Pizza Hut restaurant in Kerman in March of 1993. The tone of the meeting was cordial, and both the Latino representatives and the officials of the district seemed genuinely interested in developing a map that would improve Latino representation.

Unfortunately, the demography of the district did not lend itself to the creation of Latino majority districts. As the plots at figures 17 and 18 suggest, the Latino population of the District was quite widely dispersed with relatively few concentrations; moreover, (an irony that can be frequently noticed in areas of similar demography) the areas of concentration included disproportionate numbers of non-citizens, while voting Latinos were more widely scattered throughout the jurisdiction.

In November of 1993, this writer produced two draft districting plans. Plan 1 provided for three majority Latino districts: Area 2 with 69.81 percent Latino total population (66.55 percent Latino 18-plus); Area 4 with 54.09 percent total Latino population (49.24 percent Latino 18-plus); and Area 5 with 61.78 percent total Latino population (57.41 percent Latino 18-plus). Given the large numbers of non-citizens in the Kerman area, however, only Area 2 could be said to be at all likely to produce a Latino representative. Plan 1 appears as figure 19 and table 10.

The consultant's Plan 2 provided for only two majority Latino districts: Area 2 with 69.81 percent total Latino population (66.55 percent Latino 18-plus); and Area 5 with 64.58 percent Latino (61.14 percent Latino 18-plus). The contrast between the two plans was essentially between Plan 2's enhancement of the immediate likelihood of electing two Latinos and Plan 1's longer-term prospect of building the organization necessary to elect three Latino representatives. Plan 2 appears as figure 20 and table 11.

In an atmosphere of good will on both sides, Kerman Unified School District's Trustees chose to implement Plan 1 at their December 1993 meeting.

Figure 17. Kerman Unified School District, plot of Hispanic Population

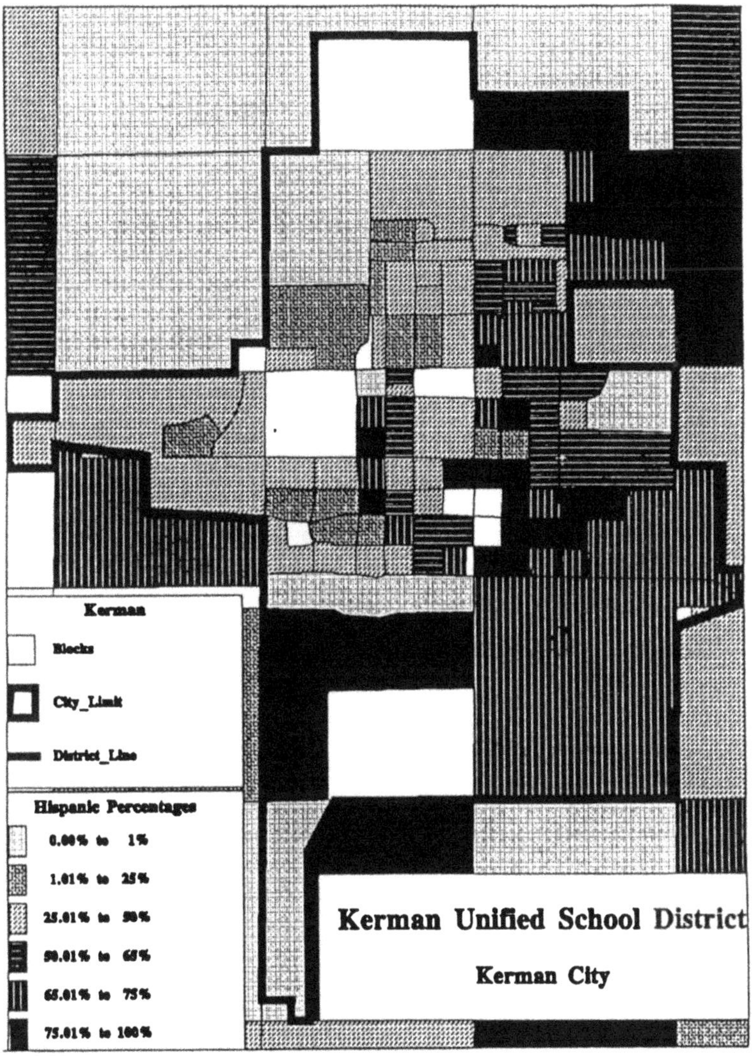

Figure 18. Kerman Unified School District, Hispanic Voting Age Population

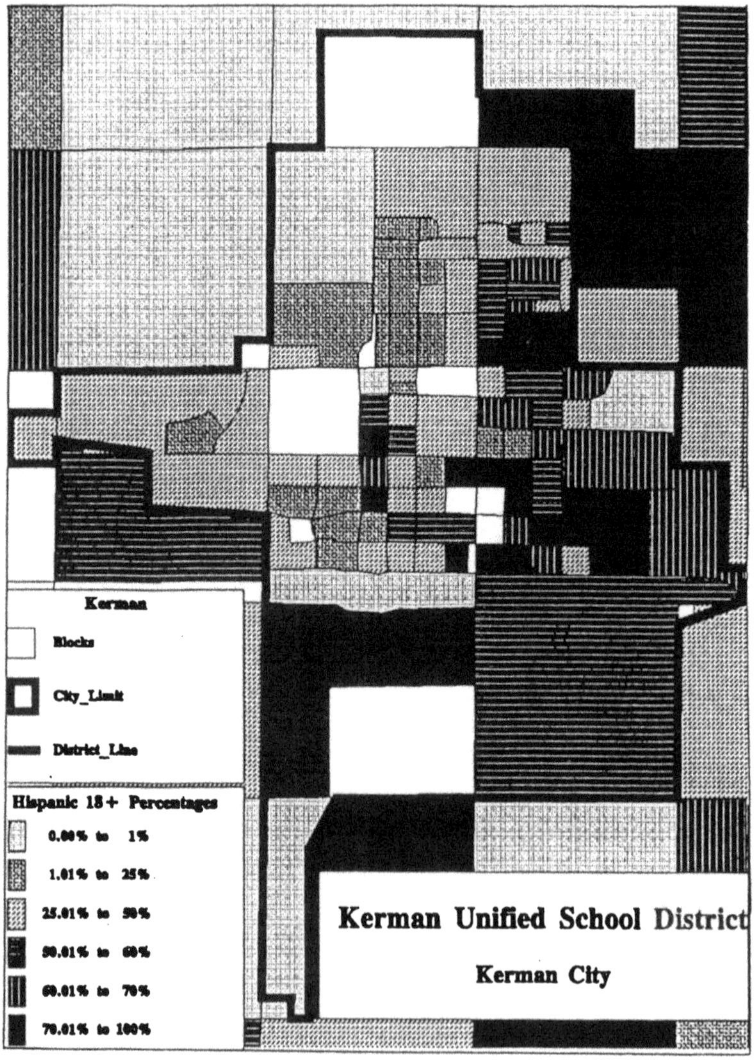

Figure 19. Kerman Unified School District, Plan 1

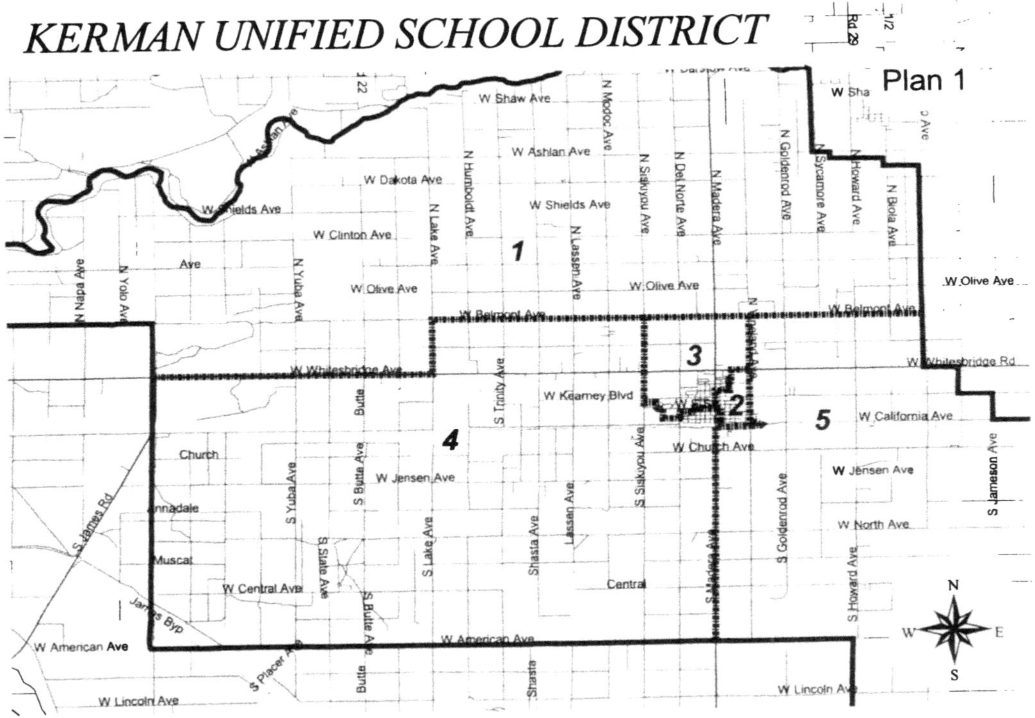

Table 10. Kerman Unified School District, Plan 1

	Area 1	%	Area 2	%	Area 3	%	Area 4	%	Area 5	%	Totals	%
Persons	2,352		2,355		2,381		2,383		2,321		11,792	
Hispanic	1,080	45.92	1,644	69.81	910	38.22	1,289	54.09	1,434	61.78	6,357	53.91
NH White	1,180	50.17	528	22.42	1,337	56.15	1,033	43.35	854	36.79	4,932	41.82
NH Black	1	0.04	2	0.08	8	0.34	2	0.08	5	0.22	18	0.15
NH Amer. Ind.	6	0.26	7	0.30	15	0.63	9	0.38	4	0.17	41	0.35
NH Asian	73	3.10	172	7.30	108	4.54	44	1.85	18	0.78	415	3.52
NH Other	13	0.55	2	0.08	3	0.13	5	0.21	6	0.26	29	0.25
Total 18+	1,679		1,423		1,610		1,574		1,538		7,824	
18+ Hispanic	703	41.87	947	66.55	530	32.92	775	49.24	883	57.41	3,838	49.05
NH 18+ White	921	54.85	366	25.72	982	60.99	761	48.35	631	41.03	3,661	46.79
NH 18+ Black	1	0.06	2	0.14	5	0.31	2	0.13	2	0.13	12	0.15
NH 18+ Amer. Ind.	5	0.30	4	0.28	14	0.87	5	0.32	2	0.13	30	0.38
NH 18+ Asian	42	2.50	103	7.24	77	4.78	28	1.78	14	0.91	264	3.37
NH 18+ Other	7	0.42	1	0.07	2	0.12	3	0.19	6	0.39	19	0.24

"NH" = "Not of Hispanic Origin"

Area Deviations (Ideal Area: 2358)

	Area 1	Area 2	Area 3	Area 4	Area 5
Population	2,352	2,355	2,381	2,383	2,321
Deviation	-6	-3	23	25	-37
	-0.27%	-0.14%	0.96%	1.04%	-1.59%

Figure 20. Kerman Unified School District, Plan 2

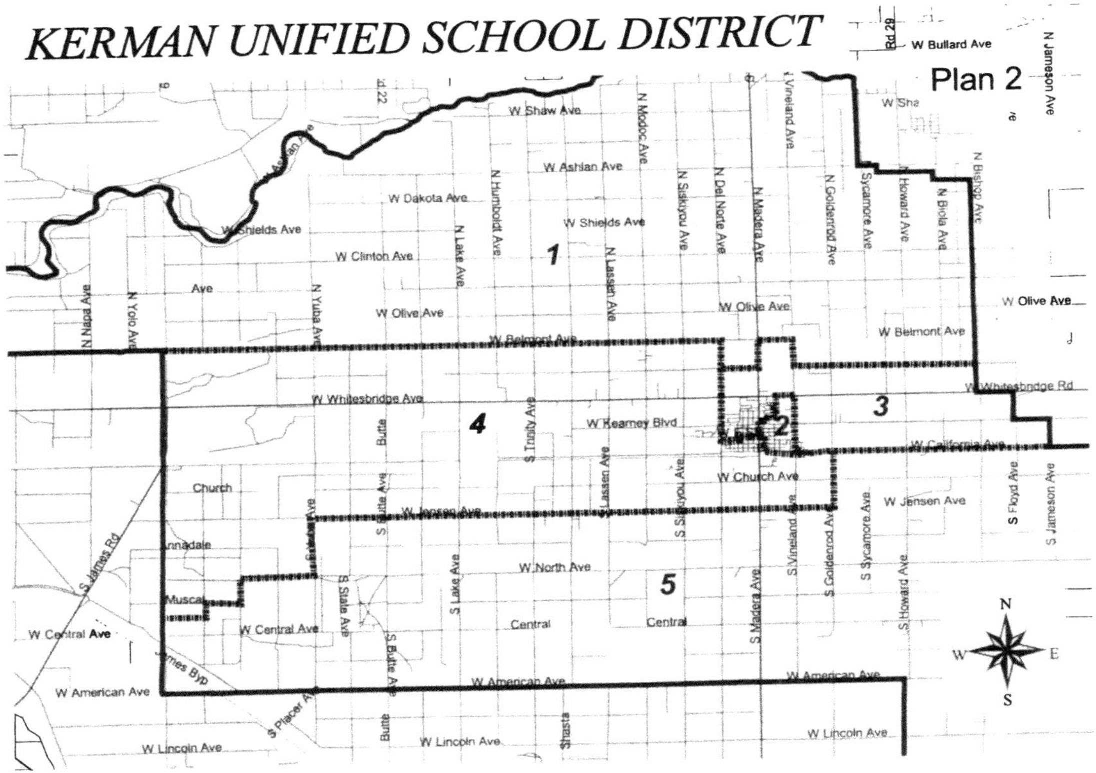

Table 11. Kerman Unified School District, Plan 2

	Area 1	%	Area 2	%	Area 3	%	Area 4	%	Area 5	%	Totals	%
Persons	2,336		2,355		2,390		2,365		2,346		11,792	
Hispanic	1047	44.82	1,644	69.81	1,001	41.88	1,150	48.63	1,515	64.58	6,357	53.91
NH White	1,198	51.28	528	22.42	1,265	52.93	1,148	48.54	793	33.80	4,932	41.82
NH Black	1	0.04	2	0.08	8	0.33	2	0.08	5	0.21	18	0.15
NH Amer. Ind.	5	0.21	7	0.30	14	0.59	11	0.47	4	0.17	41	0.35
NH Asian	73	3.13	172	7.30	98	4.10	48	2.03	24	1.02	415	3.52
NH Other	13	0.56	2	0.08	4	0.17	6	0.25	4	0.17	29	0.25
Total 18+	1,668		1,423		1,658		1,562		1,513		7,824	
18+ Hispanic	680	40.77	947	66.55	608	36.67	678	43.41	925	61.14	3,838	49.05
NH 18+ White	934	56.00	366	25.72	960	57.90	841	53.84	560	37.01	3,661	46.79
NH 18+ Black	1	0.06	2	0.14	5	0.30	2	0.13	2	0.13	12	0.15
NH 18+ Amer. Ind.	4	0.24	4	0.28	12	0.72	7	0.45	3	0.20	30	0.38
NH 18+ Asian	42	2.52	103	7.24	70	4.22	30	1.92	19	1.26	264	3.37
NH 18+ Other	7	0.42	1	0.07	3	0.18	4	0.26	4	0.26	19	0.24

"NH" = "Not of Hispanic Origin"

Area Deviations (Ideal Area: 2358)

	Area 1	Area 2	Area 3	Area 4	Area 5
Population	2,336	2,355	2,390	2,365	2,346
Deviation	-22	-3	32	7	-12
	-0.95%	-0.14%	1.34%	0.28%	-0.53%

School District Analysis Project

In the spring of 1994, this writer, working with a voting rights attorney, performed analyses of a dozen more Fresno County school districts that wished to determine if they were vulnerable under Section 2 of the Voting Rights Act. Of these districts, the smallest was comprised of 666 total persons, with a Latino population of 51.50 percent, and the largest was comprised of 13,744 persons with a 40.69 percent Latino population and a 16.94 percent African American population. Only two of these jurisdictions moved to single-member districts, both as a result of the decision to unify. But by virtue of the unification process, several elementary schools in the original study were absorbed into district systems. Riverdale Joint Union High School District made the decision to unify in May of 1994, after reviewing the demographic study of the district provided by this writer. The District, with a total population of 7,487 and a Latino population of 4,143 (55.34 percent), chose to move to a seven-district system. Three of the seven districts were solidly Latino: Area E with 79.47 percent Latino population and 77.22 percent Latino 18-plus population; Area F with 78.81 percent Latino population and 76.56 percent Latino 18-plus population; and Area G with 89.91 percent Latino population and 88.21 percent Latino 18-plus population. A fourth district, Area D had a Latino population of 54.01 percent but fell to 49.93 percent Latino 18-plus. The remaining three districts had Latino populations of 30.18 percent, 28.15 percent and 28.37 percent. The map and data for this plan appear as figure 21 and table 12. Because a small portion of Kings County (one of four Section 5 preclearance Counties in California) was contained within the District,[35] the whole plan had to be submitted to the Justice Department for preclearance. Both the districting plan and the unification plan were submitted to the Justice Department in July of 1994 and were precleared without incident.

Caruthers Union High School District also chose to unify and to create four trustee areas roughly based on the elementary schools contained within the district: the district containing Alvina Elementary is 46.7 Latino (42.4 percent Latino 18-plus) and elects one trustee; the district containing Monroe Elementary is 53.8 percent Latino (48.2 percent Latino 18-plus) and elects one trustee; the district containing Raisin City Elementary School is 58.7 percent Latino (53.1 percent Latino 18-plus) and elects one trustee; and the area containing

Figure 21. Riverdale Unified School District, Final Plan

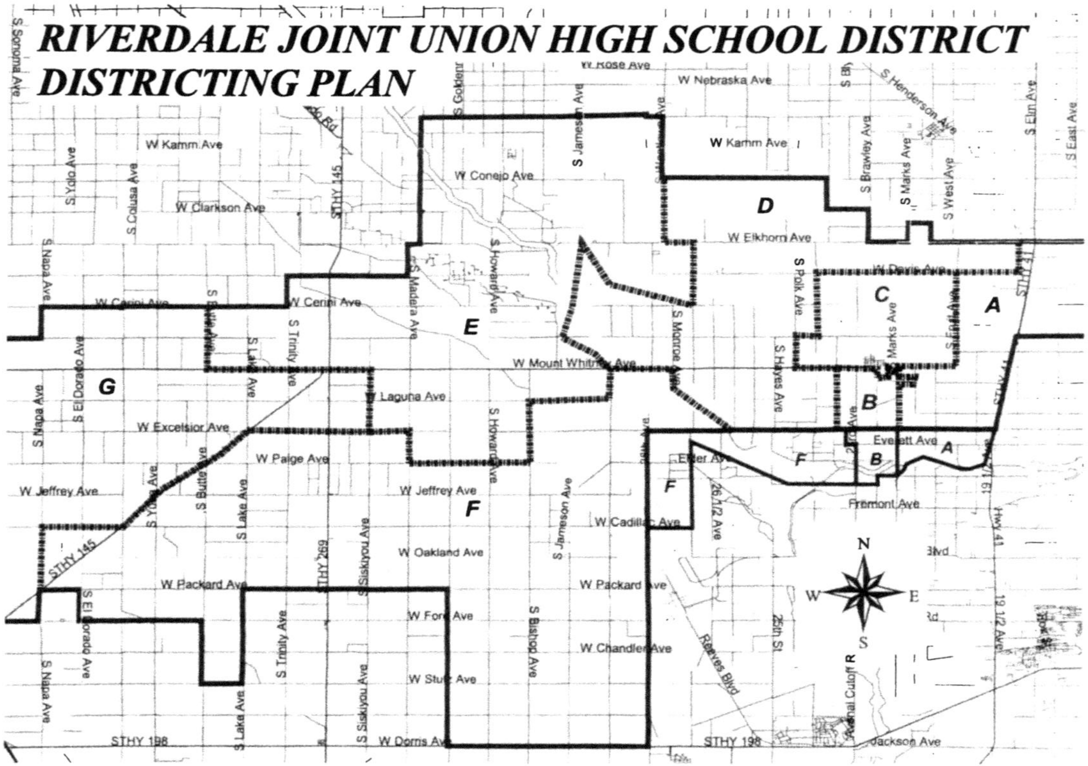

Table 12. Riverdale Unified School District, Final Plan

	Area A	%	Area B	%	Area C	%	Area D	%	Area E	%	Area F	%	Area G	%	Totals	%
Persons	1100		1087		1054		1085		1018		1043		1100		7487	
Hispanic	332	30.18	306	28.15	299	28.37	586	54.01	809	79.47	822	78.81	989	89.91	4143	55.34
NH White	711	64.64	723	66.51	739	70.11	313	28.85	172	16.90	213	20.42	110	10.00	2981	39.82
NH Black	22	2.00	28	2.58	1	0.09	160	14.75	1	0.10	8	0.77	1	0.09	221	2.95
NH Amer. Ind.	12	1.09	2	0.18	8	0.76	6	0.55	0	0.00	1	0.10	0	0.00	29	0.39
NH Asian	15	1.36	25	2.30	7	0.66	19	1.75	21	2.06	0	0.00	2	0.18	89	1.19
NH Other	8	0.73	3	0.28	0	0.00	1	0.09	15	1.47	0	0.00	0	0.00	27	0.36
Total 18+	731		747		744		715		663		640		721		4961	
18+ Hispanic	185	25.31	177	23.69	178	23.92	357	49.93	512	77.22	490	76.56	636	88.21	2535	51.10
NH 18+ White	508	69.49	529	70.82	556	74.73	231	32.31	120	18.10	145	22.66	82	11.37	2171	43.76
NH 18+ Black	13	1.78	18	2.41	0	0	108	15.10	1	0.15	4	0.63	1	0.14	145	2.92
NH 18+ Amer. Ind.	10	1.37	2	0.27	6	0.81	5	0.70	0	0.00	1	0.16	0	0.00	24	0.48
NH 18+ Asian	12	1.64	18	2.41	4	0.54	13	1.82	20	3.02	0	0.00	2	0.28	69	1.39
NH 18+ Other	3	0.41	3	0.40	0	0.00	1	0.14	10	1.51	0	0.00	0	0.00	17	0.34

"NH" = "Not of Hispanic Origin"

Area Deviations (Ideal Area: 1070)

	Area A	Area B	Area C	Area D	Area E	Area F	Area G
Population	1100	1087	1054	1085	1018	1043	1100
Deviation	30	17	-16	15	-52	-27	30
	2.80%	1.59%	-1.50%	1.40%	-4.86%	-2.52%	2.80%

Caruthers Elementary School District is 40.6 percent Latino (36.2 percent Latino 18-plus) and elects four trustees. This plan was adopted in December 1996. An election had not been held in these districts as of this writing.

CONCLUSION

The aftermath of Dinuba continued for several years. As these cases suggest, Dinuba left in its wake a score of troubled jurisdictions, each scanning the horizon for possible voting rights challenges, each expending public funds to move one or more steps toward districts. All of this turmoil and alarm resulted in few actual districtings. One reason, in this writer's view, is that the *Shaw* decision was misunderstood, both by potential plaintiffs and potential defendants. Potential defendants, such as the Tulare jurisdictions, felt much less threatened after *Shaw*. The demographics showed that only an extreme reach for Latino voters could guarantee a majority-minority district. Not feeling pressed, officials took additional time to study the issue and ultimately let the voters decide. Potential plaintiffs who had been encouraged by Joaquin Avila and other Latino activists had difficulty (again based on demographics) finding any clear Section 2 violations. There would still be an occasional plum, like the next case study, Hanford. But Hanford was serendipitous: under normal circumstances it never could have been considered ripe for a voting rights challenge and as it turned out, it was to be Joaquin Avila's last major case.[36]

For those jurisdictions that did move to districts the electoral results have been only mixed, proving once again that it takes more than a move to districts to create viable minority candidacies.

NOTES

1. Avila was joined by co-counsels, the Lawyers' Committee for Urban Affairs of San Francisco, and also by McCutchen, Doyle, Brown and Enerson. The Lawyers' Committee newsletter, commenting on the case, noted: "Unlike the South, where minority communities have successfully used the Voting Rights Act of 1965 to gain access to the political process, many minorities in California continue to be shut out of the electoral process as the result of discriminatory electoral practices. In a state where minorities make up nearly half of the population, relatively few minority members have been elected to public office. Of the almost 3000 elected representatives on California city councils, county boards, the state legislature, and other public offices, less than

one-tenth of those offices are held by minorities. See *Lawyer's Committee News*, Fall 1991, Volume 4, Number 3, 1.

2. *Reyes v. City of Dinuba.*

3. Later, after researching the issue, the City retreated from its commitment to hold an election to obtain voter certification of the districts. The City's new position was that, since the State Elections Code provides for five-member city councils, either elected at-large or by single-member districts, no conflict with state law was involved. The fact is that because registered voters choose, at incorporation, their city's form of representation, only registered voters (by election) can change it.

4. See "Council to OK Districts Tuesday," *The Dinuba Sentinel*, May 20, 1993, 3.

5. See "Council Rejects $817,654 Claim," *The Dinuba Sentinel*, August 26, 1993, 1.

6. Mark Grossi, "Valley cities forced to take notice of voting rights lawyer," *The Fresno Bee*, August 30, 1992, sec. B, 1.

7. Ibid.

8. See Lewis Griswold, "Fear of Lawsuits Motivates Council to Recommend District Elections," *Visalia Times Delta*, May 1, 1993. The article notes that the desire by racial and ethnic minorities for better political representation may be driving a trend toward single-member districts elsewhere in California, "But it's the desire to avoid a lawsuit that has apparently prompted Visalia's steps in the same direction."

9. Indeed, all but two members of the Task Force seemed to have been committed to the district concept almost from the start.

10. Representative testimony before the Task Force was that of Councilman Basil Perch, who said he believed it inevitable that Visalia, with a 25 percent Hispanic population but no Hispanic council members, would become the target of a lawsuit. "I don't want to spend taxpayers money that way," Perch said, "We should be big enough to run in districts." See Lewis Griswold, "Fear of lawsuits motivates council to recommend district elections," *Visalia Times Delta*, May 1, 1993, sec. 1C.

11. See Lewis Griswold, "Council defends district positions," *Visalia Times Delta*, November 2, 1993. "Two of you supported, one of you is wavering and two don't support it," said Cameron Davis, Chairman of the Task Force that recommended the district elections measure voters will consider today. "You agreed to support it. What happened?"

12. See Letisia Martinez, "District elections: divisive or beneficial?" *Visalia Times Delta*, November 1, 1993, sec. 1B. "Officials say north Visalia residents tend to cast fewer ballots than residents of other Visalia

neighborhoods. Low citizenship rates and education levels and higher poverty rates have contributed to dismal turnouts among minorities in that community. . . . some supporters of district elections say the measure has not received much attention, making it difficult for people to generate opinions, much less enthusiasm for voting. In part that might be because even its supporters have done little to campaign for Measure C. Even though Hispanic leaders said district elections are needed to help Visalia elect its first Hispanic council member, they issued no news releases, called no news conferences, staged no public forums and ran no advertisements for Measure C."

13. Ibid. "I don't think that the redistricting issue should be construed as something that will benefit a certain ethnic group in this community," said Reyes Laragoza, a member of the Task Force that recommended district elections. "It's a measure that will benefit everyone in this community." Manual Garcia, a Visalia dentist, said Hispanic organizations probably did not campaign for districts because they did not want Measure C to be perceived as an "ethnic issue." "I think it would have been more beneficial if non-minorities were involved in a campaign," Garcia said.

14. In the same election, Merced voters also rejected a measure to move from at-large to voting districts.

15. The cases of two other Central Valley cities, Hanford and Corcoran are treated in individual chapters.

16. Legislation allowing hospital districts to create multi-member districts and to create districts by a vote of the Board was pending in the State Legislature. Ultimately, the Legislature rejected the multi-member district concept, rendering this plan obsolete.

17. Florence Adams, Claremont, to Ms Anne M. Larson, Director, Community Relations and Development, Tulare District Hospital, Tulare, July 16, 1993.

18. Craig Moyle, "Hospital puts district voting on ballot," *Tulare Advance-Register*, June 23, 1994.

19. Jama Ballinger, "Tulare voting-district measures draw yawns," Tulare Advance-Register, November 7, 1994.

20. See "Yes, No on At-large Elections in Sanger," *The Fresno Bee*, October 28, 1991.

21. Merry Henry, the trustee from the Centerville area was a homemaker and mother of children who had gone through the system; June Heinrichs, another mother of children who had gone through the system lived in a predominantly working class Hispanic area in Sanger; Charles Johnson, a retired school principal, was a resident of a primarily Anglo area of the City of Sanger; Walter Cucuk, an agribusiness man, represented the Lone Star and

John Wash area; Jim Daily, a service technician, represented the Fairmont area; Roland Nelson, without fixed employment at the time, represented the Del Rey area; and Bill Collins, a former school administrator was a resident of a mixed Anglo/Hispanic area of Sanger.

22. See especially the article "Sanger School Board Aims for District Elections," *The Fresno Bee*, April 26, 1992. Merry Henry, the chair of the trustee board, claimed to be unaware that MAPA was on the brink of filing a lawsuit. District superintendent, Bob Jones, also claimed that the threat of litigation "was not the impetus to change." He did admit, however: "But that's always a likelihood and a reasonably prudent man could see that it was a distinct possibility." Merry Henry also admitted: "We are doing it to comply with the Voting Rights Act and to make sure all the voters' rights are protected."

23. The Board was represented by Marguerite Mary Leoni of Nielsen, Merksamer, Parrinello and Naylor.

24. See "Report on the Redistricting of Sanger Unified School District," submitted by Gregory M. Perez with assistance provided by Robert Quiroz, April 9, 1993. Perez claimed that under his proposed plan, "the Latino community . . . will have a substantially better opportunity to participate in the political process and to either elect candidates of their choice or to have an influence in determining the outcome of given elections."

25. The exact percentage of Hispanic 18-plus, according to the 1990 census, was 49.69 percent; but the presence of many non-citizens in that population meant that the percentage of eligible Hispanics was much less.

26. The consultant had agreed to analyze plans and suggestions provided by citizens.

27. The Del Rey Area was approximately 80 percent Hispanic in population.

28. Tanis Ybarra, Roy Mendoza and Alonso Gomez, Sanger, to Florence Adams, Claremont, March 27, 1993.

29. Ibid. Ybarra commented: We know that this would create at least two major Hispanic districts. This would also provide us with the opportunity to see how the other two districts within the Sanger city limits would look like. We know that one district would be very low Hispanic and the other might be a district that we could work with."

30. Del Rey was under-populated by nearly 2,400 persons. See Florence Adams, Claremont, to Mr. Tanis Ybarra, Mr. Roy Mendoza and Mr. Alonso Gomez, Sanger, April 12, 1993.

31. Thus, Area 2, as it existed in 1993, had a positive deviation of 127.67 percent from the ideal area population.

32. The district had been divided using parallel lines, with election at-large, but with candidates resident in each of five areas. In terms of 1990 populations, Area 1 had a negative deviation of 61.29 percent; Area 2 a negative deviation 63.20 percent; Area 3, a positive deviation 54.98 percent; Area 4, a positive deviation of 97.08 percent; and Area 5, a negative deviation of 27.58 percent.

33. Interestingly, the City of Kerman had a much better record of electing Hispanics and, at the time of the districting was represented by a Latino mayor, Trinidad Rodriguez.

34. Assisted by Daniel K. Fischle, the deputy superintendent, and Lloyd Wamhof, the administrator of state and federal programs.

35. The Kings County portion of Riverdale Joint Union High School District, excluding the Lemoore Naval Air Station census block, is 386 persons, 93 of whom are persons of Hispanic origin.

36. See Carla Hall, "4 of 21 MacArthur Grants Go to Californians," *Los Angeles Times*, June 18, 1996, sec. A3. According to Avila, the MacArthur Grant was most welcome as he had not been paid a legal fee since 1994.

CHAPTER 5

The Justice Department as a Player: Hanford, California

This chapter provides an account of the involvement of a California City with the Voting Rights Act as applied by the U.S. Department of Justice in the period 1992-94. It is the story of a small jurisdiction that found itself ill-equipped to deal with the powerful Justice Department. The outcome was a forced agreement by the City to replace its at-large electoral arrangements with single-member districts.

The City of Hanford (1990 population of 33,327) is the largest City in Kings County (1990 population of 107,500). In the 1992 elections, 13,745 voters were registered in Hanford. Located in the Central Valley, Hanford, like those jurisdictions mentioned in the previous chapter and like many others in the general area, had experienced an increase in its Latino population between 1980 and 1990. Unlike those jurisdictions, however, Hanford, by virtue of being located in Kings County, fell under the jurisdiction of Section 5 of the Voting Rights Act.

Kings County had come under the "triggering" provisions of the Voting Rights Act in September of 1975, retroactive to November 1, 1972. The circumstance that triggered the application was the expanded coverage of the 1975 extension of the Voting Rights Act to include language minorities (Alaskan natives, Asian Americans, persons of Spanish origin and native Americans). Under Title II of the expansion, a jurisdiction (1) that had more than five percent of voting age citizens that belonged to a single language minority group; (2) in which less than half the voting age citizens cast votes in the 1972 presidential election; and (3) in which the election was only conducted in English was subject to coverage, as were jurisdictions that maintained a test or device that inhibited voting. Kings County met the first and third criteria and, furthermore, in 1972, of 40,002 voting age persons in the County,[1] only 19,545 or (48.86 percent) voted in the 1972 presidential election.[2] Although such circumstances in the Southern United States might argue for the existence of formal or informal mechanisms of discrimination, it is highly questionable that discrimination explains any substantial part of the difference between eligible voter numbers and the actual vote. Rather, the explanation is to be found in the presence within Kings County of a large armed services base, Lemoore Naval Air Station, that housed approximately 2,817 persons on the base itself[3] and likely many more in surrounding housing. A huge majority of service men, including many previous California taxpayers, register out-of-state in order to escape the California income tax.

It appears, however, that Kings County and its municipalities were not much affected by the application of the Voting Rights Act during the 1970s and 1980s. Although the state legislative and Congressional redistrictings that affected Kings County in the 1970s and 1980s were reported for preclearance to the U.S. Department of Justice, Kings County and its municipalities apparently made no official submissions during those years. In fact, in interviews conducted by this writer, city officials of the City of Hanford claim that they were never informed by the County of reporting requirements; and, a formal Declaration by Mr. Michael Noland, city attorney for the City of Hanford supports this contention. Mr. Noland says:

> In about early summer of 1992, I received a telephone call from Kings County Counsel, Mr. Denis Eymil, informing me that the City of Hanford was subject to Section 5 of the federal Voting Rights Act. He suggested I meet with him and members of his staff so that they could provide me with additional information regarding Section 5. . . . At the meeting Mr. Eymil stated that Kings County, and hence all jurisdictions in the County including the City of Hanford, had been subject to Section 5 since September 23, 1975, retroactive to November 1, 1972. Mr. Eymil further informed me that changes made by the City which affect voting had to be precleared by the federal District Court in Washington, D.C., or the United States Department of Justice before they could be implemented. Mr. Eymil then specifically mentioned to me that the annexations of territory

> that had been accomplished by the City since November 1, 1972 may be the types of changes which required preclearance.[4]

Thus, in October of 1992, the City of Hanford submitted a request for preclearance to the U.S. Department of Justice for 72 annexations made to the City since November 1, 1972. The acting assistant attorney general of the Civil Rights Division in the U.S. Department of Justice wrote to the City in April of 1993 refusing preclearance for all inhabited annexations that had been enacted by the City in the period since that date. The letter stated:

> Because the City failed to seek preclearance of the annexations . . . in a timely manner upon their adoption, we must review the cumulative effect of the annexations at this time. . . . Based on the data available to us, the city's population, excluding the persons residing in the annexed areas [i.e. those denied preclearance] is 16,224, of whom 5,831 (35.9 percent) are Hispanic. The annexations . . . add approximately 14,977 persons as city residents, only 3,346 of whom (22 percent) are Hispanic. Thus, the effect of these annexations is to decrease the Hispanic proportion of the city's pre-annexation population by approximately 6.5 percentage points, from 35.9 percent to 25.4 percent.[5]

Thus, the first charge against Hanford was that its annexations diluted Latino population: areas with more Anglo residents than the pre-existing City's norm had resulted in reducing the overall percentage of Latino population.

The second charge was that the annexations, together with its at-large election system, had undermined the political effectiveness of Latino voters. In the same letter, the assistant attorney general noted:

> Our analysis of the information available to us suggests that Hispanic voters have preferred Hispanic candidates in recent elections, but have been unable to elect those candidates due to an apparent pattern of polarized voting. In these circumstances [i.e. at-large elections with a plurality win requirement] the reduction in the Hispanic share of the city's population, as effected by the residential annexations, which have been implemented in past elections, appears to have diminished whatever opportunity would exist for Hispanic voters in

> the pre-annexation city to elect representatives of their choice to the City Council.[6]

The letter concluded that, until the City had acted to obtain pre-clearance, the annexations would be invalid and the participation of the inhabitants of the annexations in the political life of the city would be prohibited: "Municipal residents of areas annexed after Section 5 coverage date may not participate in municipal elections unless and until the annexations receive Section 5 preclearance."[7]

How could the City obtain pre-clearance? Would it be obliged to dis-annex the offending territory? The assistant attorney general suggested a deal: if Hanford would scrap its at-large electoral arrangements and replace them with single member districts, then the difficulty would disappear and the annexations would be pre-cleared. The letter went on:

> Annexations that result, as here, in a significant decrease in the minority proportion of a city's population have such a proscribed effect, and, therefore, may satisfy Section 5 only if the method used for electing the city's governing body "fairly reflects the strength of the [minority] community as it exists after the annexation," City of Richmond v. United States, 422 U.S. 358, 370-71 (1975). . . . [8]

By modern standards, Hanford is far from any sophisticated metropolitan ideal: its city staff is small and its understanding of Census data is quite limited. Unsurprisingly Hanford's submission to the U.S. Department of Justice was found to be in substantial error. What is significant to note, however, is that the errors were not in favor of Hanford's position at all: this writer, the City's demographer, retained in the wake of the rejection of the annexations by the Justice Department, proved that the Latino percentage of the annexed areas was significantly *higher* than the City's own submission and that the difference between the Latino percentage of the annexed areas and that of the pre-annexation city was smaller than the City had submitted. The difference between the City's submission and the true and corrected submission is shown in table 13. See also figure 22 for a map of the pre-annexation and post-annexation City.

The City had retained one of California's leading voting rights attorneys, Marguerite M. Leoni of Nielsen, Merksamer, Parrinello, Mueller and Naylor, to resubmit its annexations for preclearance. A

Table 13. Hanford, California—The Difference Between the City's Original Submission and the Consultant's Analysis

City's Original Submission as Analyzed by the Attorney General

	Total	Hispanic	Hisp. %
City Pop. Total 1990 Census	31,201	9,177	29.40
Annexations	14,977	3,346	22.00
City Excluding Annexations	16,224	5,831	35.90

Decrease in Hispanic Proportion of Population: 6.5%

Request for Reconsideration Submission

	Total	Hispanic	Hisp. %
City Pop. Total 1990 Census	30,897	9,131	29.55
Annexations	10,021	2,356	23.51
City Excluding Annexations	20,876	6,775	32.45

Decrease in Hispanic Proportion of Population: 2.9%

Figure 22. Pre- and Post-Annexation Hanford

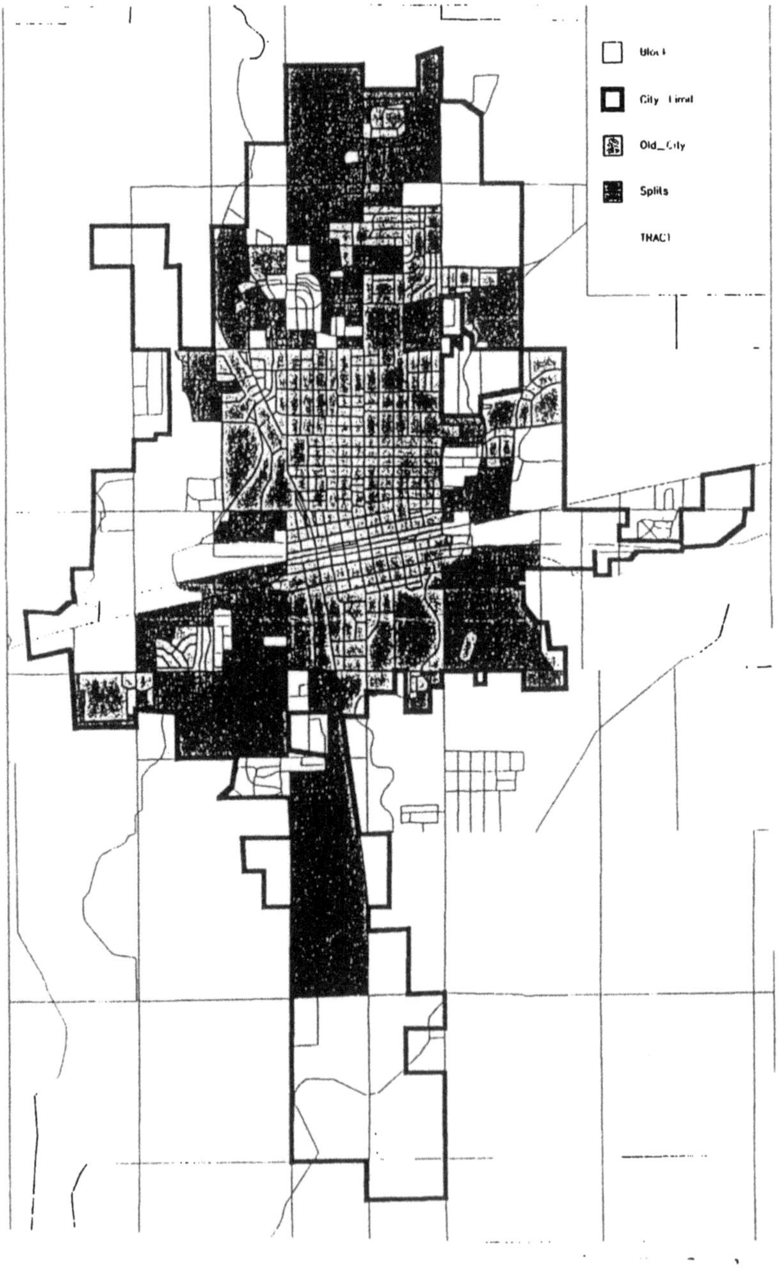

substantial effort (including very considerable costs) was invested by the City in preparing the legal and demographic materials. In August of 1993, the City sent off its Request for Reconsideration to the Department of Justice. The City based its case on several grounds. The first was that there had been substantial errors, resulting from the City's "inexperience" in making preclearance submissions and the complexity of compiling accurate demographic data. Second and more important was the claim that Hanford annexations were free of discriminatory purpose or effect. Third was the claim that the small difference between the Latino portion of the total post-annexation population of the City and of the pre-annexation city had been eliminated by Latino population growth. And, finally, there was an assertion that the electoral successes of Latino candidates afforded a proof that Hanford's post-annexation electoral system fully reflected the voting strength of its Latino citizens.

To prove the non-discriminatory purpose and effect of the annexations, the City adduced several arguments. They showed that only 14 of the 57 annexations in dispute had more than 10 residents at the time of annexation; indeed, only four of the annexations had more than 50 persons at the time of annexation. Second, the City showed that most of the annexations had a Latino population percentage that was significantly *greater* than the Latino population percentage of the City when the annexation took place: indeed, only one of the four annexations with more than 50 residents had a Latino percentage less than that of the City at the time (see table 14). In view of these facts, the City protested that it was wholly inappropriate to charge the City with selective annexation of low minority areas with the purpose of diluting minority voting strength in the City.

Turning to the issue of whether the annexations had reduced Latino voting strength, the City argued that the Latino population of King's County had been growing faster than the Anglo population throughout the period of the annexations. Using information from the California State Department of Finance and combining it with the City Planning Department's data on housing units, the City sought to show that Latino population differentials between the pre-annexation city and the post annexation city had steadily been eroded. The City claimed that the differential had been "essentially eliminated" and that "any differential that may exist is *de minimis* and insignificant."[9] The City then extended the argument from Latino population to persons eligible to vote within that population: an analysis of Latino eligibles (i.e., citizens who are 18

Table 14. Hanford, California—Annexations With More Than 50 Residents

Date	Annexation No.	Total Pop. at Time of Annexation	Total Hispanic Pop. at Time of Annexation	% Hispanic at Time of Annexation	% Hispanic in City
11/3/72	18	12	4	33.33%	1970 Census
9/24/73	21	288	102	35.42%	22.78%
9/10/73	22	140	53	37.86%	
7/23/74	30	200	71	35.50%	
10/9/73	31	13	5	38.46%	
11/26/74	36	170	31	18.24%	
11/26/74	37	33	12	36.36%	
9/24/74	38	40	3	7.50%	
5/19/80	80	13	5	38.46%	1980 Census
10/7/86	90	16	1	6.25%	24.08%
9/29/87	91	32	10	31.25%	
6/16/87	93	50	18	36.00%	
1/19/88	94	1987	484	24.36%	
9/18/90	98	17	3	17.65%	1990 Census
					29.55%

years of age or older) showed that there was only a 1.73 percent difference between the eligibles in the pre-annexation city and citywide; and, moreover, that the general growth trends affecting the Latino population would have worked to eliminate even that small difference.

Perhaps the most impressive of the arguments in Hanford's "Request for Reconsideration" concerned the actual record of Latino candidates. The City, although admitting that only one Latino had been elected in the post-annexation period, emphasized that that candidate had won support from precincts in all parts of Hanford: he placed first, second or third in nine of Hanford's twelve precincts in a field of six candidates, the other five of whom were non-Latinos. The City also showed that other minorities—an Asian and an African American—had run successfully in the City and had been repeatedly reelected in the post-annexation period. Moreover, the City showed that Latino candidates had registered successes in elections in other jurisdictions overlapping with the City or including City precincts: Latino candidates had won election to the school board and to the Board of Supervisors, some carrying the City of Hanford by large majorities composed of both Latino and non-Latino precincts. The City concluded: "Viable minority candidates have had a respectable win record in Hanford which is presumptively inconsistent with the existence of legally significant racial block voting."[10]

The Civil Rights Division of the U.S. Department of Justice was unimpressed. Instead, it found the arguments made by Joaquin G. Avila persuasive. Mr. Avila filed suit against the City on the same day that the City Council decided to enact a single-member district system. The City received an objection letter from the Justice Department dated April 5, 1993 regarding its annexation submission. On April 20, 1993, at the next regular council meeting after the letter was received, city attorney, Michael Noland, informed the City Council in closed session of the contents of the letter and also informed the Council that, according to Deputy Attorney General, Ms. Zita Johnson-Betts, that if the city enacted a single-member electoral system that was pre-cleared by the Justice Department the annexations could be simultaneously precleared. At its next regular meeting on May 4, 1993, the City Council announced its intention to begin the process for instituting single-member districts. The City's decision was reported in the *Hanford Sentinel* on May 5, 1993 along with an article on Joaquin Avila, who stated his intention to file a lawsuit against the City whether or not they opted to move to districts. The City was served with a copy of the complaint on May 7, 1993.

On February 2, 1994, Mr. Avila wrote to the Justice Department criticizing the City's correspondence regarding the Request for Reconsideration. Avila's arguments emphasized the impact of the annexations on Latino voting strength and Latino experiences in the City of Hanford. Avila's first point regarding the impact of annexations on Latino voting strength was to distinguish four population bases: total population, eligible voter population, city-wide voter registration, and registered voter population. Avila took issue with the City's methodology and conclusions in each of these categories. He was particularly critical of the City's attempt to estimate trends in its population:

> The City seeks to apply a 56 percent Latino growth rate to the City of Hanford, however . . . the application of a County-wide estimate to individual city blocks is suspect, especially since many of the census blocks within the City experienced different total population and Latino population growth rates between 1980 and 1990. Such an application does not meet the heavy burden imposed by applicable Federal precedent on parties seeking to supplement the official census figures. . . . The necessity for applying this evidentiary burden in the present administrative proceeding is even more compelling given the unique Section 5 burden of proof imposed upon the submitting jurisdiction.[11]

Avila provided a partial listing of census blocks emphasizing those that had lost population. He asked the attorney general to reject the population estimate submitted by the City. Avila's critique of population projections was used to support his conclusion that the Attorney General should also reject the City's claim that the difference between the percent of Latino eligible voters in the pre-annexation City and those in the post annexation city had declined to a *de minimis* level. Avila's central argument, however, seems to have been that, even if the eligible voter population difference was as small as 1.73 percent, it could not be ruled insignificant. In support of this view, he cited annexations from the cities of Houston, Jasper, Victoria, and San Antonio in Texas, and the City of Fayetteville in North Carolina, many of which included percentages less than or only a little greater than those in Hanford.

The bulk of Avila's letter to the Justice Department dealt with "Latino experiences in the City of Hanford," citing the testimony of Laura Yrigollen, whose husband, Albert, was a plaintiff in the original voting rights lawsuit filed by Avila. Citing her "vivid memories" about "the disparate treatment of Latinos in the Hanford public schools," experience of discrimination in the housing market, and "a prevailing sense of disenfranchisement," Avila argued that her experience and beliefs were themselves reasons for forcing Hanford to abandon its at-large electoral arrangements:

> She believes that voting in both elections was polarized along racial lines—she ran against a white candidate in both instances—and that she was unable to gather any meaningful support from the non-Latino community. Ms. Yrigollen believes that the Latino community has, and continues to be, disregarded as a political force in Hanford, and, as a result, Latinos' lack representation in city government and in other local political organizations. Based upon her observations, both the Democratic and Republican parties consistently endorse only white candidates in city and county elections. Neither party solicits membership, participation, or involvement of the Latino community, although both organizations and their candidates will seek Latino support during election years.[12]

Avila concluded his paraphrase of this individual's experiences and beliefs by asserting that she believed that Latino disenfranchisement was fostered not only by the at-large election system, but also by the organized political parties in the area. Avila's letter concluded:

> As a community member, Ms. Yrigollen has been involved in the Latino community's effort to change the at-large election to a district based election system. Her efforts have met with opposition from certain elements of the community in Hanford who are apprehensive about the presence of Latinos in elected positions because of the perception that Latinos are not educated and do not speak English fluently. . . . Ms. Yrigollen believes, based upon her experiences, that the current at-large election system has prevented the consistent election of Latinos to public office. As a result, Latinos do not have a voice and a representative on the Hanford City Council who can advocate issues directly related to the Latino community. Clearly, the experiences of Ms. Yrigollen demonstrate that the Latino community

in Hanford does not have a meaningful opportunity to participate in the political process and elect candidates of its choice.[13]

Apparently Avila and Yrigollen's arguments were persuasive. Two days later, on February 4, 1994, the Justice Department issued a letter refusing the City's Request for Preclearance of the annexations. The Justice Department concluded that "while the city has provided new information with regard to a number of matters, our conclusion remains that the annexations have diminished Hispanic voting strength in the context of an election system that fails to fairly reflect Hispanic voting strength in the enlarged city."[14] Not any districting plan would do: the Justice Department made clear that at least one of the districts be a "majority-minority" Hispanic district.

On February 7, 1994, the City complied with the Justice Department's mandate and began proceedings to move to single-member districts. Three districting plans were developed and presented for the City Council's review. See maps at figures 23, 24 and 25. As the accompanying statistics demonstrate (see tables 15, 16 and 17), one district in each plan was designed to be 55 percent Latino in population while a second district in each plan was designed to provide the Latino community with the potential for "influence," having a 34 to 35 percent Latino population. A variety of options were provided to divide the balance of the City.

The City held several public informational meetings and special City Council meetings to receive public comment on the draft plans. Then, on March 15, 1994, the City Council passed two resolutions: one adopting a five single-member district plan; and one providing for the implementation of the district plan.

The adopted plan and accompanying data can be seen as figure 26 and table 18.[15] In late May, the Justice Department accepted the district system: Deval Patrick, the new head of the Civil Rights Division, stated that "our analysis indicates that this system will fairly recognize Hispanic voting strength in the enlarged city" and that the proposed district plan "resolves the concerns that formed the basis for our objection under Section 5."[16] With this letter the original objection to the residential annexations was withdrawn and "no objection" was interposed "to the change in method of election, districting plan, implementation schedule or the elimination of the referendum requirement."[17]

It is hard to resist the conclusion that the Justice Department was over-reacting in this case. Certainly, the numbers involved are quite tiny, as the tables, supra, suggest. The annexation areas were not very different in terms of 1990 census data from the original city; and if the city is even only partly right about the direction of population trends, these differences either have been eliminated or are being rapidly eroded by the growth of Latino population.

Similarly, it is difficult to accept the Department's statement that Hanford had suffered from polarized voting behavior. Only if there is an exclusive focus on the very weakest Latino candidates can one see evidence of polarization. Strong Latino candidates, including Councilman Brieno who did not live in the downtown barrio, had a record of drawing votes from all segments of the community.

Perhaps most unimpressive is Mr. Avila's attempt to use the experiences and beliefs of a single individual, the wife of the plaintiff in his suit, to provide a basis for the claim of "political disenfranchisement." Ms. Yrigollen was clearly one of those very weak candidates who had been unable to appeal across ethnic lines and to find support in the Anglo community.[18] Yet this circumstance was adduced as an argument for moving to single-member districts and seems to have weighed heavily with the Justice Department.

Regardless of the merits of specific arguments, however, the Hanford case raises some important questions and concerns. Foremost, perhaps, is the question whether a city with fewer than 14,000 registrants and approximately 20,000 citizens 18 years of age or older, should be forced into the use of single-member districts. What is clear, however, is that the tensions between the Anglo and Latino communities have been exacerbated by the move to districts, which is seen by many in Hanford as an attempt by activist Latinos to impose ethnic representation through Federal mandate. What will be the fate of candidates such as Councilman Brieno and will they be able to appeal across ethnic lines? The movement to districts is a controversial process and federally imposed requirements could trouble the natural progress of Latino candidates into Hanford's political arena.

If districts could work against Latino candidates in this way, there is also the possibility that they may reduce the political base on which some Latino candidates currently rely. The "majority-minority" district in the map with its 54 percent Latino percentage may not be the best site for the development of Latino candidacies. It is an area of low income housing where educational levels are also low and where the

Figure 23. Hanford, California Plan 1

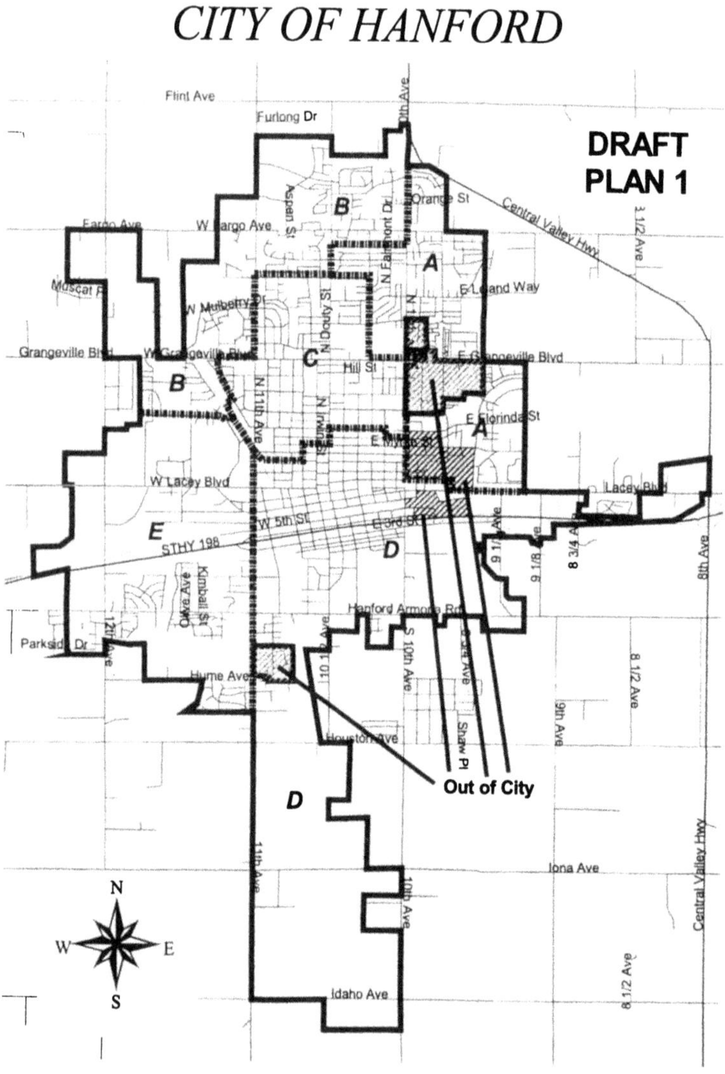

Table 15. Hanford, California, Plan 1

	District A	%	District B	%	District C	%	District D	%	District E	%	Hanford	%
Persons	6,025		6,077		6,378		5,974		6,019		30,473	
Hispanic	1,417	23.52	841	13.84	1,364	21.39	3,295	55.16	2,063	34.27	8,980	29.47
NH White	4,104	68.12	4,812	79.18	4,707	73.80	1,804	30.20	3,339	55.47	18,766	61.58
NH Black	253	4.20	160	2.63	125	1.96	667	11.17	380	6.31	1,585	5.20
NH Amer. Ind.	27	0.45	30	0.49	48	0.75	32	0.54	30	0.50	167	0.55
NH Asian	202	3.35	227	3.74	122	1.91	163	2.73	188	3.12	902	2.96
NH Other	22	0.37	7	0.12	12	0.19	13	0.22	19	0.32	73	0.24
Total 18+	4,166		4,284		4,695		3,826		3,982		20,953	
18+ Hispanic	823	19.76	507	11.83	856	18.23	2,026	52.95	1,243	31.22	5,455	26.03
NH 18+ White	3,033	72.80	3,489	81.44	3,635	77.42	1,281	33.48	2,370	59.52	13,808	65.90
NH 18+ Black	139	3.34	100	2.33	71	1.51	392	10.25	216	5.42	918	4.38
NH 18+ Amer. Ind.	21	0.50	23	0.54	37	0.79	20	0.52	20	0.50	121	0.58
NH 18+ Asian	143	3.43	159	3.71	89	1.90	99	2.59	123	3.09	613	2.93
NH 18+ Other	7	0.17	6	0.14	7	0.15	8	0.21	10	0.25	38	0.18

"NH" = "Not of Hispanic Origin"

District Deviation (Ideal District: 6,095)

	District A	District B	District C	District D	District E
Population	6,025	6,077	6,378	5,974	6,019
Deviation	-70	-18	283	-121	-76
	-1.14%	-0.29%	4.65%	-1.98%	-1.24%

Figure 24. Hanford, California Plan 2

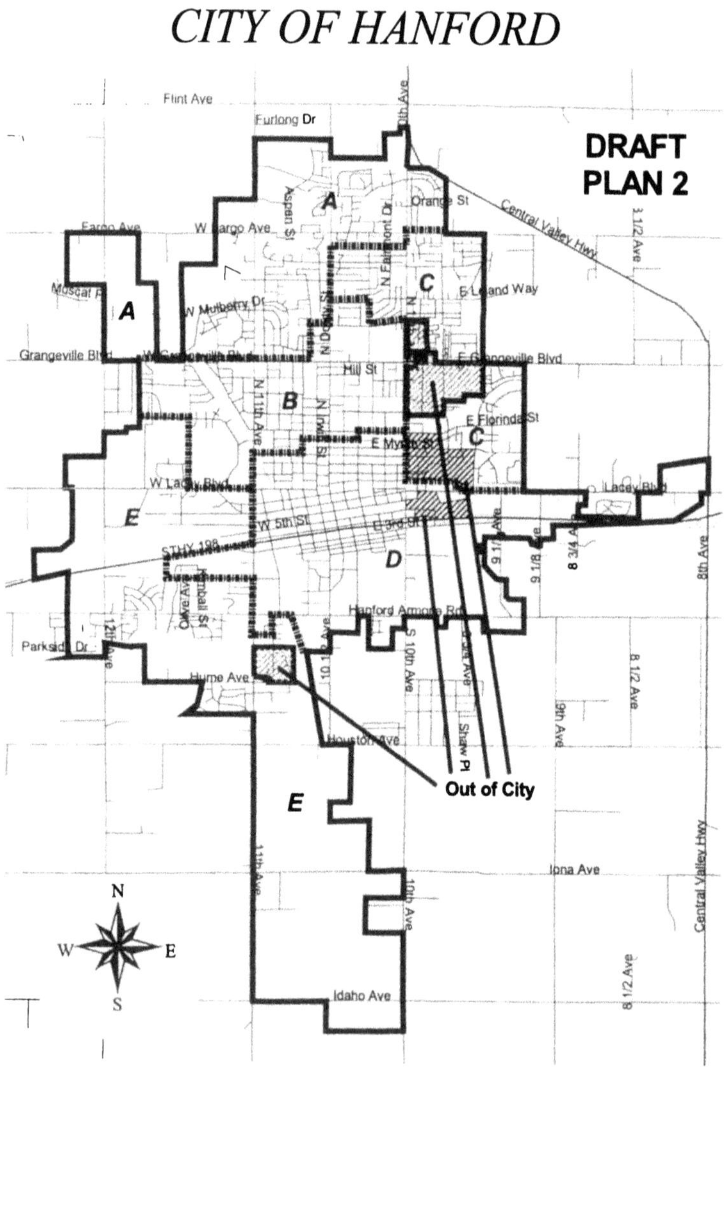

Table 16. Hanford, California, Plan 2

	District A	%	District B	%	District C	%	District D	%	District E	%	Hanford	%
Persons	5,989		6,353		6,163		5,883		6,085		30,473	
Hispanic	806	13.46	1,388	21.85	1,413	22.93	3,239	55.06	2,134	35.07	8,980	29.47
NH White	4,852	81.02	4,570	71.93	4,232	68.67	1,852	31.48	3,260	53.57	18,766	61.58
NH Black	138	2.30	148	2.33	257	4.17	602	10.23	440	7.23	1,585	5.20
NH Amer. Ind.	34	0.57	41	0.65	27	0.44	29	0.49	36	0.59	167	0.55
NH Asian	152	2.54	194	3.05	212	3.44	152	2.58	192	3.16	902	2.96
NH Other	7	0.12	12	0.19	22	0.36	9	0.15	23	0.38	73	0.24
Total 18+	4,273		4,632		4,279		3,819		3,950		20,953	
18+ Hispanic	486	11.37	867	18.72	820	19.16	2,010	52.63	1,272	32.20	5,455	26.03
NH 18+ White	3,565	83.43	3,499	75.54	3,136	73.29	1,331	34.85	2,277	57.65	13,808	65.90
NH 18+ Black	85	1.99	86	1.86	143	3.34	360	9.43	244	6.18	918	4.38
NH 18+ Amer. Ind.	25	0.59	32	0.69	21	0.49	21	0.55	22	0.56	121	0.58
NH 18+ Asian	107	2.50	140	3.02	152	3.55	90	2.36	124	3.14	613	2.93
NH 18+ Other	5	0.12	8	0.17	7	0.16	7	0.18	11	0.28	38	0.18

"NH" = "Not of Hispanic Origin"

District Deviations (Ideal District: 6,095)

	District A	District B	District C	District D	District E
Population	5,989	6,353	6,163	5,883	6,085
Deviation	-106	258	68	-212	-10
	-1.73%	4.24%	1.12%	-3.47%	-0.16%

Figure 25. Hanford, California Plan 3

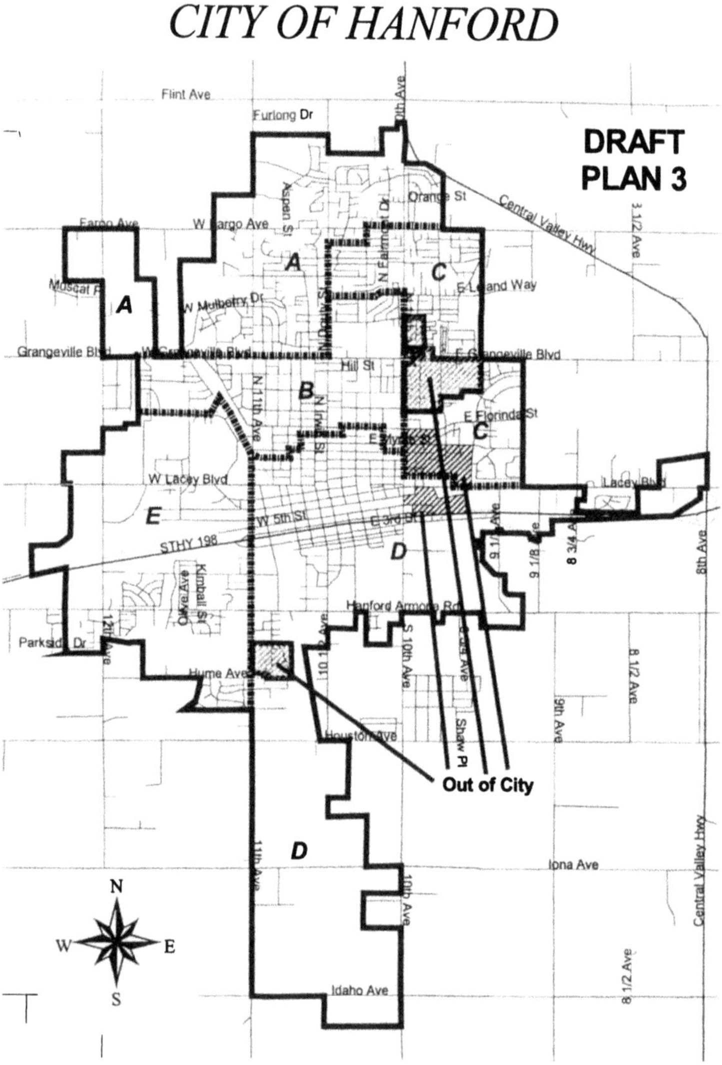

Table 17. Hanford, California, Plan 3

	District A	%	District B	%	District C	%	District D	%	District E	%	Hanford	%
Persons	5,963		6,423		6,023		5,971		6,093		30,473	
Hispanic	843	14.14	1,396	21.73	1,388	23.04	3,289	55.08	2,064	33.87	8,980	29.47
NH White	4,784	80.23	4,639	72.22	4,132	68.60	1,812	30.35	3,399	55.79	18,766	61.58
NH Black	140	2.35	144	2.24	255	4.23	664	11.12	382	6.27	1,585	5.20
NH Amer. Ind.	38	0.64	43	0.67	25	0.42	31	0.52	30	0.49	167	0.55
NH Asian	150	2.52	189	2.94	201	3.34	163	2.73	199	3.27	902	2.96
NH Other	8	0.13	12	0.19	22	0.37	12	0.20	19	0.31	73	0.24
Total 18+	4,245		4,681		4,166		3,818		4,043		20,953	
18+ Hispanic	505	11.90	874	18.67	807	19.37	2,025	53.04	1,244	30.77	5,455	26.03
NH 18+ White	3,518	82.87	3,542	75.67	3,049	73.19	1,278	33.47	2,421	59.88	13,808	65.90
NH 18+ Black	85	2.00	84	1.79	142	3.41	390	10.21	217	5.37	918	4.38
NH 18+ Amer. Ind.	27	0.64	36	0.77	19	0.46	19	0.50	20	0.49	121	0.58
NH 18+ Asian	105	2.47	136	2.91	142	3.41	99	2.59	131	3.24	613	2.93
NH 18+ Other	5	0.12	9	0.19	7	0.17	7	0.18	10	0.25	38	0.18

"NH" = "Not of Hispanic Origin"

District Deviations (Ideal District: 6,095)

	District A	District B	District C	District D	District E
Population	5,963	6,423	6,023	5,971	6,093
Deviation	-132	328	-72	-124	-2
	-2.16%	5.39%	-1.17%	-2.03%	-0.03%

Figure 26. Hanford, California Adopted Plan

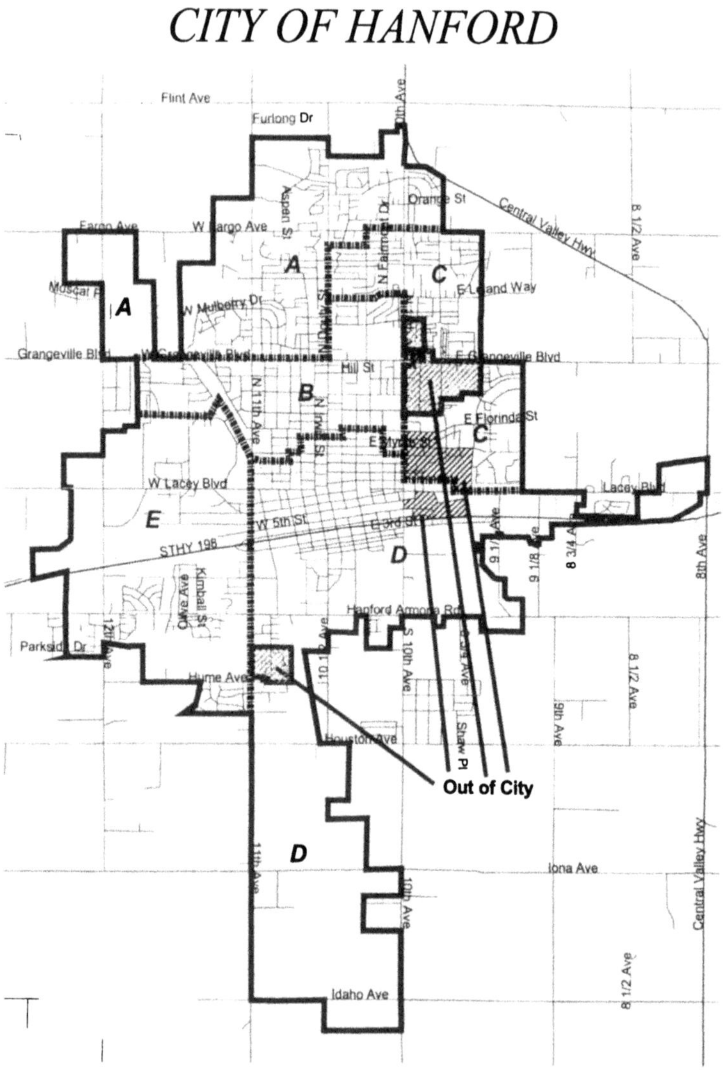

Table 18. Hanford, California, Adopted Plan

	District A	%	District B	%	District C	%	District D	%	District E	%	Hanford	%
Persons	5,963		6,423		6,023		5,971		6,093		30,473	
Hispanic	843	14.14	1,396	21.73	1,388	23.04	3,289	55.08	2,064	33.87	8,980	29.47
NH White	4,784	80.23	4,639	72.22	4,132	68.60	1,812	30.35	3,399	55.79	18,766	61.58
NH Black	140	2.35	144	2.24	255	4.23	664	11.12	382	6.27	1,585	5.20
NH Amer. Ind.	38	0.64	43	0.67	25	0.42	31	0.52	30	0.49	167	0.55
NH Asian	150	2.52	189	2.94	201	3.34	163	2.73	199	3.27	902	2.96
NH Other	8	0.13	12	0.19	22	0.37	12	0.20	19	0.31	73	0.24
Total 18+	4,245		4,681		4,166		3,818		4,043		20,953	
18+ Hispanic	505	11.90	874	18.67	807	19.37	2,025	53.04	1,244	30.77	5,455	26.03
NH 18+ White	3,518	82.87	3,542	75.67	3,049	73.19	1,278	33.47	2,421	59.88	13,808	65.90
NH 18+ Black	85	2.00	84	1.79	142	3.41	390	10.21	217	5.37	918	4.38
NH 18+ Amer. Ind.	27	0.64	36	0.77	19	0.46	19	0.50	20	0.49	121	0.58
NH 18+ Asian	105	2.47	136	2.91	142	3.41	99	2.59	131	3.24	613	2.93
NH 18+ Other	5	0.12	9	0.19	7	0.17	7	0.18	10	0.25	38	0.18

"NH" = "Not of Hispanic Origin"

District Deviations (Ideal District: 6,095)

	District A	District B	District C	District D	District E
Population	5,963	6,423	6,023	5,971	6,093
Deviation	-132	328	-72	-124	-2
	-2.16%	5.39%	-1.17%	-2.03%	-0.03%

Latino population has a large proportion of non-citizens and those who are under age. More favorable to Latino candidacies are lower middle class and middle class areas of the City where Latino populations are less dominant, but where individuals with the financial and social assets necessary to candidacy are more likely to live. The creation of two districts—the "majority-minority" and the so-called "influence" district—in Hanford's new plan tends to split into two the political base from which candidates such as Councilman Brieno would launch their bid for office. And although in the November 1994 election, Council District D, the majority-minority district elected Dennis Sanchez,[19] the only Latino candidate in a three-way race, the result could easily be reversed had there been two or more Latino candidates and only one Anglo candidate. Mr. Sanchez won with only 49.03 percent of the vote. The other two districts up for election, District E (the Latino "influence" district, and District A failed to yield any Latino candidacies. The Anglo incumbents in Districts B and C filed unopposed for the 1996 election.

Finally, it is debatable whether Hanford's Latino population—a total of 8,980 persons representing only 29.47 percent of the City's population—justified the big gun tactics of the Justice Department and the Draconian solution of a mandated districting plan. Taken individually, none of the annexations could be considered significantly dilutive of Latino voting power. Only when taken together and examined against the backdrop of the 1990 census was the Department able to raise a Section 5 issue; and only in the context of a Section 5 issue could a Joaquin Avila have found it possible to adduce the experiences and beliefs of Laura Yrigollen as in any sense relevant. Thus, at the end of any analysis one returns to the question: Why is Kings County subject to Section 5 preclearance? Was there in 1972, and was there in 1992, any really compelling evidence of discrimination in voting? Definitive answers to these questions require much further research; but it is a stretch to compare the discriminatory tactics of the Democratic establishment against blacks in the old South to the political and social situation of Latinos in Kings County.

NOTES

1. *General Population Characteristics, California*, 1970 Census of Population, U.S. Bureau of the Census. In the 1965 Act, the word "person" was

used; however, in the 1975 expansion the word "citizen" was substituted for the word "person" due to concern over the ever-increasing non-citizen Hispanic population in the West and Southwest. It is not clear whether an attempt was made to factor out non-citizens in the case of Kings County. Only 456 voting age persons made the difference between inclusion and exclusion.

2. *Statement of Vote*, General Election, November 3, 1992, Secretary of State, State of California.

3. 1970 Census of Population.

4. Declaration of Michael Noland in Support of Objections to Bill of Costs, *Yrigollen v. City of Hanford*, CV-F-93 5303-OWW/NEW June 3, 1994.

5. James P. Turner, Acting Assistant Attorney General, Civil Rights Division, U.S. Department of Justice, to Michael J. Noland, Esq., April 5, 1993, 2.

6. Ibid.

7. Ibid., 3.

8. Ibid.

9. *Request for Reconsideration by the City of Hanford, California of the April 5, 1993 Objection Letter Pertaining to its Submission Under Section 5 of the Voting Rights Act for Preclearance of Annexations November 1, 1972-October 30, 1992*, dated August 27, 1993 and *Supplement* dated December 3, 1993.

10. Ibid.

11. Joaquin Avila, Esq., to Steven H. Rosenbaum, Chief, Voting Section, Civil Rights Division, Department of Justice, February 2, 1994, 2.

12. Ibid., 6.

13. Ibid.

14. James P. Turner, Acting Assistant Attorney General, Civil Rights Division, U.S. Department of Justice to Marguerite Mary Leoni, Esq., Mill Valley, CA, February 4, 1994, 3.

15. Because of the lawsuit, the City of Hanford did not go to the voters for approval to implement the plan as required by the General Law of California.

16. Deval L. Patrick, Assistant Attorney General, Civil Rights Division, U.S. Department of Justice, undated letter (received on May 31, 1994) to Marguerite Mary Leoni, Esq., Mill Valley, California, 2.

17. Ibid.

18. The Yrigollens, who lived in the racially mixed area considerably to the west of the Hispanic barrio, moved to the predominantly Anglo north Hanford during the case.

19. In 1982, Sanchez had run for county board of supervisors and won the primary against a field of three non-Hispanics. He lost the election in the runoff.

CHAPTER 6

A Majority Minority City: Corcoran, California

Can the impact of the Voting Rights Act be felt before any formal challenge is made? What is a "majority-minority" district? How cohesive is the Hispanic community? Should small communities be pressured into district systems? What happens when a defined minority becomes a majority? This case study attempts to shed light on these questions.

The resolution of the Dinuba case, as we have already seen, was a shock to many jurisdictions all through the Central Valley. To many city and district managers the exaction of over $200,000 in costs from a hospital district of only 13,000 persons stood as a warning of the trouble that similar litigation might wreak in their own budgets. To Hispanic groups and to voting rights activists, of course, the decision was a signal to broaden their challenge; and to Joaquin Avila and other voting rights attorneys who might handle such litigation, the award of costs and attorney's fees served as a financial inducement. It was against this supercharged atmosphere that our next case study opens.

Corcoran, a city of 8,335 in population (excluding a prison population of approximately 5,000), lies in the Central Valley between the 99 and 5 freeways, about mid-way between Fresno and Bakersfield. It is roughly 35 miles from Dinuba and 150 miles from Watsonville. As of the 1990 census, its Hispanic population stood at 5,029 persons or 60.34 percent of the total. When news of Hanford's predicament reached Don Pauley, Corcoran's City Manager, a cause for alarm seemed all too clear. As a municipality within Kings County, Corcoran was, like its neighbor, Hanford, subject to Section 5 preclearance provisions of the Voting Rights Act. Corcoran had almost three times the percentage Hispanic population of Hanford, yet the latter was being forced to move to districts by a Justice Department decision.

Pauley consulted with the members of the City Council only to find a clear majority opposed to districts. Most members of the Council felt that the City was "just too small" to develop what they tended to term "wards."

Pauley next consulted with attorneys in the voting rights field. From them he drew the conclusion that prudence required an attempt to move to single-member districts. Annexations made to the City since November 1, 1972 had been considered non-dilutive and were precleared by the Justice Department; however, according to the attorneys, the City still was vulnerable to a Section 2 challenge to its current at-large arrangements, a circumstance that could lead to substantial legal costs and a possible adverse decision. Pauley's resolution to take this counsel was strengthened when Robert Quiroz, who worked with Gregory Perez and who was also serving as an aide to Joaquin Avila, visited the City offices and suggested that a suit was likely.

At first glance, Corcoran appeared to have grown rapidly in the 1980s: the 1980 census population of 6,454 grew by the addition of a further 6,910 persons. The 1990 census totals, however, are misleading from a voting rights perspective: 5,029 of the growth is accounted for by the addition of a state prison, whose residents cannot vote. Moreover, there are 1,561 non-citizens in Corcoran: 531 of these are inmates of the Corcoran state prison, but there are 1,030 non-citizens in the general, non-prison population of the City (see the map of Corcoran at figure 27, with the Corcoran State Prison located at the bottom right hand corner). Corcoran's Hispanic population, by far the most rapidly growing element of the City, was quite widely dispersed throughout the different areas of Corcoran: there were substantial concentrations at almost all parts of its compass excepting only the extreme northeast and the very center of the City (see the map of Hispanic population and of Hispanic counts at figures 28 and 29). Much the same is true of the voting age population (see maps of Hispanic 18-plus population and Hispanic 18 plus counts at figures 30 and 31). Aside from the Hispanic population, there are relatively small numbers of other minorities, with no strong groupings of either Asians or African Americans.

Figure 27. Map of Corcoran, California.

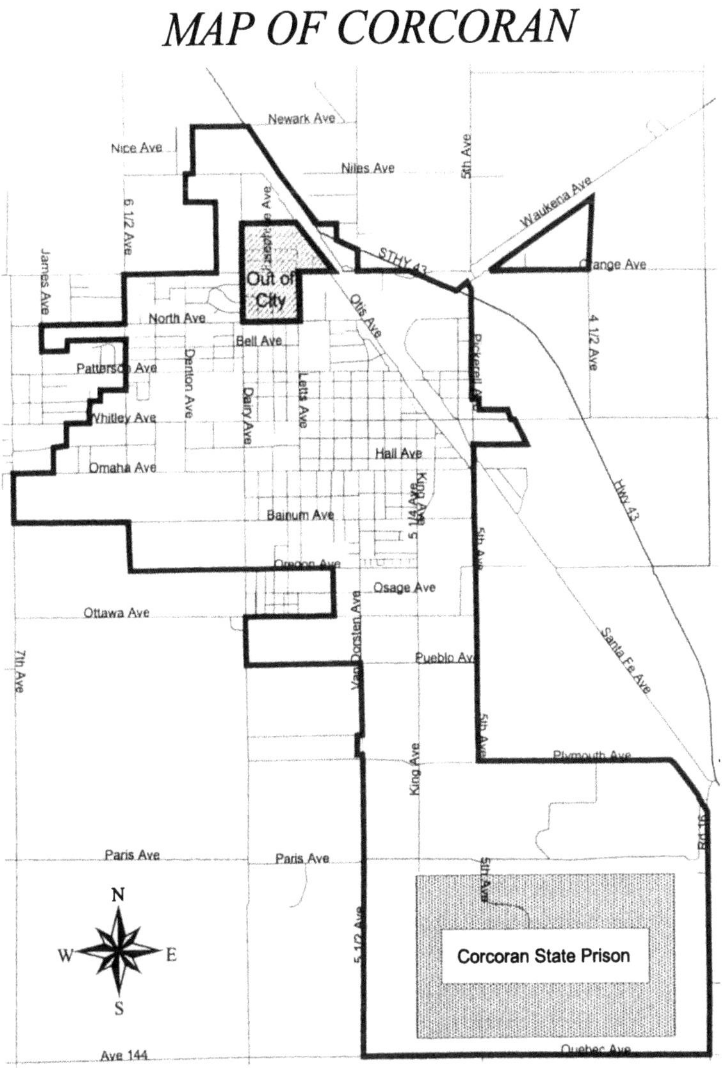

Figure 28. Corcoran, California, Plot of Hispanic Population Percentages.

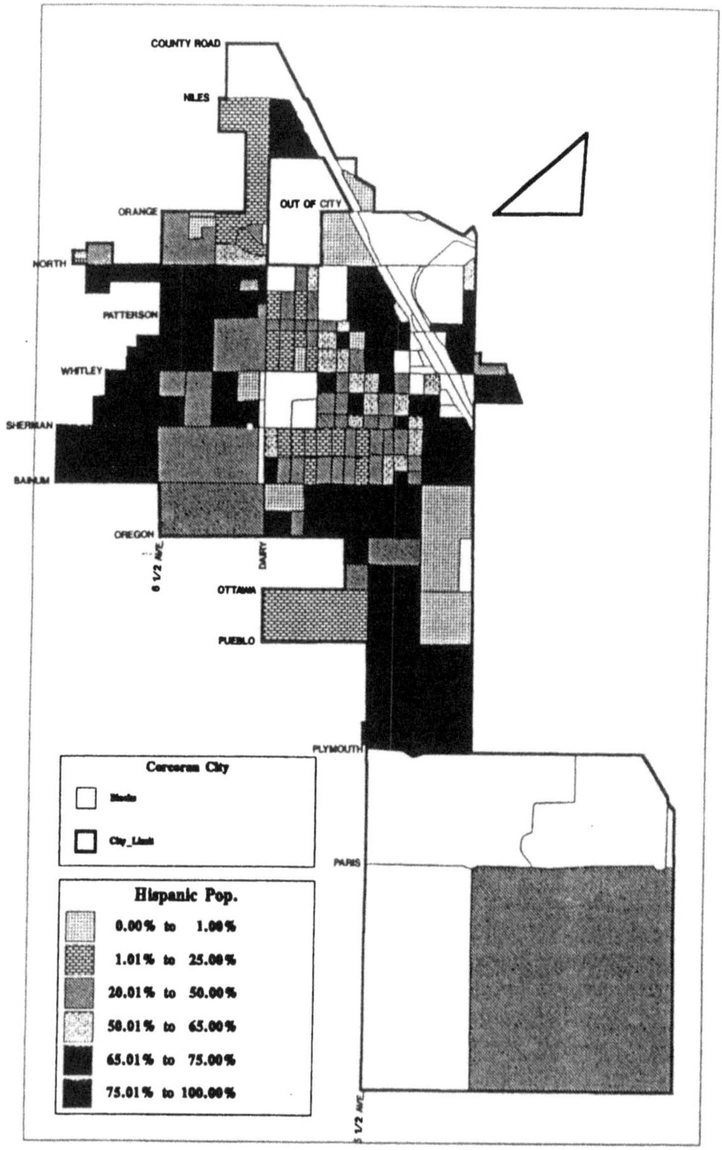

Figure 29. Corcoran, California, Plot of Hispanic Population Counts.

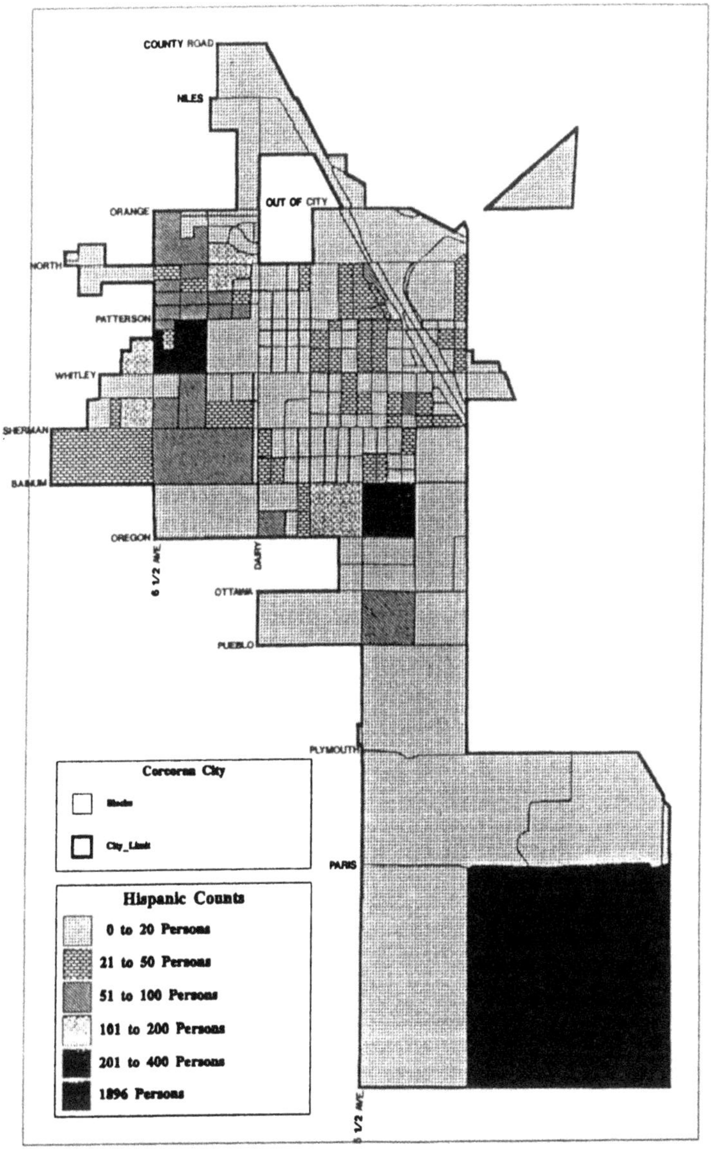

Figure 30. Corcoran, California, Plot of Hispanic Voting Age Population Percentages

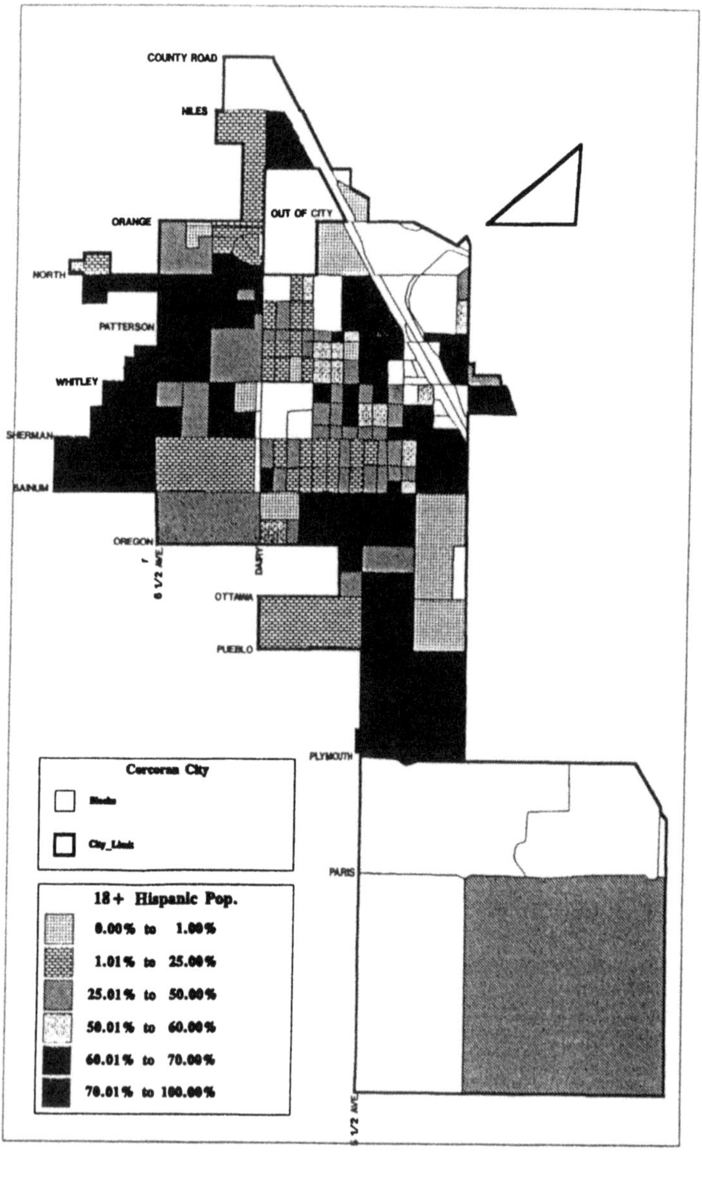

Figure 31. Corcoran, California, Plot of Hispanic Voting Age Population Counts.

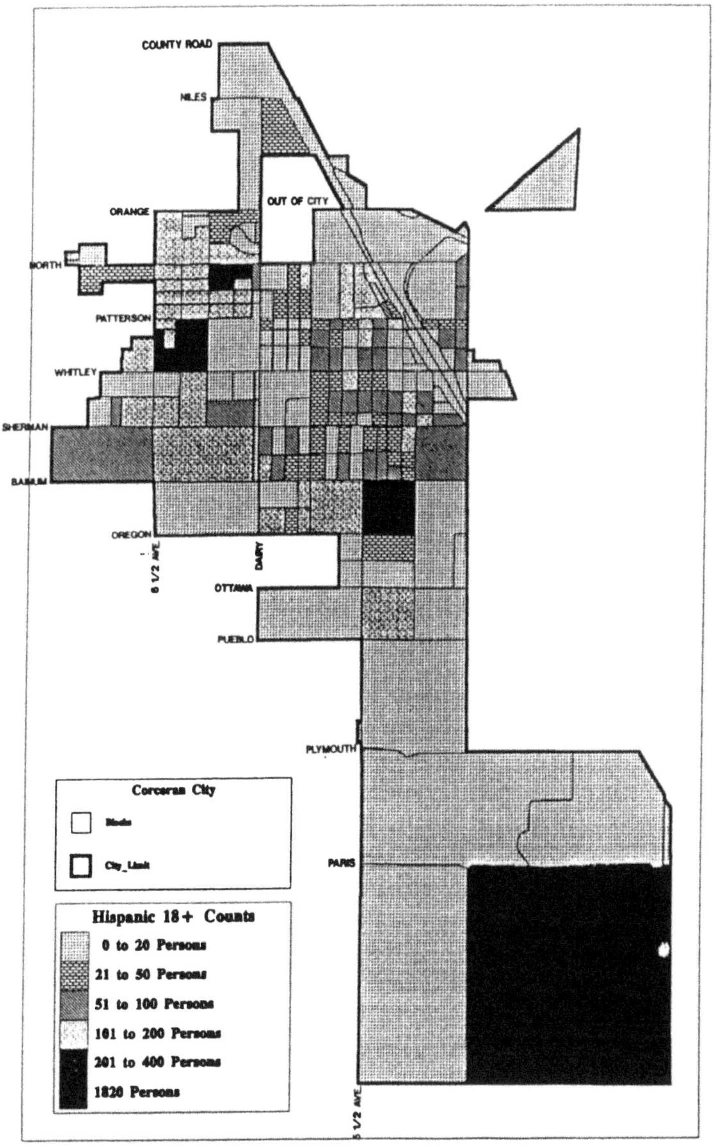

In 1993, the City was represented by a five-member city council, including two Hispanic representatives (one elected in 1990, the other in 1992). The terms of city council members were staggered (3 members elected in presidential election years, two in gubernatorial election years).

In order to change from an at-large to a single-member district system, Corcoran (like all general law cities in California) is required by the election code to place an ordinance on the ballot for voter approval or rejection. The ordinance must describe the districts and their boundaries.

After substantial deliberation, the Council retained a demographer for development of a five-district, single-member districting plan. Under advice from a voting rights attorney and this writer, serving as the City's demographer, the Council determined that the districting plan had to be the result of an open public process.

The city manager's task was politically daunting. On the one hand, he faced a Council majority fully committed to the current at-large system; on the other, he faced challenge from local Hispanic groups (principally the Hispanic Leadership Roundtable and the Corcoran League of Voters) which were threatening to call on the talents of Hispanic voting rights attorneys.

The City's demographer began work for Corcoran in September of 1993 and, as a first step, created a block level database using 1990 census information. In October, the demographer delivered a report to the City, "Preliminary Report to the Citizens of Corcoran on the Districting Process," containing a brief discussion of the database, demography of the city at large, and data on the distribution of the Hispanic population. Meetings between the City's demographer and the Hispanic Leadership Roundtable and the Corcoran League of Voters allowed members of these groups to provide their insights and to make a case for particular district boundary lines. On the basis of these meetings, the City's demographer developed three plans for council review (see copies of the plans and their statistics at figures 32, 33 and 34 and tables 19, 20, and 21). Each plan created three majority voting age Hispanic districts, while maintaining relatively low total deviations.

A council meeting on November 1, 1993, provided the occasion for a public presentation of the three plans to the Council and interested citizens. Council members, although expressing individual concerns, agreed to move forward with a public hearing on the three plans on November 15. Prior to that meeting, however, the Hispanic Leadership

Roundtable and the Corcoran League of Voters met with the City's demographer and urged changes, focusing in particular on modifications that would reduce the Hispanic concentration in District 3 of Plan 3. When the demographer presented such a modification at the meeting of November 15, however, the Hispanic Leadership expressed concern that the concentration had been too much weakened. In an effort to avoid impasse, the demographer suggested an expenditure of $1,275.00 to permit official Census Bureau "splits" of blocks that would provide additional flexibility for population adjustments. A final public meeting took place on December 6. The meeting had been preceded by various maneuvers involving detailed adjustments to satisfy the Hispanic Leadership and the Corcoran League. Even so, the meeting saw further proposals for adjusting districts in order to advantage particular Hispanic candidacies. When different groups within the Hispanic Leadership were found to be at odds concerning the proposal, the City Council recessed in order to allow the Hispanics to discuss the problem among themselves. At last, the leader of the Hispanic Leadership Roundtable, Mr. Angel Martinez, agreed to a final version of a five-district plan. This plan (see the map at figure 35 and the data at table 22) creates five reasonably compact and fully contiguous single-member districts. Three of the districts contain a majority of Hispanic voting age persons: District 3, 73.75 percent; District 4, 67.19 percent; and District 5, 74.33 percent. In these districts, Hispanic persons also constitute a majority of the voting age citizens: District 3, approximately 67.9 percent; District 4, 60.2 percent; and District 5, 65.5 percent. The plan was fully documented and submitted for preclearance under Section 5 of the Voting Rights Act on December 30, 1993.

Soon after the City's submission for its request for preclearance, however, Robert Quiroz of Perez and Associates, who represented himself and Perez and Associates as a technical arm of Joaquin Avila, had submitted directly to the Justice Department (apparently with the support of one of the Hispanic members of the Council) an alternative plan. The plan provided for four majority Hispanic districts. Mr. Quiroz and supporters among Corcoran's Hispanic leadership believed that the plan would quickly assure a majority of Hispanics on the City Council, an outcome that they regarded as appropriate and just, given the fact that a majority of Corcoran's total population is Hispanic. Behind this rationale, however, there seems to have been another motive.

Figure 32 Corcoran, California, Plan 1

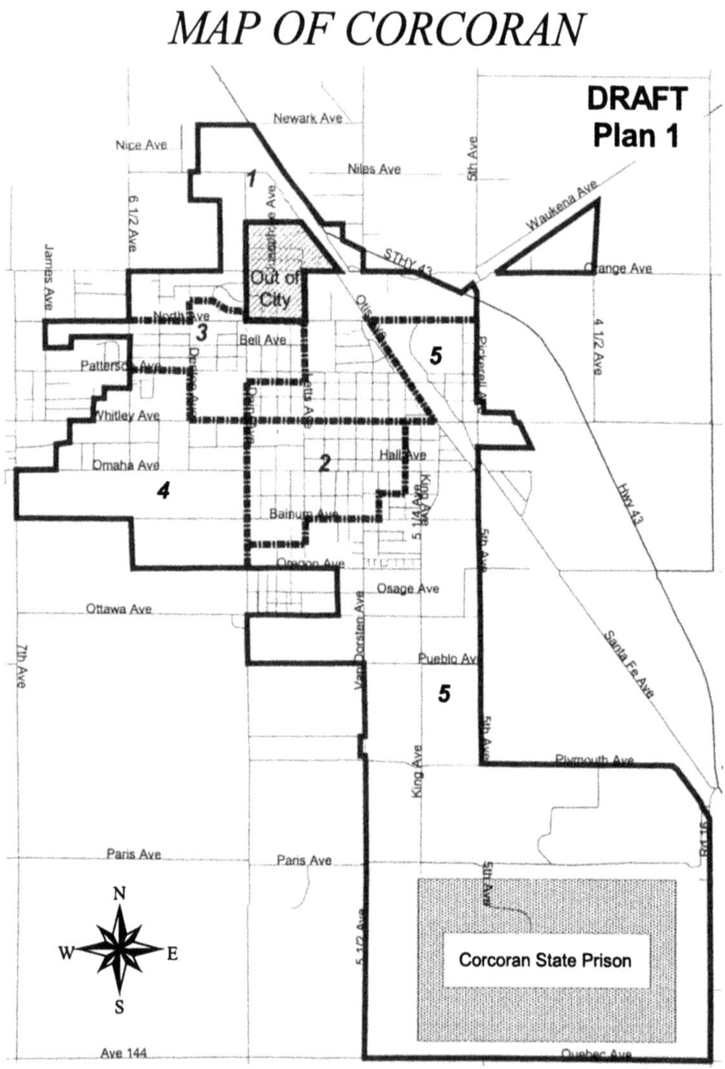

Table 19. Corcoran, California, Plan 1

	District 1	%	District 2	%	District 3	%	District 4	%	District 5	%	Corcoran	%
Persons	1,650		1,670		1,665		1,712		1,638		8,335	
Hispanic	879	53.27	707	42.34	1,156	69.43	1,100	64.25	1,187	72.47	5,029	60.34
NH White	712	43.15	898	53.77	438	26.31	487	28.45	342	20.88	2,877	34.52
NH Black	19	1.15	18	1.08	55	3.30	110	6.43	90	5.49	292	3.50
NH Amer. Ind.	16	0.97	13	0.78	6	0.36	4	0.23	13	0.79	52	0.62
NH Asian	14	0.85	26	1.56	3	0.18	8	0.47	3	0.18	54	0.65
NH Other	10	0.61	8	0.48	7	0.42	3	0.18	3	0.18	31	0.37
Total 18+	1,082		1,149		1,047		1,008		931		5,217	
18+ Hispanic	541	50.00	429	37.34	703	67.14	587	58.23	629	67.56	2,889	55.38
NH 18+ White	504	46.58	675	58.75	304	29.04	351	34.82	232	24.92	2,066	39.60
NH 18+ Black	12	1.10	14	1.22	31	2.96	58	5.75	57	6.12	172	3.30
NH 18+ Amer. Ind.	8	0.74	11	0.96	2	0.19	4	0.40	9	0.97	34	0.65
NH 18+ Asian	11	1.02	16	1.39	2	0.19	5	0.50	3	0.32	37	0.71
NH 18+ Other	6	0.55	4	0.35	5	0.48	3	0.30	1	0.11	19	0.36

"NH" = "Not of Hispanic Origin"

District Deviations (Ideal District: 1,667)

	District 1	District 2	District 3	District 4	District 5
Population	1,650	1,670	1,665	1,712	1,638
Deviation	-17	3	-2	45	-29
	-1.02%	0.18%	-0.12%	2.70%	-1.74%

Figure 33. Corcoran, California, Plan 2

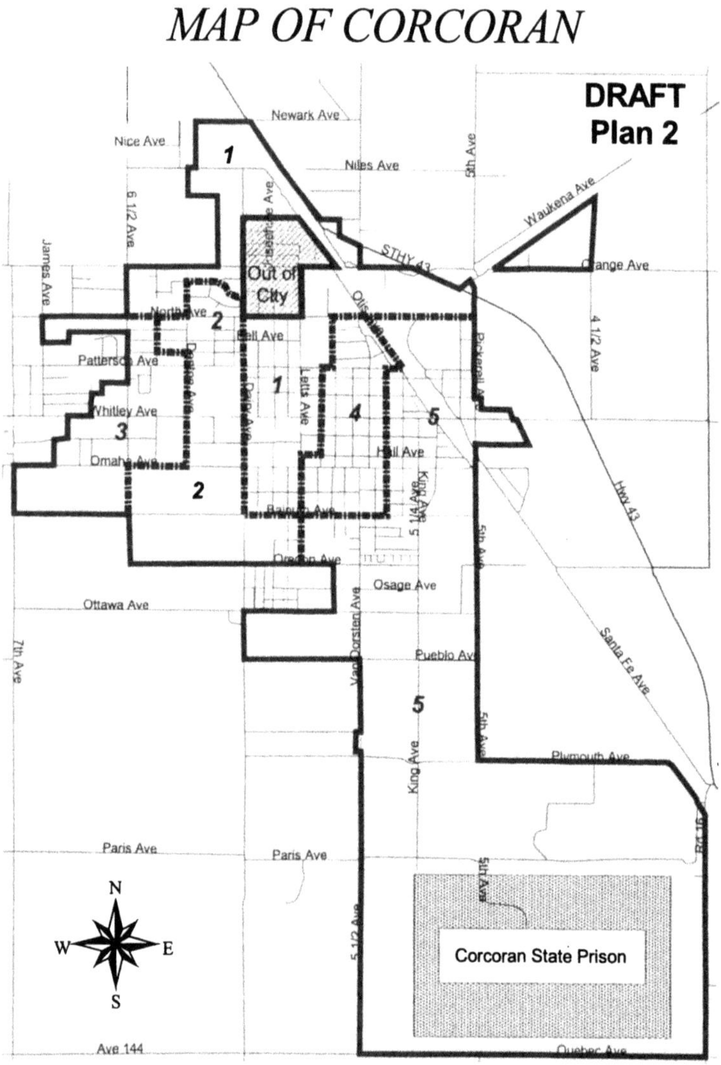

Table 20. Corcoran, California, Plan 2

	District 1	%	District 2	%	District 3	%	District 4	%	District 5	%	Corcoran	%
Persons	1,696		1,630		1,636		1,708		1,665		8,335	
Hispanic	590	34.79	1,035	63.50	1,249	76.34	955	55.91	1,200	72.07	5,029	60.34
NH White	1,044	61.56	502	30.80	277	16.93	702	41.10	352	21.14	2,877	34.52
NH Black	26	1.53	72	4.42	94	5.75	11	0.64	89	5.35	292	3.50
NH Amer. Ind.	21	1.24	9	0.55	4	0.24	8	0.47	10	0.60	52	0.62
NH Asian	8	0.47	11	0.67	5	0.31	19	1.11	11	0.66	54	0.65
NH Other	7	0.41	1	0.06	7	0.43	13	0.76	3	0.18	31	0.37
Total 18+	1,165		1,015		946		1,127		964		5,217	
18+ Hispanic	362	31.07	620	61.08	681	71.99	579	51.38	647	67.12	2,889	55.38
NH 18+ White	761	65.32	346	34.09	199	21.04	515	45.70	245	25.41	2,066	39.60
NH 18+ Black	17	1.46	36	3.55	54	5.71	9	0.80	56	5.81	172	3.30
NH 18+ Amer. Ind.	12	1.03	6	0.59	6	0.63	6	0.53	7	0.73	37	0.65
NH 18+ Asian	6	0.52	6	0.59	4	0.42	13	1.15	8	0.83	37	0.71
NH 18+ Other	7	0.60	1	0.10	5	0.53	5	0.44	1	0.10	19	0.36

"NH" = "Not of Hispanic Origin"

District Deviations (Ideal District: 1,667)

	District 1	District 2	District 3	District 4	District 5
Population	1,696	1,630	1,636	1,708	1,665
Deviation	29	-37	-31	41	-2
	1.74%	-2.22%	-1.86%	2.46%	-0.12%

Figure 34. Corcoran, California, Plan 3

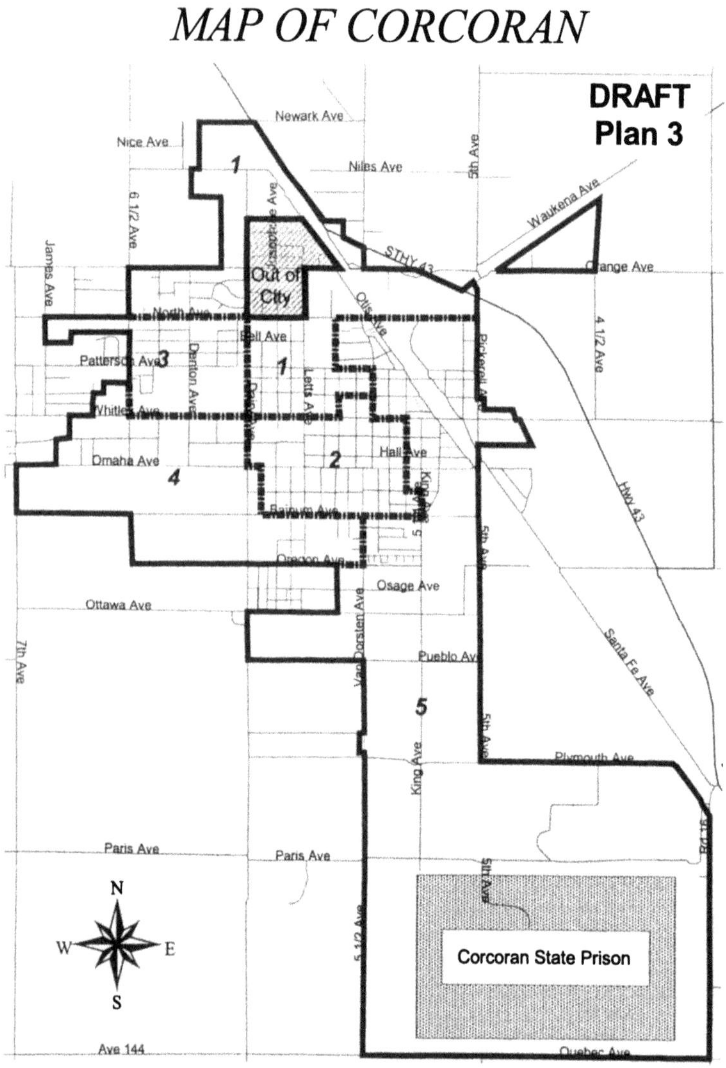

Table 21. Corcoran, California, Plan 3

	District 1	%	District 2	%	District 3	%	District 4	%	District 5	%	Corcoran	%
Persons	1,660		1,656		1,681		1,676		1,662		8,335	
Hispanic	684	41.20	680	41.06	1,389	82.63	1,010	60.26	1,266	76.17	5,029	60.34
NH White	925	55.72	919	55.50	191	11.36	550	32.83	292	17.57	2,877	34.52
NH Black	19	1.14	17	1.03	86	5.12	92	5.49	78	4.69	292	3.50
NH Amer. Ind.	17	1.02	12	0.72	6	0.36	8	0.48	9	0.54	52	0.62
NH Asian	7	0.42	20	1.21	2	0.12	14	0.84	11	0.66	54	0.65
NH Other	8	0.48	8	0.48	7	0.42	2	0.12	6	0.36	31	0.37
Total 18+	1,110		1,141		986		1,004		976		5,217	
18+ Hispanic	426	38.36	415	36.37	798	80.93	538	53.59	712	72.95	2,889	55.38
NH 18+ White	650	58.56	685	60.04	131	13.29	399	39.74	201	20.59	2,066	39.60
NH 18+ Black	12	1.08	14	1.23	47	4.77	50	4.98	49	5.02	172	3.30
NH 18+ Amer. Ind.	8	0.72	10	0.88	3	0.30	7	0.70	6	0.61	34	0.65
NH 18+ Asian	6	0.54	13	1.14	2	0.20	8	0.80	8	0.82	37	0.71
NH 18+ Other	8	0.72	4	0.35	5	0.51	2	0.20	0	0.00	19	0.36

"NH" = "Not of Hispanic Origin"

District Deviations (Ideal District: 1,667)

	District 1	District 2	District 3	District 4	District 5
Population	1,660	1,656	1,681	1,676	1,662
Deviation	-7	-11	14	9	-5
	-0.42%	-0.66%	0.84%	0.54%	-0.30%

Figure 35. Corcoran, California, Final Plan

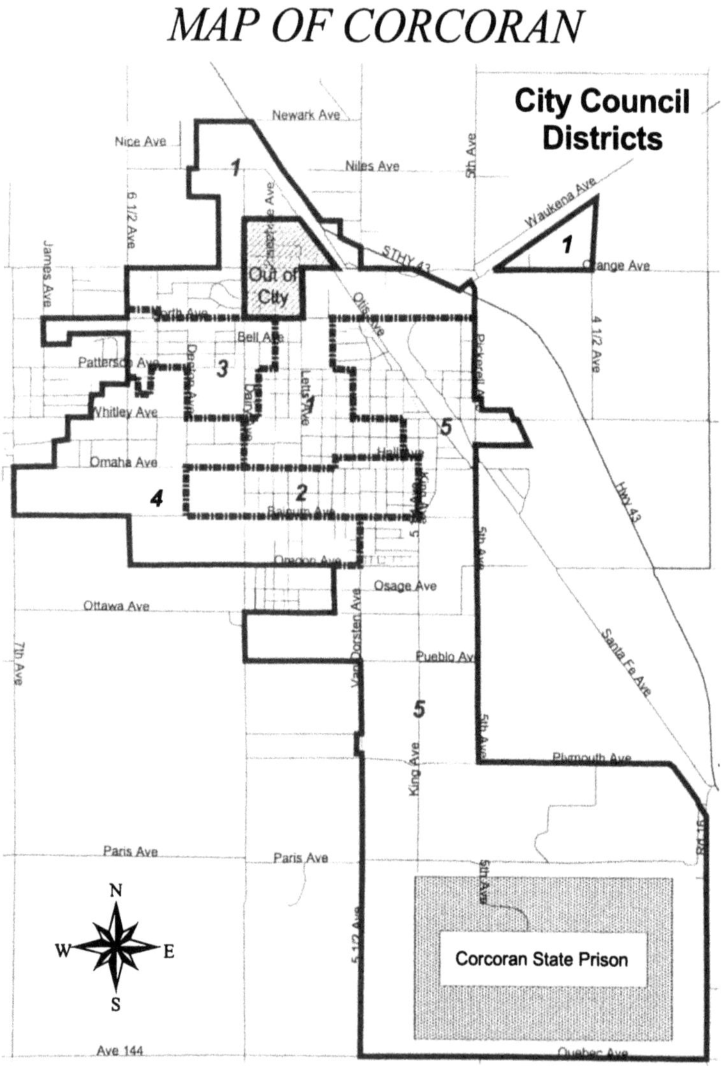

Table 22. Corcoran, California, Final Plan

	District 1	%	District 2	%	District 3	%	District 4	%	District 5	%	Corcoran	%
Persons	1,667		1,669		1,648		1,655		1,696		8,335	
Hispanic	634	38.03	617	36.97	1,248	75.73	1,218	73.60	1,312	77.36	5,029	60.34
NH White	979	58.73	965	57.82	306	18.57	346	20.91	281	16.57	2,877	34.52
NH Black	12	0.72	56	3.36	76	4.61	72	4.35	76	4.48	292	3.50
NH Amer. Ind.	21	1.26	10	0.60	5	0.30	7	0.42	9	0.53	52	0.62
NH Asian	11	0.66	17	1.02	5	0.30	10	0.60	11	0.65	54	0.65
NH Other	10	0.60	4	0.24	8	0.49	2	0.12	7	0.41	31	0.37
Total 18+	1,106		1,139		1,014		957		1,001		5,217	
18+ Hispanic	393	35.53	363	31.87	746	73.57	643	67.19	744	74.33	2,889	55.38
NH 18+ White	680	61.48	725	63.65	211	20.81	256	26.75	194	19.38	2,066	39.60
NH 18+ Black	7	0.63	29	2.55	44	4.34	44	4.60	48	4.80	172	3.30
NH 18+ Amer. Ind.	10	0.90	10	0.88	2	0.20	6	0.63	6	0.60	34	0.65
NH 18+ Asian	8	0.72	10	0.88	5	0.49	6	0.63	8	0.80	37	0.71
NH 18+ Other	8	0.72	2	0.18	6	0.59	2	0.21	1	0.10	19	0.36

"NH" = "Not of Hispanic Origin"

District Deviations (Ideal District: 1,667)

	District 1	District 2	District 3	District 4	District 5
Population	1,667	1,669	1,648	1,655	1,696
Deviation	0	2	-19	-12	29
	0.00%	0.12%	-1.14%	-0.72%	1.74%

One of the two Hispanic members of the Council had resigned for personal reasons at about the time of the submission of the request for preclearance. To replace this member, the Council had appointed an Hispanic who resided in one of the majority Hispanic districts created by the submitted plan. Opponents of this Hispanic, seeing the plan as being likely to confirm his presence on the Council at the first election, now sought to overturn it via the Perez-Quiroz plan.

The City's demographer pointed up deficiencies in the Perez-Quiroz plan, including its overall deviation of 5.64 percent and its lack of contiguity; (District 5 in the plan is made of two separate population areas that are not territorially linked). The City's demographer, noting that there were only two effective Hispanic voting age districts in the plan, also drew attention to the fact of splintering both white and mixed neighborhoods in two of the districts. Given significantly lower turnout rates for Hispanic eligible voters, the Perez plan was criticized by the City's demographer as being potentially dilutive of Hispanic voting strength. The Request for Preclearance was submitted on an emergency basis ("Expedited Review Request") and pre-clearance was granted for the City's proposed plan to be put on the June 1994 ballot. The City wanted to tell the voters about the stakes involved, so it provided a newsletter in both English and Spanish and announced a public meeting to be addressed by the City's demographer and a consultant on issues of representation. The aim was to make a balanced case for the single-member districts.

Controversy developed, however, over the Council's stance. The majority was adamant that it had not endorsed the districting plan but simply fostered a public process by putting the plan on the ballot, allowing the voters of Corcoran to decide. To Corcoran's Hispanic leadership, however, this was inadequate, for they believed that the City Council must endorse the plan in order for it to have a chance of passage. In June of 1994, Corcoran's voters rejected the district system by an overwhelming majority, 62.2 percent to 37.8 percent.

Concerned over the failure of the district system to succeed with the voters and the renewed threat of a Section 2 suit, Pauley explored the concept of a four-district system with an at-large mayor, cumulative voting and other alternatives to strict single-member districts. But the controversy died down and, to date, no litigation has been attempted to force the City into the use of single-member districts.

At this writing, there were two Hispanic members of the City Council: Ruben Quintanilla, who had been appointed to the Council in the Spring of 1994 in opposition to the wishes of many in the Hispanic community who wanted Ms. Toni Baltierra appointed; and Ray Lerma, who had been very active in the attempt to move to districts. In November of 1996 six candidates had filed for two seats. Incumbent John Rachford was elected to the Board of Supervisors and was retiring from the Council; and, incumbent Ruben Quintanilla had filed for the seat to which he was appointed. Of the six filed candidates, only one, besides Councilman Quintanilla, was Hispanic.

This case history permits consideration of a number of important issues. First, it is clear that the impact of the Voting Rights Act, and of litigation under it, can be felt by jurisdictions even *before* there is any formal challenge or filing of suits. Corcoran took the step toward single member districts because of the fear of future litigation and in order to avoid the astronomical costs that had been imposed on other jurisdictions in its area.

Second, the controversy between the City's demographer and the voting rights demographer, Mr. Quiroz, illustrates the lack of objective grounds for deciding what is a "majority" Hispanic district or what configuration of districts is most likely to assure the election of Hispanic candidates. To Mr. Quiroz, districts with little more than 50 percent citizen Hispanic voting age population were acceptably "safe:" his plan provided for a District 4 with 69.01 percent Hispanic population, and 65.65 percent Hispanic voting age population; but, these figures drop to 53.24 percent for *citizen* Hispanic voting age population and, when the typically lower Hispanic registration and turnout are taken into consideration, this district could easily fall below 50 percent. Similarly, Mr. Quiroz's District 2 is only 63.82 percent Hispanic, 57.62 percent Hispanic voting age population and falls to 51.9 percent in *citizen* Hispanic voting age population. Clearly, it is impossible to decide in absolute terms what a "true majority-minority district" is, absent not only a calculation of citizenship and turnout but also much more complete understanding of the effectiveness of political organization, the availability and willingness of candidates, and the intention and ability of the community to support them. Much of the debate between demographers has the character of an abstract duel over meaningless statistics; the real forces that determine elections are at the level of community politics.

A third issue concerns the cohesiveness of the Hispanic community and its ability to represent its needs with one voice. A plan that was fully acceptable to the Hispanic leadership at one moment was rejected the next, apparently because of the perception that the "wrong Hispanic" might be elected. Like any other group, Hispanics differ in their judgments as to the merits of candidates, even those from their own community.

A further issue concerns the utility of moving from an at-large scheme to single-member districts in a community as tiny as Corcoran. One concern has to do with the efficacy of districts in a community where almost any active candidate can visit almost every household in the City personally in the course of a campaign. The democratic rationale for districts, which in large cities tends to unite Hispanic and non-Hispanic critics of at-large arrangements, is altogether lacking in Corcoran. Indeed, the push for districts by the Hispanic leadership groups seems to have stirred ethnic tensions in Corcoran well beyond any previous point.

From another perspective, too, the Corcoran case raises doubt about single-member districts. If Hispanics are, as claimed by the leadership groups, about to become a voting majority in the City, why do they need districts for political protection, or for fairness, or to prevent discrimination, or to assure true representation, or indeed, for any of the purposes for which districts have been advanced as the sole solution? After all, a voting majority of Hispanics, if committed to ethnic voting, could assure the election of an all-Hispanic city council. At that point, districts would become no more than a protection for the non-Hispanic minority. Thus, one needs to know at what point in the transition from minority to majority status districts become redundant as a means of protecting Hispanic voting power and become, instead, an obstacle to the assertion of Hispanic majority rights.

CHAPTER 7

The Arizona Cases: Phoenix

In this chapter we trace the difficulties of protecting minority concentrations from an expanding white suburban population and the problems of adjusting a plan to the competitive demands of Hispanics and African Americans. The design of the adopted plan is especially interesting because it employs the device of a narrow corridor, and thus is similar in kind—if not in bizarre degree—to the affirmative action gerrymanders struck down by the Court in *Shaw v. Reno* and other more recent decisions.

DISTRICTING PHOENIX

In 1982, the City of Phoenix faced a movement to force the city to convert from its at-large electoral arrangements to a single-member district system. As identified by the 1980 Census, Phoenix had a population of 790,045, of whom 14.7 percent were Hispanic. In part, the pressure for districts came from union groups, especially the Firemen's Union; but, in larger part, it reflected a sense in several areas of Phoenix that they were underrepresented by a "downtown elite." Maryvale, South Phoenix, Paradise Valley and Northwest Phoenix believed themselves overlooked by the existing system. As the *Phoenix Republic* reported on December 21, 1983:

> The Maryvale and south Phoenix chorus has been for increased political power. Residents maintain they never have had much of it with city council members elected at-large. Paradise Valley residents simply want to be in a district by themselves, and northwest Phoenix

have been upset about municipal services since being annexed in 1979.

On December 1, 1982, therefore, the City's 303,805 registered voters confronted a Yes or No choice in a special election on Proposition 200, an initiative increasing the City Council from six to eight members, requiring that these eight members be nominated and elected from eight geographical districts, and providing for a mayor who would continue to be elected at-large.[1] The Charter Amendment also provided that each district must have a substantially equal number of "electors."

Approval by the voters led immediately into a legal tangle over the meaning of the term "elector." Litigation[2] eventually determined that the term meant "persons eligible to vote;" and the language of the ordinance, emphasizing the words "substantially equal," was held to require achievement of a high degree of general population equality, defined as "total number of persons," as counted by the U.S. Bureau of the Census in 1980. The first major problem in drawing the new districts, therefore, was to meet the two differing population criteria. A second major problem in drawing the new districts arose from the origins of Proposition 200 and the sense of community identity that had driven it. As the *Phoenix Republic* reported on January 16, 1983:

> Despite the differences, what all of the [districting] concepts have in common is community identity. The new city council districts need to reflect existing informal communities, Phoenix residents said loudly and clearly at four public meetings. . . . Some envision Phoenix as a flower with eight petals. Others see it partitioned into vertical or horizontal strips. Some want the city divided into wedges; others are content to go along with the urban-village plan. Still others have ideas about using mountains, the Salt River or the Freeway as dividing lines. Despite the differences, what all of the concepts have in common is community identity . . . .The obvious centers mentioned again and again are the already closely knit areas of Maryvale, South Phoenix, Northwest Phoenix and Paradise Valley.

Although community identity is always an important feature of local districting, the history of Phoenix appeared to give unusually strong emphasis to it—resulting in further conflict with the dual population criteria. In other words, it was impossible to develop equipopulous districts, using either definition of equality, without splitting self-conscious communities.

The minority population of Phoenix had grown significantly in the previous two decades and was growing even further in some areas of south Phoenix. The Southwest Voter Registration Project, which had been active in the redistricting of the Arizona State Legislature, made clear its intention to play an aggressive role in assuring Justice Department enforcement of voting rights protections. Conscious above all of the needs of their own ethnic community, the Hispanic leadership gave little priority either to meeting the dual population criteria or to respecting the drive by the different geographic communities for their own boundary lines. Moreover, the process was complicated by the need to acknowledge the different--indeed, occasionally competing--claims of Phoenix's black community.

Adding to these pressures in the districting process was the insistence of the Phoenix Council on the use of additional "good government" criteria. At a minimum, the Council wanted four additional attributes in district design:

1. "Compactness and Contiguity." The Council wished to assure ease of voter access to all parts of each district, to assure substantial territorial contiguity, and to make the districts as "plain and straightforward in shape" as possible.
2. "Fit with Legislative Districts." The Council sought a high degree of correspondence with the boundaries of the new state legislative districts, both for the convenience of elected officials and for improved voter understanding of the political system. (There was also a recognition here that the new legislative districts had recently survived the tests both of public scrutiny and Justice Department review, and, therefore, could be held to possess a high degree of legitimacy.)
3. "Recognition of Natural and Manmade Barriers." The Council was concerned to give a degree of recognition in the development of districts to features such as the Salt River, the freeway system and the major mountain ranges. The view was that these were barriers that had assisted the formation of community identity, thus helping to shape the social, political and economic life of the city.[3]
4. "Respect for Administrative Units." Precinct boundaries were viewed with an unusual degree of respect by the City Council,

> which required that they be followed in drawing the new districts, especially when they were long-established and well-recognized. The Council even was prepared to accept irregularities in district lines to preserve existing precincts.

These various requirements added several layers of complexity to the redistricting process, which was then even further complicated by high levels of political tension in the many public meetings that were held during the process.

Nevertheless, it proved possible to develop a plan (see figure 36) that won the votes of a substantial majority of the City Council, while also receiving the support of the Southwest Voter Registration Project and satisfying the aspirations of most of the community groups that appeared at the various public hearings and meetings.

Much public attention focused on the creation of two "Hispanic influence districts." District 7, with a total Hispanic percent of 35.9 percent and an 18-plus Hispanic population of 32.0 percent, comprised all of Southwest Phoenix (and most of Legislative District 22, which supposedly had been designed to achieve Hispanic representation). Bounded on the east by Central Avenue and on the south by South Mountain Park, the district extended to the western limits of the city. District 8, with a total Hispanic population of 36.1 percent and an 18-plus Hispanic population of 33.0 percent, was bounded on the east and the south by the city limits, on the west by Central Avenue, and on the north by Thomas and McDowell Roads. In both districts, the black percentages were also high: in District 7, blacks accounted for 10.5 percent; and in District 8, blacks accounted for 19.4 percent.

The plan was submitted to the Justice Department and was pre-cleared without objection. To the knowledge of this writer, who was the principal technical consultant throughout the process, there were no complaints by Hispanics or other minorities regarding the process or its outcome.

The City Council, which had hoped for relatively little change in the politics of the city was taken aback by the first elections within the new district lines. Incumbents lost or nearly lost, and groups--particularly the Firemen's Union and public employees in general--who had long complained against the rule of the downtown business elites proved their power under the new system. By the end of the 1980s, only one councilmember from the old at-large system, Calvin Goode, a black representative from District 8, survived on the council.

Figure 36. Phoenix Districting Plan

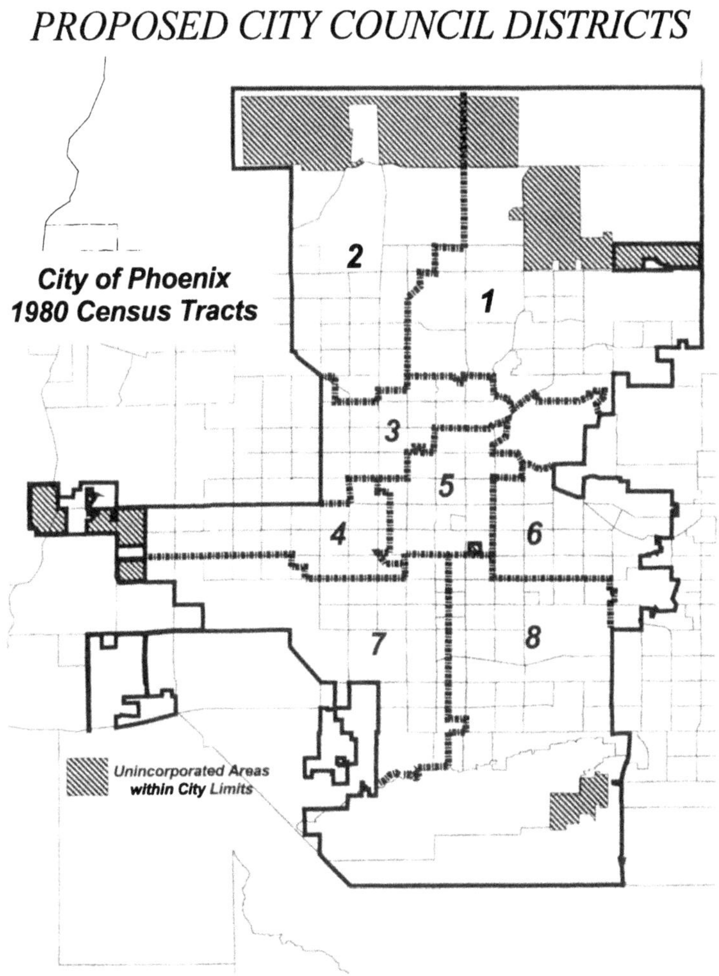

Beyond these changes in personnel, the new districts seem to have accomplished other, more fundamental, changes. Thus, senior city staff, who had experience of both electoral forms, noted that the districts were attracting new groups to council hearings and stimulating new kinds of behavior by members elected to the Council. In particular, the effort to win approval by district constituents led council members to press for increased staff, to emphasize district projects (at the expense of city-wide projects and programs) and, in general, to develop their skills as "ombudsmen" and representatives of the particular needs of their individual districts, which had become their only crucial political base.

REDISTRICTING PHOENIX

The 1990 census reported more than twenty percent growth in Phoenix's population, adding nearly 200,000 persons to its 1980 population to make a new total of 984,281. The two most marked aspects of this growth were: first, the large increase in non-minority population in Phoenix's affluent, northern areas[4] and in the extreme south (the Ahwatukee area); and second, the growth of the minority population—the black population from 38,893 or 4.9 percent in 1980 to 51,090 or 5.2 percent in 1990, and the Hispanic population from 115,780 or 14.7 percent in 1980 to a new total of 197,159 or 20.0 percent. The bulk of the minority population was still found to the south of Indian School (where there was total population sufficient to create slightly more than three districts); whereas north of Indian School, the minority population was much lighter (in an area where there was sufficient population to create nearly five districts).

In January of 1991, this writer was retained as principal technical consultant to the City's redistricting. The process began with interviews with councilmembers, the mayor, city staff and others, in which an effort was made to outline major criteria, to determine an appropriate approach, and to identify basic building blocks for districts.[5] In late February, the consultant produced a map of all the community associations registered with the city and designed citizen redistricting kits for use by interested members of the public. In early March, also, map overlays were completed of Phoenix's Village areas and elementary school districts. On March 26, an initial plan was presented to the City Council that incorporated features derived from public hearings. Six further public hearings were held in early April. In early

April, also, several citizen kit plans were analyzed and a further report was submitted to the City Council. On April 24, a presentation was made to the City Council on four acceptable options for redistricting the City and a memorandum recommending technical emendations to whichever plan the Council adopted was also submitted. Following this testimony, additional options were presented by citizen groups, after which the Council adopted the plan recommended by the consultant. An obvious complication of the redistricting was the aggressive stance of the Justice Department and of several minority groups and voting rights activists. The process was occurring in the wake of a number of controversial voting rights cases, including the findings in *Gomez v. Watsonville* and the Southern California case of *Garza v. Los Angeles County* which had struck down an incumbent-protection plan in order to implement a plaintiff's plan that maximized Hispanic power. Moreover, the rules that had emerged from the Court's key ruling in *Thornburg v. Gingles* seemed to emphasize a requirement that majority-minority districts be formed when minority groups were large enough and sufficiently concentrated to form a majority of the population in single-member districts.[6] The most pressing legal and technical question seemed to center on the degree to which the minority populations of Districts 7 and 8 should be enhanced. Was it sufficient to maintain the minority percentages that had successfully elected the minority incumbents in these districts? Or should steps be taken toward "maximized minority districts," as urged by some activists in the minority communities?

In addition to the federal mandates respecting total population and minority representation, the Phoenix City Council committed itself to achieving districts that would meet other planned criteria. These were:

> *Community Identity*. The initial districting of Phoenix had made clear the unusual importance that Phoenicians gave to their Village concept, their community associations, and their elementary school districts. The Council, therefore, insisted that "community identity" be an important consideration in district design and that every effort be made to support and build further the local sense of community. For the same reasons, the Council emphasized the importance of incorporating as boundaries, wherever possible, the well recognized street geography of the city.[7]

Existing Jurisdictional Boundaries. The Council thought that the districts that had been in existence since 1984 had given the City effective representation for most of a decade and, therefore, should be respected to the extent possible in the development of new districts. Although accepting that the federal mandate for equality of population was forcing a basic re-design, the Council wanted to preserve at least some of the basic logic of the existing plan and, wherever possible, to continue at least the core of existing councilmanic districts, if not their actual boundaries.[8] The Council also wanted to give at least some recognition to other jurisdictional boundaries and asked the consultant to work with existing whole precincts.

Population Growth. The high-growth districts were said to place a substantial burden of constituent representation on their councilmembers, who urged, therefore, that the districts attempt to anticipate future population growth. Thus, to the extent that the new districts deviated from population equality, the Council wished such deviations to be in line with projected future growth patterns.

Voter Recognition and Voter Access. The Council wished the districts to be easily recognized by voters and to be fully compact and contiguous.

On the consultant's recommendation, the city staff contacted all of the minority organizations within the City and in the greater Phoenix metropolitan area, alerting them to the redistricting process and offering information and assistance.[9] The new data showed that the two existing "minority districts"--represented by Mary Rose Wilcox, an Hispanic, and Calvin Goode, an African American--could be significantly improved in terms of their minority population. Indeed, it would be possible to draw them to assure large majorities of Hispanic and black population; but to do so would involve separating them from the predominantly white area of Ahwatukee, which had developed at the southernmost end of the City (Districts 7 and 8 overlay Ahwatukee, a rapidly growing white area of relatively high income. The clear projection was that this area would grow more rapidly than its neighboring minority areas). A further complication was that District 4's Hispanic population had increased to nearly 28 percent of its total, and if the aim was to increase the Hispanic percentage in Districts 7 and 8, a reach into the territory of District 4 would become necessary; yet, to do this might prevent the further development of District 4 as a "minority influence" district. A further complication was the fact that District 8, with an Hispanic population of 39 percent and a black population of only 14.2 percent, was represented by an African American, a fact that led some Hispanic groups to suggest adding to the District's Hispanic numbers.

Convinced that a plan with two minority districts must be maintained, the consultant soon saw that the Ahwatukee issue would loom as the most troublesome in the redistricting process. On April 19, the consultant reported:

> We have continued to research the Ahwatukee issue. . . . The necessity of creating two minority districts forces the issue of separating Ahwatukee from the area of heavy minority population north of South Mountain. Our original recommended plan provided for such a separation; and, apart from a very few objections, it has not been contested. Moreover, most of the Citizen Kit plans have accepted the necessity of the Ahwatukee separation. . . . We now conclude that there is simply *no substitute* for separation. Indeed, we believe that Ahwatukee's projected population growth virtually mandates separation, if escalating ethnic dilution and the associated legal and constitutional problems are to be avoided.

The consultant knew that a plan providing for two solid majority-minority districts could be created and would win approval from the City Council, including the votes of the two minority representatives. Increasingly, however, controversy focused on the character of the "bridge" between Ahwatukee and the non-minority district to the north of Districts 7 and 8.

At this point,[10] the two minority groups entered the process, one suggesting that the Ahwatukee issue be ignored, the other asserting a voting rights claim that the Ahwatukee separation must be as narrow as technically feasible. The Southwest Voter Registration Project ignored the Ahwatukee problem to create three "minority districts:" a District 4 with a total minority population of 29 percent (Hispanic population 23.58, black population 5.42); a District 7 with a total minority population of 54 percent (Hispanic population of 45.5 percent, black population of 8.54 percent) and a District 8 with a minority population of 55 percent (Hispanic population of 41.28 percent, black population of 14.19). The City Attorney's view was that this recommendation would not survive pre-clearance in the Department of Justice; and, since it retained the rapidly growing white population of Ahwatukee in Calvin Goode's district, that councilmember vigorously opposed it.

The Phoenix Chapter of the Arizona Hispanic Community Forum (AHCF) presented an alternative to the consultant's proposed District 6 strip for purposes of the Ahwatukee separation. AHCF pointed out that "there presently exist neighborhoods in the proposed one mile strip between 40th and 48th Streets that are predominantly minority, specifically Hispanic and black. This strip, some call it 'the barbell,' will not provide members of those neighborhoods with a true opportunity for representation." Instead of the one-mile wide strip advocated by the consultant, AHCF urged:

> . . . a five foot strip running south from Sky Harbor Airport along the municipal boundaries of Tempe and Guadalupe, to Guadalupe Road, thence west to follow the eastern and southern boundary of South Mountain Park, and to follow the continuation and boundary of the South Mountain Village. . . . This will allow the minority community to have a true opportunity for representation on the Phoenix City Council.

Although the consultant recommended against it, the Council incorporated the five-foot wide Ahwatukee strip in the consultant's recommended plan. The resulting shape is seen at figure 37. The full plan is seen at figure 38. It is worth mentioning that "the Ahwatukee strip" was later used as precedent by the Arizona Legislature in the design of a similarly dis-contiguous legislative district.

All eight council seats were up for election following the redistricting. Mary Rose Wilcox (with 72.58 percent of the vote) and Calvin Goode (with 58.72 percent of the vote) were re-elected easily. The only casualty was Linda Naldolski, incumbent of District 6 with the Ahwatukee corridor. This district changed hands once again in 1993. Also in 1993, two Hispanics and two African Americans ran for the seat of retiring African American councilman Calvin Goode. African American Cody Williams won the seat. In 1995, Solomon Leija, an Hispanic, was narrowly defeated in a runoff with Anglo Doug Lingner (51.18 percent to 48.82 percent) in a race to replace retiring Hispanic incumbent Mary Rose Wilcox. Leija led in the primary 42.5 percent to 38.27 percent. Council District 5, the "minority influence"

Figure 37. Phoenix Ahwatukee Corridor

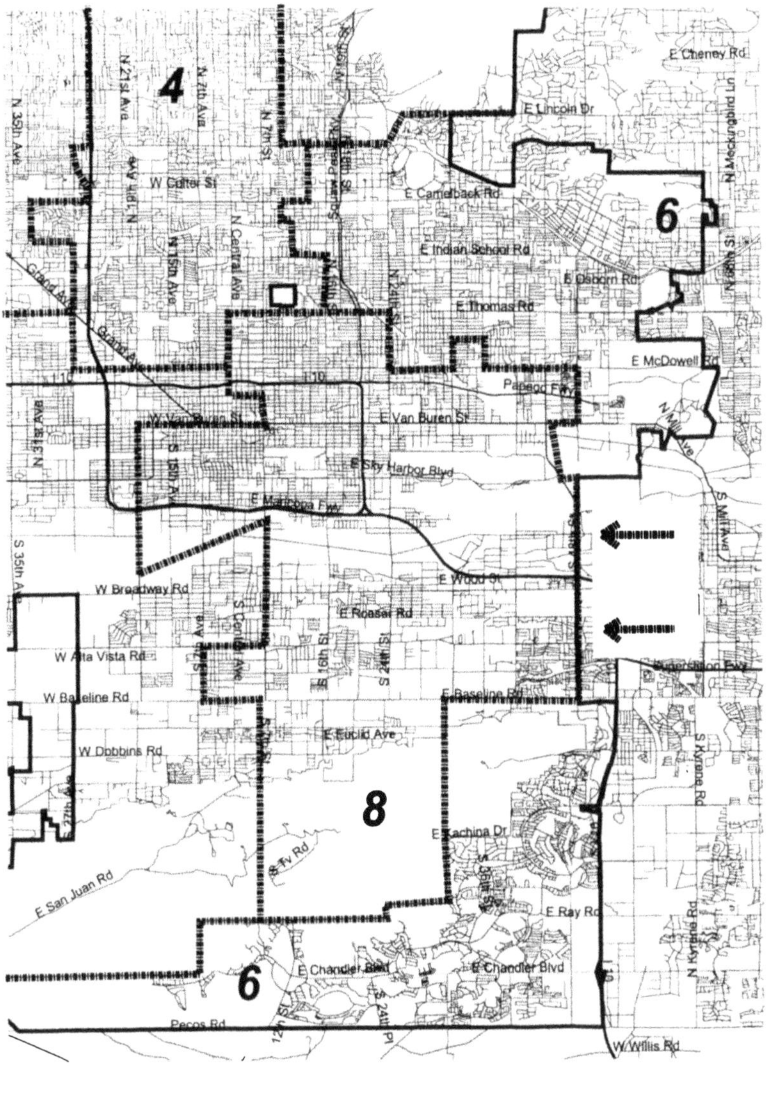

Figure 38. Phoenix Redistricting Plan.

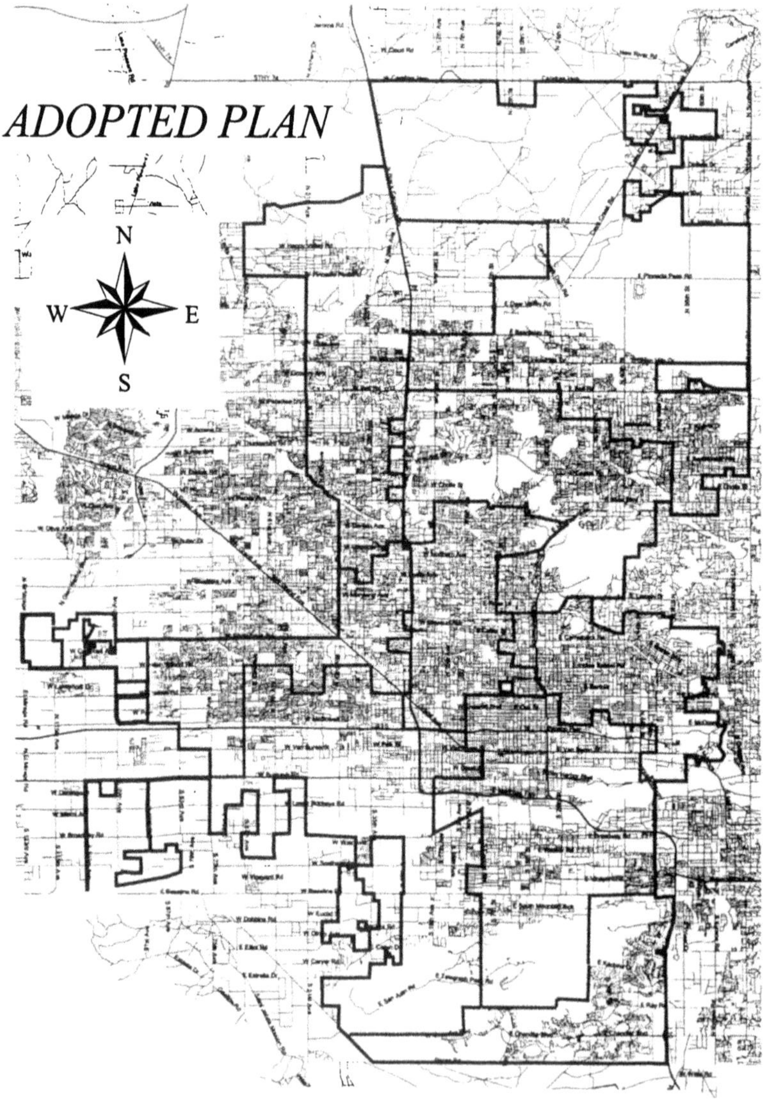

district produced only one minority candidacy in the two elections following the redistricting.

The Ahwatukee corridor served to preserve minority representation in District 8. Unlike the districts struck down in North Carolina, Georgia and Texas, which were drawn solely to create minority districts, Phoenix's District 8 was compact and contiguous. The bizarre district in this case linked two Anglo communities in order to preserve a minority community of interest from being swamped by the addition of a predominantly Anglo area. Whether it will be necessary to continue the linkage in 2001 remains to be seen. What will be the impact of the *Vera* and *Hunt* decisions on Justice Department actions regarding creation of minority districts and preservation of neighborhoods?

NOTES

1. For news coverage, see the *Phoenix Gazette*, November 30, 1992.

2. *American Continental Corporation vs. Donna Culbertson*, Superior Court, Division II, Arizona, No. C-479271.

3. Anyone who looks at a map of Phoenix can recognize the major features of its physical and man-made geography. Especially impressive as physical barriers to communication are the South Mountain and the Phoenix Mountain Preserve. The Black Canyon Freeway serves as a major north-south communication link; and the Hohokam Expressway and 48th Street constitute the major transportation corridor to the east of the city – indeed, the only internal city link between Ahwatukee and the airport and Phoenix Gateway area. The failure of political geography to catch up with the rapid development of the city's transportation complex is suggested by the fact that the three other major freeways – Papago, Squaw Peak, and Maricopa – do not follow precinct lines.

4. It was in Districts 1 and 2, at the City's northern end, that the population surge had been most marked. District 1, with a population of 178,483 had developed a positive deviation from the new ideal of 45.1 percent. District 2 with a population of 149,362 had a positive deviation of 21.4 percent.

5. The consultant set forth an understanding of the tasks that should be involved in the redistricting in a Preliminary Report to the City Council on February 5, entitled, "The Redistricting Process in Phoenix." This report set out the detail of the planned approach and timetable; it also covered the criteria to be used, including a full discussion of the federal mandates regarding equal population and minority representation.

6. Of course, the Court also required evidence that the minority typically voted together and was politically cohesive, and further, that the white majority was sufficiently cohesive, or voted together as a block enough, that it usually defeated the minority preferred candidate. In Phoenix, the presence of two minority incumbents on the Council, suggested that the initial districts would not be subject to Section 2 challenge; but even this fact was brought into question by the Court's express statement in *Gingles* that the 1982 amendments to the Voting Rights Act "plainly demonstrated that proof that some minority candidates have been elected does not foreclose a Section 2 claim." The *Gingles* majority opinion had held further that a challenged redistricting plan, "if it works to dilute the minority vote, . . . cannot be defended on the ground that it sporadically and serendipitously benefits minority voters."

7. This emphasis was further brought out in public hearings and public meetings in different parts of the City. These gave evidence of a very strong popular aspiration to protect Villages, neighborhood associations and school districts in the drawing of councilmanic lines. Representatives of both village and elementary school districts appeared at many of the meetings, as did numbers of persons representing neighborhood associations. The necessity of cutting their communities, forced by the federal mandates concerning equality of population and minority representation, was never accepted by some participants, who saw these mandates as proof of gross federal interference at the local level.

8. Perhaps it does not need to be remarked that this criterion is not remote from the aim of incumbent protection.

9. Citizen kits were specially messengered to the Southwest Voter Registration Project and other minority organizations.

10. That is to say, very late in the process, just before the April 19 hearing.

CHAPTER 8

The Arizona Cases: Glendale

Municipalities such as Glendale and Peoria, Arizona (the next two case studies) posted percentage increases in population that far exceeded percentage changes in state population. Moreover, for cities that are required to redistrict (Peoria) or that have the option to redistrict (Glendale) after a mid-decade census, preserving a stable core for districts is very challenging. Another challenge to successful redistricting is brought about by the aggressive annexation policies of both cities, a policy that has affected significantly their growth and growth potential.

The City of Glendale, located in the western portion of Arizona's Maricopa County and part of the Phoenix metropolitan area, is a primarily residential community, many of whose residents work in Phoenix or are retirees. The City's growth has been dramatic, much more than doubling its population in the decade of the 1970s (from 36,200 to 97,200), adding a further 50,000 in the 1980s (to reach a population 148,134 in 1990), and yet a further 35,000 persons in the first half of the decade of the 1990s. In not much more than a half-century, Glendale has been transformed from a primarily agricultural to an urban community.[1]

In October of 1987, a group known as Glendale Citizens for a Responsive Government, led by citizen activists Bill and Carol Stout, filed 11,343 signatures to place an initiative on Glendale's 1988 primary election ballot.[2] The initiative required the replacement of Glendale's traditional at-large electoral system with six single-member districts. Arguments made for the proposition ranged from improvement of representation for all citizens to enhancement of representation of Glendale's Hispanic community.[3]

Glendale's City Council perceived the threat to its continued existence offered by the initiative, known as Proposition 100. It placed a competing measure, Proposition 101, on the primary ballot, providing for a modified district system. The Council's measure provided that the City would be divided into three districts, from each of which a council member would be elected in 1990, while the remaining three councilmembers would be elected at-large in 1992.

The primary election in February of 1988 saw Proposition 101, the Council's modified district system, receive 3,028 "Yes" votes, 3,216 "No" votes; while the Citizens' Measure, Proposition 100, received 4,750 "Yes" votes, and 2,223 "No" votes. Thus, Glendale's charter was amended to provide for a council elected from six single-member districts, serving four year terms, with a mayor elected at-large every two years.[4] The Charter Amendment required that each district must contain a substantially equal number of "electors," a term referring to persons eighteen years of age or older and eligible to register to cast votes.[5]

This writer was responsible for the development of Glendale's six new districts in 1988 (and for redistrictings in 1992 and 1996). The mid-decade census of 1985, which had reported a total of 122,400 residents, was already badly outdated four years later by an on-going development boom that was occurring especially in the primarily Anglo portions of north Glendale; but it provided the only uncontested official data. The census had reported that Glendale's population included 19,600 Hispanic residents, around one-third of whom were concentrated in the old downtown section of Glendale.[6] The other two-thirds of Glendale's Hispanic residents were much more dispersed, with increasing numbers moving into the residential areas north of Northern Avenue.

Given the dispersal of the Hispanic population, it was known from the beginning of the 1988 process that it would be impossible to create a district in which Hispanics (or even Hispanics combined with all other minority groups), would constitute a voting majority. This writer developed various maps showing Hispanic and other minority population and experimented on the computer with many different configurations, none of which was found to come even close to forming a "majority-minority" district. Nevertheless, although creation of such a district was impossible, Glendale's Council committed itself to enhancing minority representation through the districting process in order to add to minority opportunities to participate and influence city politics.[7]

The well-known challenges facing Hispanics in election politics—especially non-citizen population and low incidence of registration, as well as a high proportion of under voting age population—suggested that it would be especially important to create a district that would enhance their opportunities for political organization. It was in Glendale's downtown area that Hispanics had organized most effectively in the past, and it was, therefore, around that area that it was decided to focus a new "Hispanic influence" district. In terms of Glendale's councilmanic politics, however, this decision involved a direct challenge to Bob Huffman, a veteran of the Council, who was strongly committed to enhancing his electoral prospects in the course of the redistricting process and who felt keenly threatened by the prospect of adding to the Hispanic percentage in his home base.[8]

Research preparatory to the 1988 redistricting showed that Glendale had no experience of polarized voting behavior; indeed, the city seemed to have no issues that might tend to polarize the community on racial grounds. Moreover, well before the creation of the district system in 1988, an Hispanic had been elected to the Glendale city council. Nevertheless, given the known interest of the Voting Rights Section of the Justice Department in Arizona's Hispanic community and its pre-clearance authority, it was decided to conduct a process with the most extensive outreach possible to Glendale's Hispanic community.[9] Citizen kits[10] were provided to Hispanic organizations and interested Hispanic individuals; and channels of communication were kept open with the Hispanic community in all areas of the city. In effect, it was determined that everything possible would be done to encourage Hispanic involvement in the districting process.

As it turned out, however, despite these efforts, Hispanic interest in districting proved scant. Representatives of national and statewide Hispanic organizations contacted the consultant by telephone for information and warned that they were closely monitoring the process (although there was no evidence that they did, in fact, do so). An unsuccessful Hispanic candidate from the 1986 elections spoke critically of the process (but failed to develop a map or to make concrete suggestions for boundary improvements).[11] And an Hispanic from a neighboring town, who had been active in statewide Hispanic organizations, attended a meeting. With these exceptions, however, no Hispanic showed an active interest in the process.

Once a majority of the Glendale Council had shown itself prepared to override Huffman's objections to the concentration of Hispanics in a downtown-centered district, the districting task proved straightforward. The final plan (see figure 39 and table 23) provided for a district, named "Ocotillo," that encompassed an Hispanic population of 36.4 percent. Although it was known that the area was most unlikely to experience population growth, the district's population was kept below the ideal—that is, it was given a "negative deviation"—in order to avoid dilution of the Hispanic vote.

Officials from the Voting Rights Section of the U.S. Department of Justice contacted various Hispanic groups for comments; but the plan was successfully pre-cleared. In the 1990 election following the districting, three districts, including the Hispanic influence district, Ocotillo, were up for election. The incumbent of Ocotillo, Bob Huffman, defeated Hispanic candidate Bobby Gonzales, 53.7 percent to 46.3 percent. Ocotillo District had the lowest registration total, roughly half the number of registered voters found in Cholla or Barrel Districts: thus, Mr. Huffman won with 892 votes, while it took 1,219 and 1,956 votes respectively for wins in Cholla and Barrel.

The census of 1990 reported that Glendale had a new population of 148,134. A huge disparity had developed between the populations of the areas to the north of the city, where most of the development in the previous half decade had been concentrated, and the districts to the south, especially the old downtown area, which included much of the Hispanic population. Thus, the Cholla district as drawn in 1988 had grown from 19,561 to 27,962 in 1990; but the Ocotillo district, drawn in 1988 with a population of 19,600 had a 1990 population of only 21,188. The latter district, drawn in 1988 with a high negative deviation in order to accommodate the aim to maximize its minority population percentage, was now dwarfed by the primarily Anglo districts in the rapidly growing areas of Glendale.

Again, as in 1988, the chief technical task was to develop districts in compliance with both federal law and the Glendale Charter, giving priority to the federal requirements of equal population and respect for minority voting rights, but roughly equalizing the numbers of "electors." Again, it was clear that the major hurdle would be pre-clearance by the Justice Department of the submitted plan; and, therefore, once again, the process was devised to involve constant contact with Hispanic organizations and interested Hispanic individuals in Glendale and the surrounding areas. It was obvious, also, that the most careful craftsmanship would be necessary to draw the Ocotillo district to avoid "retrogression" from the percentage originally achieved for the Hispanic population in that district.

The concept of "retrogression" had been gaining legal and practical force in the years prior to 1990.[12] The 1976 case of *Beer v. United States*[13] had begun the use of the concept in a way that seemed likely to limit the reach of the Justice Department's pre-clearance authority in Section 5 cases.[14] Under the original *Beer* standard, any enhancement of minority voting strength of the existing arrangements was viewed by the Court as affording prima facie grounds for mandatory approval by the Justice Department of a new plan in Section 5 jurisdictions. This understanding of the concept, however, began to change as a result of continuing voting rights litigation: the Supreme Court affirmed a number of district court rulings that softened this interpretation of retrogression.[15] Moreover, the 1982 amendments to the Voting Rights Act resulted in a much more aggressive use by the Justice Department of the retrogression concept in its pre-clearance decisions. By 1991, therefore, it seemed clear that the Justice Department would refuse to countenance any diminution from the 36.4 percent Hispanic population that had been achieved in the 1988 plan.

The total minority population of Glendale in the 1990 Census was 31,555 persons, or 21.30 percent of the City's total population. This minority population, already widely dispersed throughout the city in 1985, had dispersed even further by 1990, with increasing numbers of minority residents buying homes in the more affluent northern parts of the city and in the rapidly growing middle class areas of Glendale's southwest portion. The Hispanics continued, of course, to be the largest minority group, but they accounted for only 15.47 percent of the City's total population (down from 16.01 percent in 1985); the eighteen-plus Hispanic population amounted to no more than 13.02 percent; and, given the proportion of non-citizen Hispanics, the total eligible Hispanic voting population was even smaller.

As a basic minimum, therefore, a chief aim of the 1992 process was to assure that the Hispanic population in the new Ocotillo district would be higher than the Hispanic population percentage of the Ocotillo District in the plan pre-cleared by the U.S. Department of Justice in 1989 (namely 36.40 percent). This aim, of course, was complicated by the fact that, as drawn in 1988, Ocotillo had been

Figure 39. Glendale, Arizona, Districting, 1988

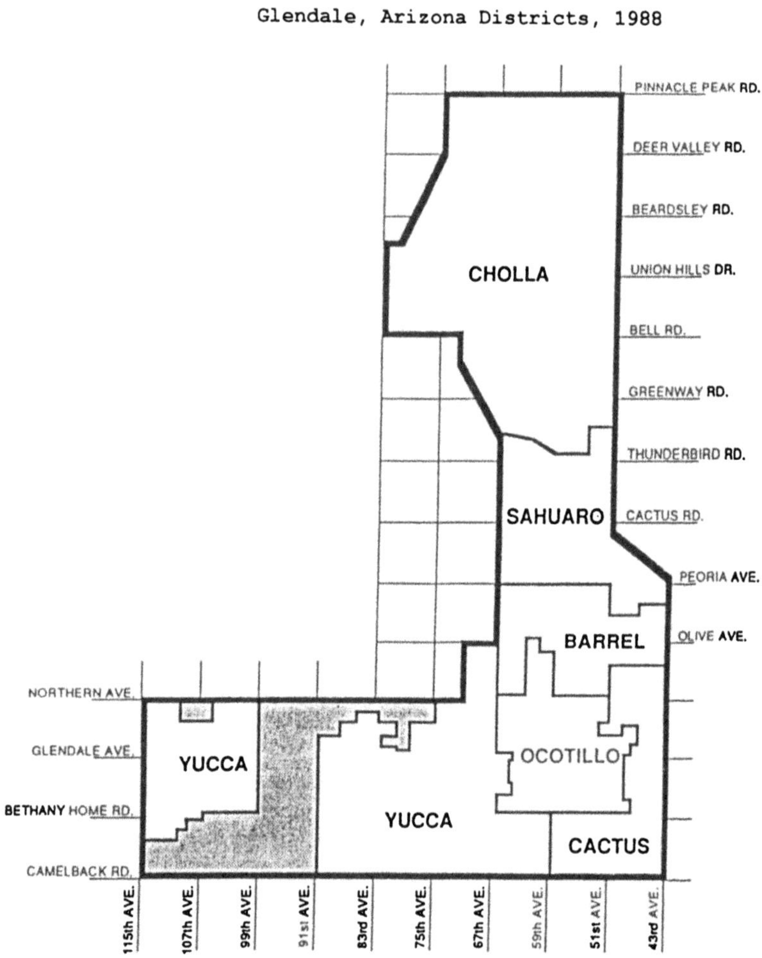

Table 23. Glendale, Arizona—Districting, 1988

	Cholla	Sahuaro	Barrel	Cactus	Ocotillo	Yucca
1985 Total Population	19,561	21,251	20,502	20,789	19,600	20,759
Deviation	-849	841	92	379	-810	349
% Deviation	-4.16%	4.12%	0.45%	1.86%	-3.97%	1.71%
1985 Hispanic Population	1,213	1,561	1,329	1,502	7,134	2,856
Percent	6.20%	7.35%	6.48%	7.22%	36.40%	13.76%

Figure 40. Glendale, Arizona, Plot of Hispanic Population, 1990 Census

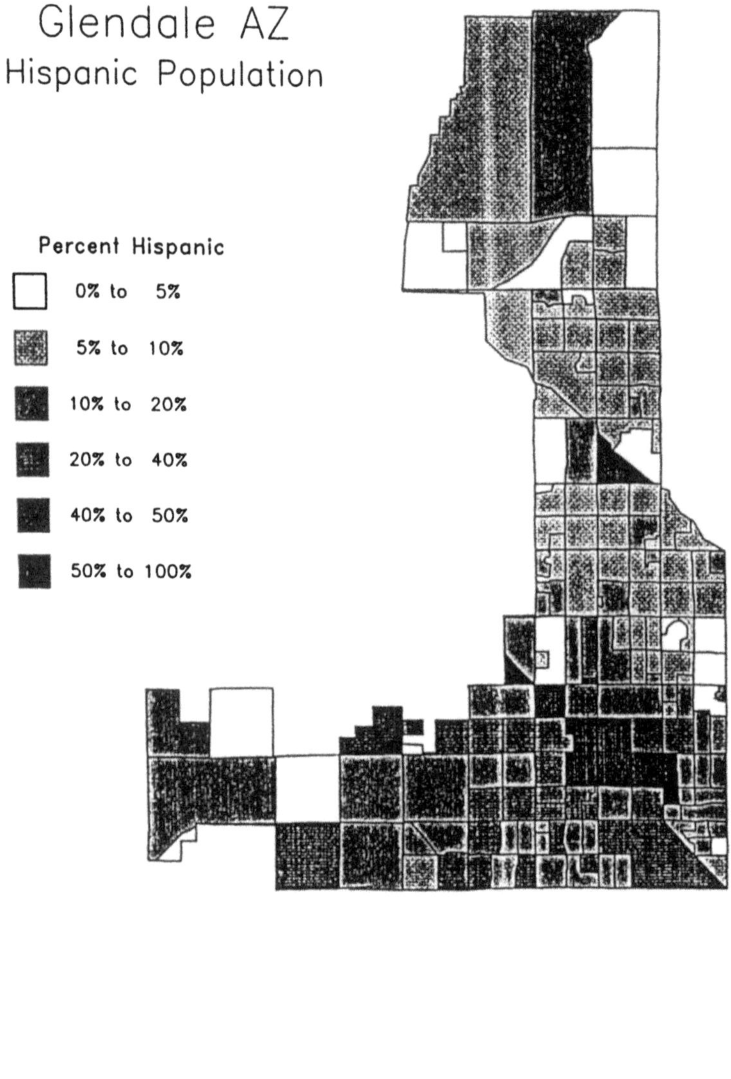

significantly deviant from the ideal population—a negative deviation of minus 3.9 percent in terms of the 1985 census figures. The 1990 census now recorded that there were 21,188 persons in the 1988-drawn Ocotillo district, or a negative deviation from the new ideal (24,689 persons) of minus 14.18 percent. Thus, in order to equalize Ocotillo with the other districts in the 1992 plan—and to bring Glendale's districting system into accord with federal population standards[16]—more than three thousand additional persons had to be added to the district.[17]

The effort to include all the important concentrations of Glendale's downtown Hispanic community in a single district and to avoid "retrogression" led to a further contortion of the boundary lines in designing a new Ocotillo in order to capture heavily Hispanic census blocks. Again, the consultant used computer-drawn maps of Hispanic concentrations (see, for example, figure 40) to assist the process of district design. As finally drawn, the new Ocotillo's Hispanic percentage of 37.33 percent compared favorably with the 36.4 percent of the Ocotillo district drawn in 1989; and, although this Hispanic percentage could have been raised slightly (perhaps by a further one or two percent) by even further contorting the district's boundaries, this would have necessitated the addition of new territory, not previously comprehended in the district and not hitherto organized by Hispanic groups. Moreover, the problems of candidate and voter recognition of the district boundaries had been most pronounced in the Ocotillo 1988 district in the 1990 election, and there was general agreement among the few Hispanics who participated in the 1992 process that their task of political organization should not be complicated further by drawing a district that would be even less compact.[18]

Given the requirement for a much larger Ocotillo, the task of improving beyond the 36.4 Hispanic percentage was bound to entail a complex series of block additions to the already irregular boundaries of the 1988 Ocotillo district. What, however, if the Justice Department insisted on using as a benchmark the Hispanic percentage of the 1988 Ocotillo as reported in the 1990 census—namely 41.95 percent? To achieve such a five percentage point increase would require gerrymandering of an extreme kind and the extension of long fingers of territory to pick up every available Hispanic precinct. Use of such a benchmark seemed clearly inappropriate on two further grounds. First, it was a percentage in a district configuration that had been achieved only by use of a negative deviation from equality (in the quite extraordinary circumstances of Glendale's late-1980s population explosion). Second, it was a percentage of a population that was now more than three thousand persons short of equality—in other words, a population that no longer afforded a constitutionally permissible basis for district representation.

In theory, it might be argued that heroic measures should be taken—that Ocotillo's lines should be contorted in any way possible—to garner as much additional Hispanic population as feasible. As a practical matter, however, the Hispanic representatives in the process believed that to do so would achieve nothing besides fragmenting the existing political base that they had developed in the Ocotillo area. In light of all of these considerations, therefore, it was decided that the benchmark appropriate in the design of the new Ocotillo should be its original 36.4 percent.

A final plan, incorporating an Ocotillo with a 37.33 percent Hispanic percentage, was approved by the Glendale Council for submission to the U.S. Department of Justice. Again, Hispanic participation in the process was minimal but there were no objections from Hispanics to the plan as presented. See map at figure 41 and data at table 24.

Nevertheless, the U.S. Department of Justice communicated to Glendale that it was not satisfied with the Ocotillo District as presented and that it required an explanation of the retrogression that had occurred from the 41.95 percent of 1990. The consultant objected that this was a percentage of a district population that was now several thousand persons short of equality—in other words, a population that no longer constituted a basis for district representation. The Department was informed, too, that at no point in the 1992 process had any criticism been voiced by Hispanics or by any other minorities of the proposed Ocotillo district. A further argument was made that the Ocotillo district as drawn comprised territory with which Hispanic groups were already familiar for purposes of political organization. Moreover, it was urged that to add new territory in a way that would substantially reconfigure the district would involve an extreme gerrymander, the chief result of which would be to complicate the tasks of political organization. Are minor statistical gains, the consultant asked, so important as to compel incorporation of unorganized territory that no known Hispanic group or individual is interested in representing? It was noted as well that Glendale's Hispanic population as a whole had declined proportionate to the City's total population.

Figure 41. Glendale, Arizona, Redistricing 1992

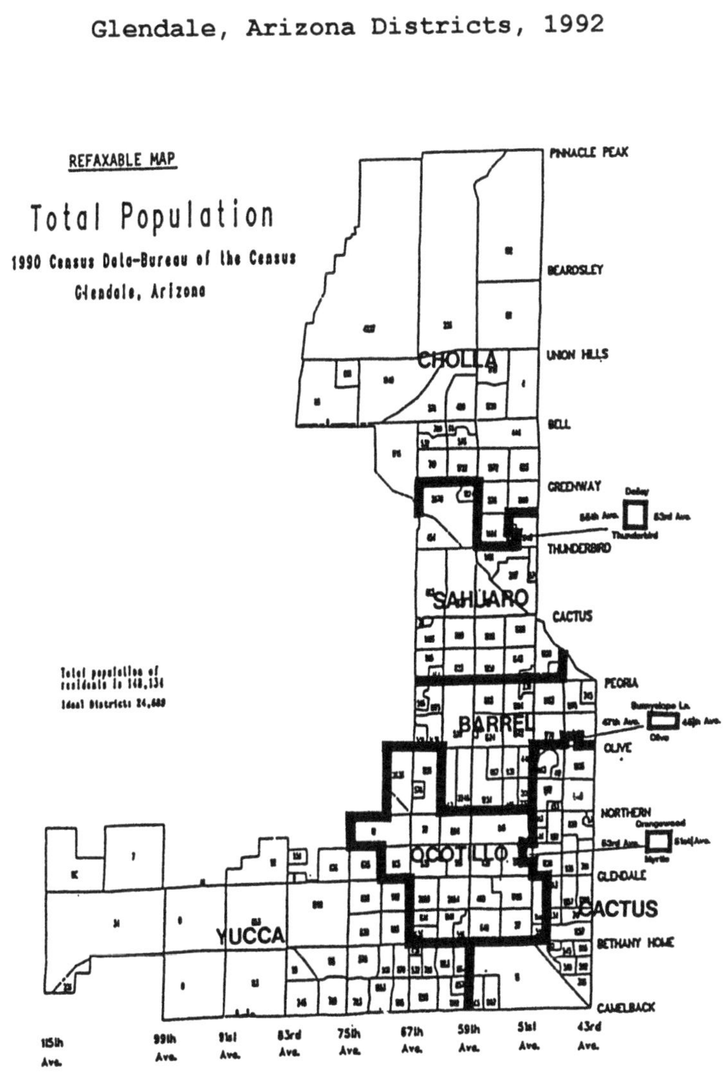

Table 24. Glendale, Arizona—Redistricting, 1992

	Yucca	%	Ocotillo	%	Cactus	%	Barrel	%	Sahuaro	%	Cholla	%	Glendale	%
Persons	23,986		24,682		25,150		25,120		25,222		23,974		148,134	
Hispanic	4573	19.07	9,213	37.33	2,599	10.33	2,915	11.60	2,036	8.07	1,575	6.57	22,911	15.47
NH White	17,556	73.19	14,161	57.37	21,055	83.72	20,313	80.86	21,925	86.93	21,569	89.97	116,579	78.70
NH Black	1173	4.89	649	2.63	621	2.47	1,066	4.24	487	1.93	264	1.10	4,260	2.88
NH Amer. Ind.	237	0.99	332	1.35	180	0.72	256	1.02	92	0.36	104	0.43	1,201	0.81
NH Asian	410	1.71	252	1.02	668	2.66	524	2.09	657	2.60	452	1.89	2,963	2.00
NH Other	37	0.15	75	0.30	27	0.11	46	0.18	25	0.10	10	0.04	220	0.15
Total 18+	16,355		17,234		18,261		19,001		17,227		16,821		104,899	
18+ Hispanic	2593	15.85	5,384	31.24	1,651	9.04	1,830	9.63	1,237	7.18	966	5.74	13,661	13.02
NH 18+ White	12,578	76.91	11,020	63.94	15,577	85.30	15,911	83.74	15,187	88.16	15,291	90.90	85,564	81.57
NH 18+ Black	730	4.46	379	2.20	438	2.40	672	3.54	309	1.79	176	1.05	2,704	2.58
NH 18+ Amer. Ind.	143	0.87	221	1.28	106	0.58	162	0.85	54	0.31	67	0.40	753	0.72
NH 18+ Asian	294	1.80	188	1.09	475	2.60	399	2.10	432	2.51	317	1.88	2,105	2.01
NH 18+ Other	17	0.10	42	0.24	14	0.08	27	0.14	8	0.05	4	0.02	112	0.11

"NH" = "Not of Hispanic Origin"

Table 24 (continued)

District Deviations (Ideal District: 24,689)

	Yucca	Ocotillo	Cactus	Barrel	Sahuaro	Cholla
Population	23,986	24,682	25,150	25,120	25,222	23,974
Deviation	-703	-7	461	431	533	-715
	-2.85%	-0.03%	1.87%	1.75%	2.16%	-2.90%

Electoral Deviations (Ideal District: 17,483)

	Yucca	Ocotillo	Cactus	Barrel	Sahuaro	Cholla
18+ Population	16,355	17,234	18,261	19,001	17,227	16,821
Deviation	-1128	-249	778	1518	-256	-662
	-6.45%	-1.42%	4.45%	8.68%	-1.46%	-3.79%

Despite these arguments, the officials in the Voting Rights Section continued to argue for a more extreme racial gerrymander over a period of several weeks. Only with the release of the Court's decision in *Shaw v. Reno*, did the Justice Department agree to pre-clear the plan.

Following the 1992 redistricting Bobby Gonzales challenged incumbent Bob Huffman again in 1994, but he withdrew prior to the election for health reasons. No other Hispanic candidates evinced any active interest in running for office.

Citing rapid growth in the north and the large populated annexation of Luke Air Force Base in the southwest, the Glendale Council chose to redistrict following the 1995 mid-decade census, as allowed under the City Charter. In the years following the previous redistricting, the Hispanic population of Glendale had climbed from 15.47 percent to 19.76 percent, but much of this increase had again occurred in the more affluent portions of the city, in districts other than Ocotillo. Again, the major obstacle was the concept of retrogression and the likely objections the Department of Justice would make to an Ocotillo District that fell short of its 1990 Hispanic total.

Despite the fact that there was little if any evidence of Hispanic mobilization in Ocotillo and despite the fact that the Council had appointed a Hispanic councilmember to the Cholla District,[19] the chief thrust of the redistricting process was again to concentrate Hispanics in "the Hispanic District" (which continued to re-elect the veteran, Councilman Huffman). Representatives of the Hispanic Forum, who briefly participated in the process, shared their view that the likely political development of the Hispanic community would come, not from Ocotillo, but from neighboring districts where more highly educated and politically active Hispanic candidates are now living. Yet, like the City's senior staff and voting rights attorney, they were so convinced of the importance of avoiding retrogression that they, also, backed a higher Hispanic total in Ocotillo.

Evidently "non-retrogressive redistricting" has become a permanent feature of Section 5 redistrictings. Less clear, however, is the benefit of non-retrogression to Hispanic political aspirations. Indeed, in the 1996 process the question was voiced by members of the Council concerning the danger of raising Hispanic percentages to such a level that meeting the non-retrogression standard would prove impossible in 2001. Thus it is possible that the standard could prove a deterrent to maximization of Hispanic concentrations.

NOTES

1. Glendale's early development was largely determined by the construction of the railroad in 1895, which linked Phoenix and Prescott to Glendale and encouraged its development as the processing center for the area's major agricultural products. Suburban development was rapid in the decades after the Second World War, a period when Glendale's Bell Road first began to expand as a commercial artery. Traffic patterns in the Metropolitan area began to encourage residential development to the north of Bell Road in the early 1970s; and, following annexation of these areas, the Paloma Corporation began development of the Arrowhead Ranch in 1983. Continuing development interest has been stimulated by construction of the Outer Loop Freeway through the Foothills area. Nearly all of Glendale's significant geographic features are man-made.

2. Based on a 5 percent random sample, the Maricopa County Recorder's office found 2,179 of the signatures invalid; but the remaining 9,164 valid signatures far exceeded the required total of 7,266 signatures, thus helping to mute or even cow opposition to the measure on the City Council and by supporters of the at-large arrangements of the existing charter.

3. The Stouts claimed to have worked closely with leaders of the Hispanic community in developing and campaigning for the initiative.

4. The charter amendment did not change the provision of the existing charter for staggered four-year terms for councilmembers, with three council seats being decided every two years. Thus, a process was established by ordinance deciding in which three districts council elections would be held in 1990, and in which three districts council elections would be held in 1992.

5. Obviously, this Charter requirement involved strong potential for conflict with federal constitutional mandates requiring equipopulous districts—"equal" in the case of these mandates being based on total population. In 1985, the City had reported 85,700 persons of age eighteen or older (namely the "electors" that the Charter Amendment required to be equalized by district).

6. This is the area south of Northern Avenue, north of Bethany Home Road, west of 51st Avenue, and east of 67th Avenue.

7. At an early point, on recommendation of the consultant, the city council publicly committed itself to the development of a district that would provide for a significant concentration of the Hispanic population in the downtown area.

8. Huffman's residence was in a racially mixed area neighboring the heavily Hispanic precincts.

9. Major Hispanic groups outside Glendale were also included in this process, because of indications that they might involve themselves in the preclearance process.

10. These were composed of: a map and data analysis of different portions of the city in terms of the 1985 Special Census; maps and data sets for suggested alternatives for district boundaries; maps showing voting age population and Hispanic voting age population in census block groups; a listing by census block group of data elements; and an explanation of the redistricting process and instructions for developing citizen plans (in English and in Spanish). The basic purpose of the kits was to permit all interested citizens, both Anglos and minorities, to develop plans of their own and/or to follow the process and to critique plans produced by the consultant. It was also decided to establish a system by which citizens would be able to fax their plans to the consultant, who would then analyze them and return them to citizens within a 24-hour period, providing written analysis and comments. Along with this effort, it was decided specially to notify all Hispanic groups in and around Glendale of the public meetings and of their opportunity for input to the process; Spanish translation was made available at all public meetings; and materials were specially delivered to Hispanic leaders who expressed interest in the process. At least two public meetings were held in each councilmanic district and these meetings were widely advertised in local newspapers and electronic media.

11. He lived well outside the downtown area.

12. Also see the discussion of retrogression in Chapter 2.)

13. *Beer v. United States*, 425 U.S. 130,1976. The case involved a New Orleans city redistricting that split a black concentration among five districts. The Supreme Court overturned rulings by the Attorney General and the Federal District Court, both of which had disapproved the districting, because of a finding that it did not diminish black voting strength. "[T]he purpose of section 5 has always been to assure that no voting procedure-change would be made that would lead to a retrogression in the position of racial minorities with respect to their effective exercise of their electoral franchise." Because the districting plan offered the opportunity for the election of at least one or, perhaps, two blacks, the Court considered the plan non-discriminatory and, thus, non-retrogressive.

14. Thus, Frank Parker, in *Minority Vote Dilution*, op. cit. p. 105, refers to the *Beer* decision as having dealt minority rights "a severe setback."

15. See, e.g. *Mississippi v. United States,* 541 F.Supp.569, 582 (DDC 1979), 444 U.S. 1050, 1980.

16. Such as those enunciated in *Connor v. Finch.*

17. Moreover, since the 1990 census data was relatively new—unlike the mid-decade data at the time of the 1988-89 districting—and since growth in Glendale in the recession years immediately following the 1990 census had been relatively slight, there was no justification for repeating the high deviations of the 1988 plan. Moreover, it was the Ocotillo district in which population of any kind had been—and had the prospect of continuing to be—at the lowest rate in Glendale.

18. It might be noted here that several members of the council were seriously concerned by the irregular character of Ocotillo's boundary as proposed and expressed sharp irritation that the federal mandate was causing disruption of Glendale's well-understood street geography. Some members of the council, also, were displeased that the consultant recommended that compliance with the federal mandate required giving Ocotillo a negative deviation: the council wished the fastest growing districts (Cholla in the north and Yucca in the southwest) to receive the negative deviations in order to reflect the future projected growth and to avoid burdening the representatives of those districts with a disproportionate constituent caseload. Not only the council, but many members of the public had urged the consultant to draw the new plan with lines that would be easily recognizable: several participants in meetings claimed that the 1988 lines of Ocotillo had not been "clean," "straightforward," or "sensible;" and that the lines had led to a degree of voter confusion, which was particularly detrimental to Hispanic and low income citizens.

19. Manuel Martinez was born and raised in Ocotillo District but had moved, first to Cactus District and then, ultimately, to the affluent north Glendale Cholla District. His migration is typical of the dispersal of Hispanics from the old "barrios."

CHAPTER 9

The Arizona Cases: Peoria

Some of the same issues raised in Glendale's districting and redistricting processes were raised at the same times in its neighboring community, Peoria. To an even greater degree than in Glendale, the Peoria processes raised sharp concerns over the costs and benefits of concentrating Hispanics in a rapidly growing suburban community.

Founded as a farming community in 1886 by settlers from Peoria, Illinois, and incorporated only in 1954, Peoria has experienced four decades of dramatic population growth. In the two decades after its incorporation, it transformed itself from a primarily agricultural to a primarily residential community; and, in the same period, it began a process of annexation that expanded its geographic reach into the northwestern portions of Maricopa County. By 1985 Peoria's population had climbed to 28,765.

The growth that Peoria experienced in the 1960s and 1970s, spectacular though it seemed at the time, was dwarfed by its growth in the latter part of the 1980s: population grew at the rate of several hundreds every month. By 1990, with a census population of 50,618, Peoria had expanded its geographic reach to encompass a total of 31 square miles and was in the midst of annexing an additional 32 square mile strip, with other annexations planned for the future.

Part of the Phoenix metropolitan area, Peoria is divided in its sparsely populated northern portion by the Agua Fria River and in the southern portion by the New River and Skunk Creek. In fact, however, most of Peoria's significant features are manmade: in the 1980s, Glendale Avenue delimited the City's southern extremity and Stagecoach Pass its northern boundary; 83rd Avenue has emerged as the most traveled north-south route, and Peoria Avenue runs centrally through its most populated areas.

Peoria is primarily a residential community with a very large retirement and nursing home population. Although metropolitan Phoenix has experienced the beginnings of traffic congestion, Peoria's commuters have relatively easy access to employment centers in Glendale and to the industrial corridors along Thunderbird and Bell Roads and Interstate 17. As in many primarily residential or suburban communities, school campuses seem to provide the most important social foci for Peoria.

According to the 1985 mid-decade special census, Peoria's population stood at 28,765 persons, of whom 5,034 (or 17.5 percent) were Hispanic. A portion of the Hispanic population was concentrated in the old downtown area; but more than half the City's Hispanics were rather widely dispersed throughout the community.

Political activists, including Bill and Carol Stout from Glendale, and some leaders of greater Phoenix's Hispanic community, began to campaign following the 1985 mid-decade census for conversion of Peoria's at-large system to a single-member-district form. This agitation resonated in several of Peoria's communities, swamped by the unending growth and feeling increasingly distant from city hall; in particular, the rapidly growing northern areas of the city seem to have felt neglected in city decision-making.

On March 21, 1989, the voters of the City of Peoria approved a districting amendment to the city charter, providing for a mayor to be elected at-large, but with six council members elected by each of six separate geographical areas. The amendment stated that candidates for the six councilmanic districts must be "residents of the district from which election is sought and must continue their residence while in office;" and it required, too, that redrawing of district boundaries "shall not remove the residence of the incumbent councilmember from the district he/she represents during the term" for which elected.

The City Council believed that the new districts must support and promote a sense of community, which they perceived to be threatened by Peoria's rapid growth. They interpreted this requirement to mean that district lines must not divide or fragment areas that had a consciousness of their own identity; and, therefore, they specified the need for public meetings to hear input on community attitudes at the neighborhood level. The Council was concerned as well, to have "clean, straight lines," to preserve precinct boundaries where possible, and to develop a final plan that would conform with the major features of Peoria's street geography.

Alerted by increasing numbers of Justice Department pre-clearance objections to the districting and redistricting plans of other jurisdictions, Peoria's Council and City Manager determined that they would undertake an aggressive effort to contact the Hispanic community to bring it into the districting process. This writer, serving as the principal technical consultant to the process, advised that a first step should be to test the development of districts with the maximum possible Hispanic population; and computer experiments were run to devise fully contiguous districts that would concentrate as many Hispanic persons as possible. One district incorporated an Hispanic population of 43.9 percent, with a positive deviation from the population norm of plus 9.63 percent. A second district incorporated 44.57 percent Hispanics, with a negative deviation from the ideal population of minus 8.06 percent. (These districts are shown as figures 42 and 43.) It proved impossible to design a full majority Hispanic district.

The plan selected and voted for by a unanimous City Council can be seen at figure 44 and is described in statistical terms in data table 25. A district, named Acacia, was drawn to coincide as closely as possible with the downtown barrio. To design this district involved departing from the use of major thoroughfares, splitting precincts, and a considerable degree of irregularity in boundary lines.

The Acacia District provided an effective basis for Hispanic political organization: its percentage of Hispanic population (36.55 percent) was only eight percent less than the maximum possible Hispanic district, and it met, as well, the federal mandate of population equality with a 3.36 percent deviation from the ideal district. Perhaps more fundamentally, from the perspective of Justice Department pre-clearance, the district met the requirements of Johnny Osuna, an incumbent twice elected under the at-large system and the recognized leader of Peoria's Hispanic population, who was consulted by personnel of the Voting Rights Section of the Justice Department for his opinion concerning the plan.

The City Council expressed pleasure with the plan on the grounds that the new districts would support and promote the sense of community. The only major cause for irritation among councilmembers was that the district lines were not as "clean and straight" as would have been possible with larger deviations from population equality or a

Figure 42. Peoria, Arizona, Maximum Hispanic District (+)

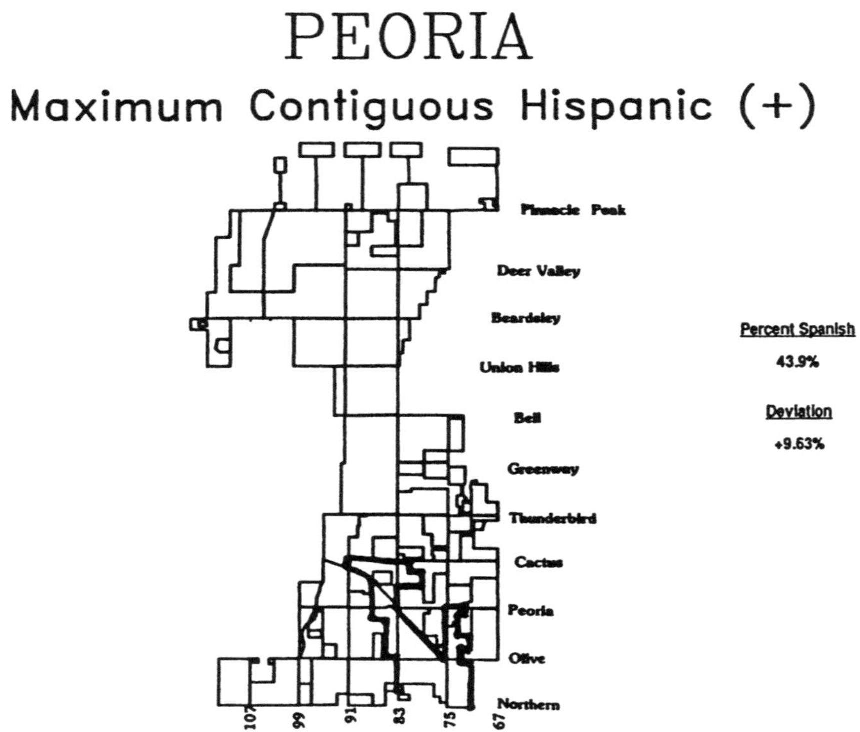

Figure 43. Peoria, Arizona, Maximum Hispanic District (-)

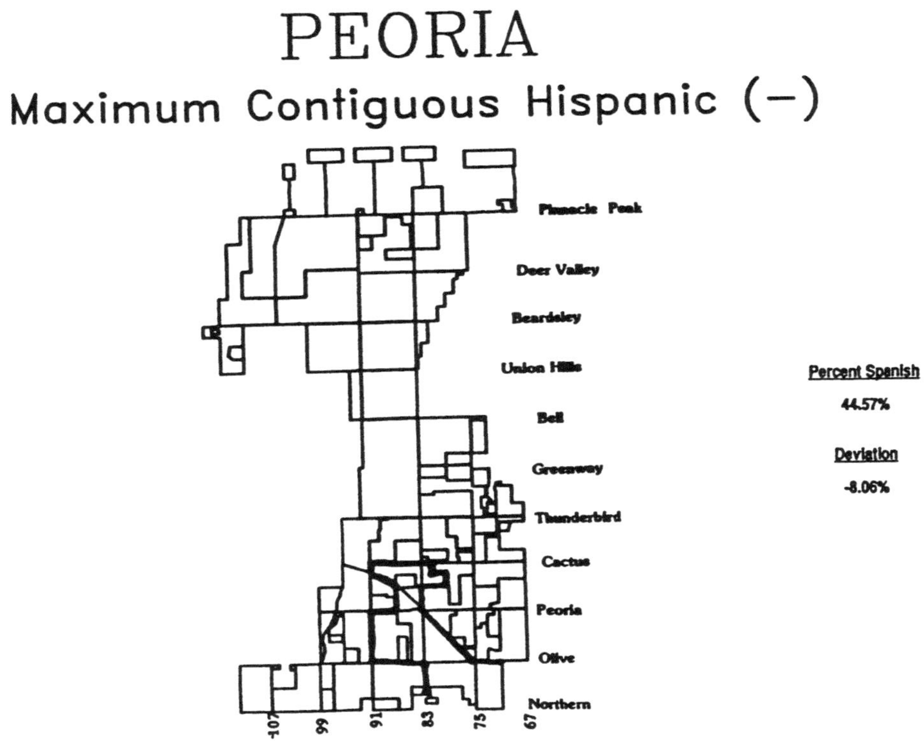

Figure 44. Peoria, Arizona, Districting, 1989

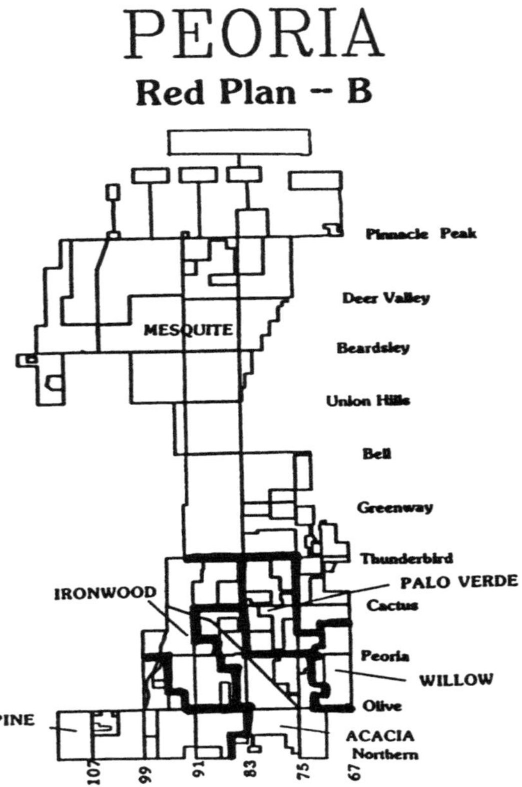

Deviations

MESQUITE	-1.11%
IRONWOOD	3.88%
PALO VERDE	-1.42%
WILLOW	-1.61%
ACACIA	3.36%
PINE	-3.09%

Percent Spanish

ACACIA	36.55%

Table 25. Peoria, Arizona—Districting, 1989. The RED Plan B

	Mesquite	%	Ironwood	%	Palo Verde	%	Willow	%	Acacia	%	Pine	%	Peoria	%
85 Persons	4,741		4,980		4,726		4,717		4,955		4,646		28,765	
85 White	4,467	94.22	4,813	96.65	4,582	96.95	4,577	97.03	4,664	94.13	4,498	96.81	27,601	95.95
85 Black	47	0.99	85	1.71	90	1.90	66	1.40	133	2.68	73	1.57	494	1.72
85 Asian	79	1.67	52	1.04	42	0.89	63	1.34	20	0.40	41	0.88	297	1.03
85 Amer. Ind.	147	3.10	28	0.56	5	0.11	8	0.17	18	0.36	5	0.11	211	0.73
85 Other	1	0.02	2	0.04	7	0.15	3	0.06	120	2.42	29	0.62	162	0.56
85 Hispanic	297	6.26	894	17.95	1,228	25.98	554	11.74	1,811	36.55	250	5.38	5,034	17.50

District Deviations (Ideal District: 4,794)

	Mesquite	Ironwood	Palo Verde	Willow	Acacia	Pine
Population	4,741	4,980	4,726	4,717	4,955	4,646
Deviation	(53)	186	(68)	(77)	161	(148)
	-1.11%	3.88%	-1.42%	-1.61%	3.36%	-3.09%

less contorted Hispanic district. The plan was submitted to the Justice Department in early 1990. It was pre-cleared without objection.

By 1990, Peoria's population had climbed to 50,618 and, despite the recession of the period, there was evidence that growth was continuing to soar. Because much of the development had occurred in the higher income areas of northern Peoria, the Hispanic population had failed to keep pace with the overall count: the 1990 census reported only 15.52 percent Hispanic population. The City's total population had climbed from 28,765 in 1985 to 50,618 in 1990; but the Hispanic population had grown from 5,034 to only 7,865, declining as a percent of the total population from 17.5 percent. The census also provided evidence that the Hispanic population of Peoria had continued to disperse away from the downtown barrio.

Acacia, with a total population of 6,186, had preserved its 36 percent Hispanic population, but it had become minus 26.7 percent deviant from the new ideal district population of 8,436; while Mesquite, the district in the rapidly growing northernmost portion of Peoria, had a population of 13,622 and was plus 61.5 percent deviant from the ideal. Palo Verde, the other northern district, was also many thousands above the new population ideal.

Again, the city planned an open, public process through all stages of the redistricting, with a special effort being made to involve Hispanics and other minority representatives.[1] Citizen redistricting kits were distributed to all interested citizens and specially delivered to Hispanic organizations.

The plan accepted by the Council provided for a new Acacia with 41.92 percent Hispanic total population and 38.4 percent 18-plus Hispanic. As figure 45 demonstrates, the effort to avoid "retrogression" in the development of this Hispanic influence district resulted in considerable further contortion of the district lines. (Data for this plan appears at table 26.) Again, this was the major concern for Peoria's City Council: several members of the Council publicly voiced their displeasure that the City's map was cut up to form this "jigsaw puzzle district."

Peoria's 1989 charter amendment provided as follows: "Should Peoria participate in a mid-decennial census conducted by the United States, the Council shall also modify district boundaries to substantially equalize population of each for the next regular election following such special census."[2] Thus, when 1995 mid-decade census reported that Peoria's population had increased from 50,618 to 74,568, the City was

Figure 45. Peoria, Arizona, Redistricting, 1991

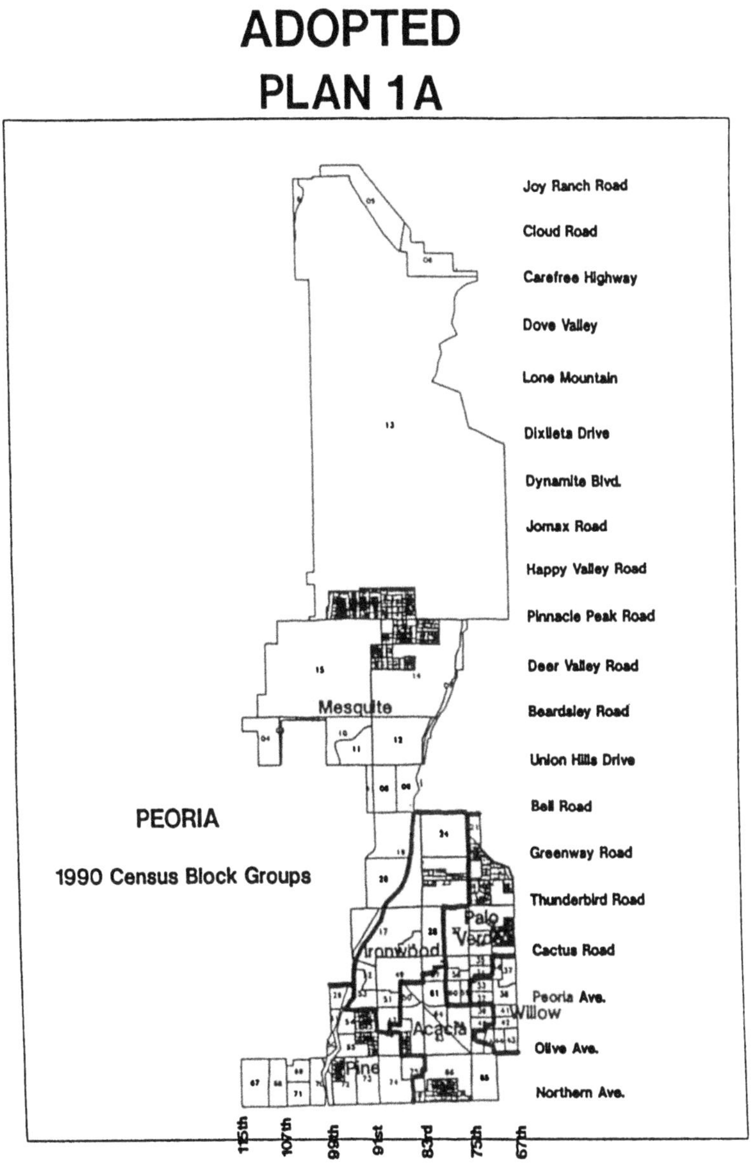

Table 26. Peoria, Arizona—Redistricting, 1991

	Mesquite	%	Acacia	%	Ironwood	%	Palo Verde	%	Pine	%	Willow	%	Peoria	%
Persons	8,534		8,340		8,456		8,464		8,447		8,377		50,618	
White	8,271	96.92	5,685	68.17	7,336	86.75	7,643	90.30	7,689	91.03	7,388	88.19	44,012	86.95
Black	83	0.97	266	3.19	188	2.22	206	2.43	176	2.08	188	2.24	1,107	2.19
Amer. Ind.	27	0.32	101	1.21	57	0.67	29	0.34	46	0.54	40	0.48	300	0.59
Asian	42	0.49	98	1.18	119	1.41	218	2.58	141	1.67	115	1.37	733	1.45
Other	111	1.30	2,190	26.26	758	8.96	368	4.35	395	4.68	646	7.71	4,468	8.83
Hispanic	247	2.89	3,496	41.92	1,437	16.99	808	9.55	732	8.67	1,136	13.56	7,856	15.52
NH White	8,138	95.36	4,394	52.69	6,680	79.00	7,217	85.27	7,349	87.00	6,911	82.50	40,689	80.38
NH Black	82	0.96	255	3.06	175	2.07	202	2.39	173	2.05	184	2.20	1,071	2.12
NH Amer. Ind.	23	0.27	83	1.00	51	0.60	27	0.32	41	0.49	32	0.38	257	0.51
NH Asian	42	0.49	82	0.98	107	1.27	208	2.46	138	1.63	104	1.24	681	1.35
NH Other	2	0.02	30	0.36	6	0.07	2	0.02	14	0.17	10	0.12	64	0.13
Total 18+	7,627		5,177		5,647		5,478		6,438		5,532		35,899	
18+ Hispanic	174	2.28	1,988	38.40	764	13.53	460	8.40	418	6.49	601	10.86	4,405	12.27
NH 18+ White	7,343	96.28	2,949	56.96	4,675	82.79	4,736	86.45	5,774	89.69	4,751	85.88	30,228	84.20
NH 18+ Black	61	0.80	133	2.57	102	1.81	125	2.28	122	1.89	95	1.72	638	1.78
NH 18+ Amer. Ind.	16	0.21	49	0.95	33	0.58	19	0.35	25	0.39	13	0.23	155	0.43
NH 18+ Asian	33	0.43	48	0.93	68	1.20	136	2.48	94	1.46	69	1.25	448	1.25
NH 18+ Other	0	0.00	10	0.19	5	0.09	2	0.04	5	0.08	3	0.05	25	0.07
Housing Units	5446		2750		3385		2879		4175		3309		21,944	

"NH" = "Not of Hispanic Origin"

Table 26 (continued)

District Deviations (Ideal District: 8,436)

	Mesquite	Acacia	Ironwood	Palo Verde	Pine	Willow
Population	8,534	8,340	8,456	8,464	8,447	8,377
Deviation	98	-96	20	28	11	-59
	1.16%	-1.14%	0.24%	0.33%	0.13%	-0.70%

again faced with redistricting. This time, the task was further complicated by the addition of a huge new tract of land, via annexation, stretching from Deer Valley Road to Lake Pleasant at the northern edge of Maricopa County.

Again, Peoria's growth had been concentrated in its northern areas, where new developments had brought in several thousand high-priced new homes. Again, also, it was the northern-most district, Mesquite, that had experienced the huge majority of the new population growth: it recorded a positive deviation of 43.36 percent.

The pattern changed, however, for Acacia (still represented by Johnny Osuna). The real numbers of Hispanics had increased slightly but had decreased as a percentage of the overall population of the district, which was now underpopulated by 2,328 persons. Indeed, it was clear from the 1995 census data that Peoria's Hispanic population was continuing to disperse away from its old downtown concentration. While Acacia and Ironwood (the second most Hispanic district in 1991) had decreased in Hispanic percentage, Willow, Palo Verde, Cholla and Pine all showed increases in Hispanic percentage. The census reported a total of 11,686 Hispanics in the city as whole, but only 4,050 of these persons continued to live in the old downtown barrio, which had been used as the core of Acacia in the initial districting.

The City's legal staff, accustomed by the redistricting process of 1991 to think in terms of problems of "retrogression" and "maintenance of influence districts," was concerned to avoid dilution of Acacia's Hispanic percent. This was the view, also, of Hispanic voting rights representatives from the greater Phoenix area. To achieve 41.92 percent Hispanic population in an enlarged Acacia, however, would involve drawing a bizarrely-shaped district that would inevitably fragment neighboring districts. This writer experimented with computer tests to produce a non-retrogressive result, as did one councilmember who used his citizen kit to conduct tests. Adding to the difficulty of this exercise was the fact that the mid-decade census was conducted by Enumeration District (ED), a very much larger unit than the census block (in fact, an aggregation of census blocks similar to the block group), making it impossible to exclude heavily Anglo blocks and to include heavily Hispanic blocks. An example of a plan that these efforts produced may be seen at figure 46 and table 27. Although the plan goes to the extreme of having two EDs in Acacia contiguous only at a point and although the district is purposely underpopulated, it falls short of the 41.92 percent of the 1991 Acacia.

Figure 46. Peoria, Arizona, Pearson Plan, 1996

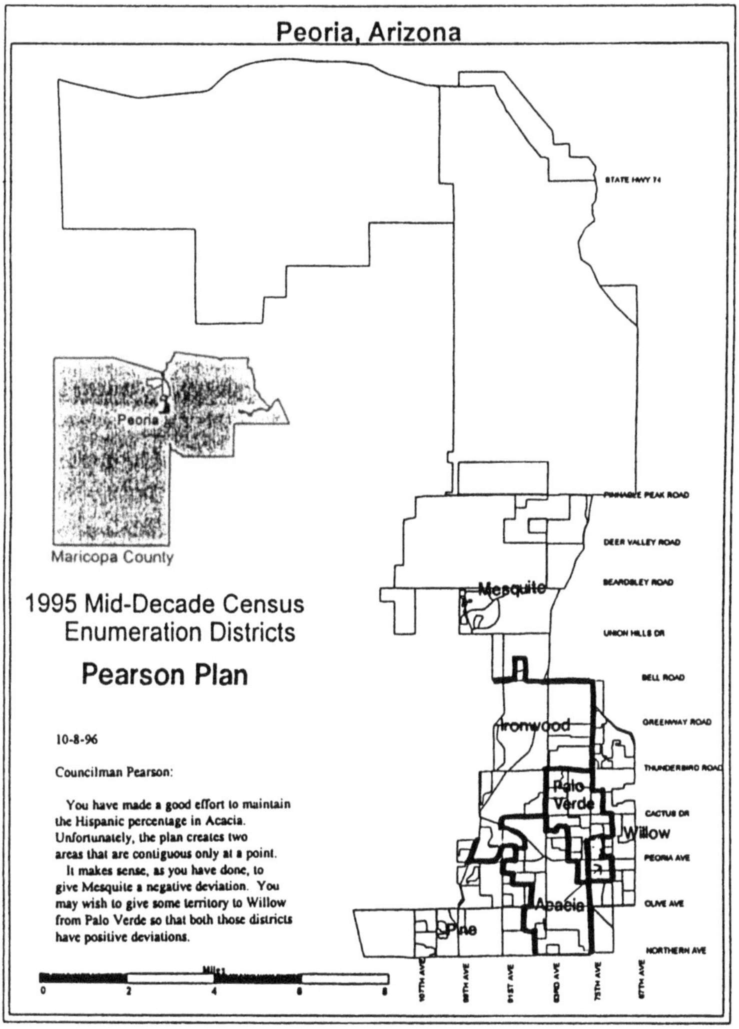

Table 27. Peoria, Arizona, Pearson Plan, 1996

	Mesquite	%	Acacia	%	Ironwood	%	Palo Verde	%	Pine	%	Willow	%	Peoria	%
Persons	12,030		12,352		12,237		13,685		12,778		11,483		74,565	
Hispanic	567	4.71	5,088	41.19	1,211	9.90	1,827	13.35	1,410	11.03	1,583	13.79	11,686	15.67
NH White	11,154	92.72	6,623	53.62	10,417	85.13	11,065	80.85	10,668	83.49	9,254	80.59	59,181	79.37
NH Black	138	1.15	308	2.49	289	2.36	369	2.70	356	2.79	238	2.07	1,698	2.28
NH Amer. Ind.	36	0.30	69	0.56	56	0.46	64	0.47	85	0.67	57	0.50	367	0.49
NH Asian	82	0.68	176	1.42	206	1.68	275	2.01	191	1.49	273	2.38	1,203	1.61
NH Other	53	0.44	88	0.71	58	0.47	85	0.62	68	0.53	78	0.68	430	0.58
Total 18+	10,333		7,950		8,708		8,925		9,760		7,794		53,470	
18+ Hispanic	363	3.51	2,953	37.14	687	7.89	1,070	11.99	796	8.16	871	11.18	6,740	12.61
NH 18+ White	9,743	94.29	4,590	57.74	7,639	87.72	7,371	82.59	8,484	86.93	6,520	83.65	44,347	82.94
NH 18+ Black	105	1.02	181	2.28	180	2.07	224	2.51	252	2.58	138	1.77	1,080	2.02
NH 18+ Amer. Ind.	27	0.26	53	0.67	41	0.47	40	0.45	61	0.63	36	0.46	258	0.48
NH 18+ Asian	61	0.59	120	1.51	133	1.53	173	1.94	126	1.29	181	2.32	794	1.48
NH 18+ Other	34	0.33	53	0.67	28	0.32	47	0.53	41	0.42	48	0.62	251	0.47

"NH" = "Not of Hispanic Origin"

Table 27 (continued)

District Deviations (Ideal Area 12,428)

	Mesquite	Acacia	Ironwood	Palo Verde	Pine	Willow
Population	12,030	12,352	12,237	13,685	12,778	11,483
Deviation	-398	-76	-191	1257	350	-945
	-3.20%	-0.61%	-1.54%	10.11%	2.82%	-7.60%

Table 28. Peoria, Arizona, Final Redistricting Plan, 1996

	Mesquite	%	Acacia	%	Ironwood	%	Palo Verde	%	Pine	%	Willow	%	Peoria	%
Persons	12,030		12,001		12,204		12,762		12,662		12,906		74,565	
Hispanic	567	4.71	4,934	41.11	1,172	9.60	1,735	13.60	1,698	13.41	1,580	12.24	11,686	15.67
NH White	11,154	92.72	6,473	53.94	10,440	85.55	10,281	80.56	10,211	80.64	10,622	82.30	59,181	79.37
NH Black	138	1.15	310	2.58	284	2.33	352	2.76	374	2.95	240	1.86	1,698	2.28
NH Amer. Ind.	36	0.30	71	0.59	85	0.70	54	0.42	54	0.43	67	0.52	367	0.49
NH Asian	82	0.68	131	1.09	169	1.38	260	2.04	257	2.03	304	2.36	1,203	1.61
NH Other	53	0.44	82	0.68	54	0.44	80	0.63	68	0.54	93	0.72	430	0.58
Total 18+	10,333		7,741		9,116		8,334		9,226		8,720		53,470	
18+ Hispanic	363	3.51	2,856	36.89	667	7.32	1,016	12.19	954	10.34	884	10.14	6,740	12.61
NH 18+ White	9,743	94.29	4,511	58.27	8,070	88.53	6,860	82.31	7,761	84.12	7,402	84.89	44,347	82.94
NH 18+ Black	105	1.02	182	2.35	185	2.03	216	2.59	258	2.80	134	1.54	1,080	2.02
NH 18+ Amer. Ind.	27	0.26	53	0.68	59	0.65	36	0.43	43	0.47	40	0.46	258	0.48
NH 18+ Asian	61	0.59	93	1.20	109	1.20	161	1.93	165	1.79	205	2.35	794	1.48
NH 18+ Other	34	0.33	46	0.59	26	0.29	45	0.54	45	0.49	55	0.63	251	0.47

"NH" = "Not of Hispanic Origin"

Table 28 (continued)

District Deviations (Ideal Area: 12,428)

	Mesquite	Acacia	Ironwood	Palo Verde	Pine	Willow
Population	12,030	12,001	12,204	12,762	12,662	12,906
Deviation	-398	-427	-224	334	234	478
	-3.20%	-3.44%	-1.80%	2.69%	1.88%	3.85%

Figure 47. Peoria, Arizona, Final Redistricting Plan, 1996

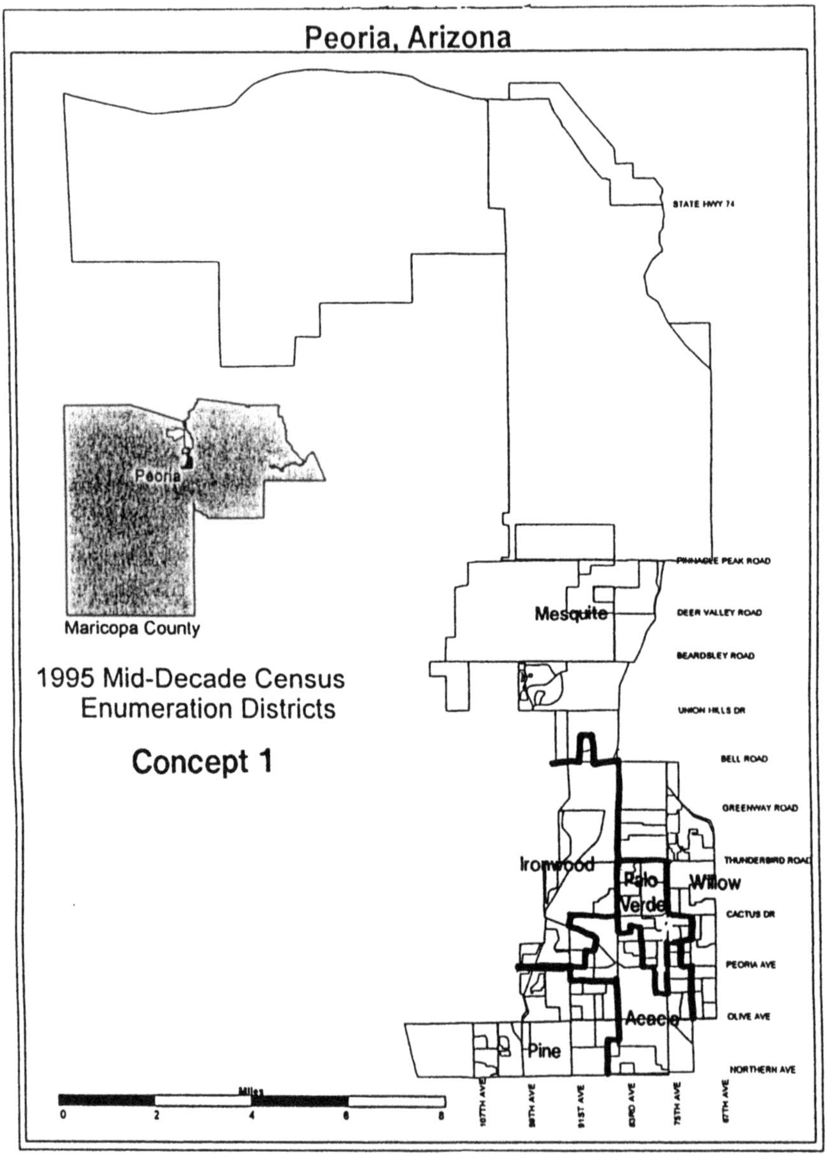

Essentially, the effort to maintain the high Hispanic percentage of the 1991 redistricting ran into conflict with the facts not only of Peoria's newly enlarged population but also of Hispanic assimilation. Even Councilman Osuna recognized the essentially nugatory testing of Acacia's boundaries against the concept of "retrogression." And, even he, reflecting the displeasure of his constituents, wished there to be no further misshapen lines in the new district plan. Yet, although it was the consultant's recommendation to abandon the 41.92 percent standard in favor of a district that would accommodate the practical needs of Hispanic political organization in the area, and even though the consultant's recommendation was undergirded by the knowledge that the Supreme Court had finally begun to acknowledge the impropriety, both constitutional and social of single-factor, race-based districting, the City's legal counsel did not wish to engage Justice on the issue.[3] The plan adopted on November 5, 1996 appears as figure 47 and table 28.

As in Glendale, a troubling question is raised: what are the gains, in terms of Hispanic representation, of specially configuring a district to concentrate Hispanics around a dwindling downtown barrio? Councilman Osuna's political base was not significantly strengthened by the 1996 process, and he would almost certainly have garnered as many (perhaps, more) votes in a less Hispanic, "retrogressive" district that encompassed ethnically mixed, but more politically active precincts. Without the emphasis on non-retrogression in Acacia District it would have been possible to add to the Hispanic percentages of districts that are gaining in Hispanic population and where there are better prospects for political mobilization and the recruitment of good Hispanic candidates. The use of the non-retrogression standard in Peoria resulted in a focus on a district that was already represented by an entrenched Hispanic incumbent (who had previously won at large) and the depreciation of Hispanic political opportunities in other areas.

NOTES

1. For news coverage of the meetings and other features of the process, see: *Daily News-Sun*, Tuesday, February 11, 1992, "Peoria Council to Choose Between Redistricting Plans;" *The Phoenix Gazette*, February 14, 1992, "Redistricting Plan OK'd in Peoria."
2. Peoria City Charter, Article II. The Council, Section 2, (C).

3. Peoria has elections in March of 1997. Candidates will have filed and the election may have to be held prior to preclearance of the plan. The City Attorney, therefore, advised the Council to maintain the Hispanic percentage to the maximum extent possible in the 1996 redistricting and to save the possible fight over retrogression for the year 2001.

CHAPTER 10

An Anglo-Driven Move to Districts: Colton, California

Are districts always to the advantage of minorities? This chapter traces the results of a districting that was masterminded by Anglo activists in an apparent effort to protect their interests from an emerging Latino majority.

Founded in 1875 and incorporated in 1887, the City of Colton covers an area of roughly 16 square miles in southern California's Inland Empire. Located on the main lines of the Southern Pacific, Santa Fe and Union Pacific railroads, and at the meeting point of freeways I-10 and I-215, Colton's access to the transportation system has permitted its emergence as a growing center of light manufacturing. In the decades 1970 to 1990, the city grew from 19,974 to 40,213 in total population: of the latter total, exactly 20,000 persons or 49.74 percent, were Hispanic; 14,937 (or 37.14 percent) were non-Hispanic white; 3,381 (or 8.41 percent) were non-Hispanic African American; and 1,546 (or 3.84 percent) were non-Hispanic Asian.

A general law city, Colton operated for most of the 20th Century under a council-city manager type of government, with four council members elected at-large and with a mayor also elected city-wide. As of 1990, city governance seemed to reflect rather well the ethnic proportions of its population, perhaps even favoring slightly the emerging Latino majority: the mayor (Frank A. Gonzales) and two councilmembers were Latino, as was the City Manager, the City Clerk, the Director of Community Development, and the Parks Superintendent. Two members of the Council were Anglos, as were the

City Attorney, the chiefs of Police and Fire, the City Engineer, the Director of Public Works, and the City Treasurer.

Nevertheless, a significant group of Colton citizens, mainly Anglos, had come to believe that the at-large system was failing to represent them and was neglecting the interests of significant portions of the City's territory. George Fulp, the leader of the group, which took the title "Colton Voters for Fair Representation," argued that districts were needed to "hold council members more responsible to their constituents."[1] Fulp claimed that many residents, particularly those living near the Price Club, close to the city boundary with Rialto, and in the ranching and rural areas of the city, felt seriously underrepresented. Fulp insisted that only single-member districts would correct long-standing political inequities in Colton: "The Council is unbalanced . . . in that the Mayor and council people reside in one part of town."[2] He insisted that, for most of the preceding twenty years, all five elected city officials, whether Latino or not, had come from a single area, namely "the upper middle portion of the City," leaving "the four corners of Colton" without effective representation. Fulp claimed to be opposed to the status quo because "the powers that be" had kept "their people" in government for too long. "Under a ward system," Fulp claimed, "you have people who know the areas where they reside and that area's needs and desires but they also carry the responsibility of the entire city."[3] Fulp was also quoted as claiming that the biggest benefit of the district system was that it would encourage more people to run for office. In citywide elections, he charged, only people who could afford to put up signs and send out mailers for the whole city could run; in districts, with their smaller territories, people with lesser funds could campaign door-to-door in their own neighborhoods.[4]

The organizing committee of Colton Voters For Fair Representation—composed of George Fulp, Margaret Binford, and Louie Aboytes—began the circulation of a petition to create six councilmanic districts from each of which only one resident council member could be elected, together with a mayor elected city-wide. The petition urged creation of the six "neighborhood districts" for the following reasons:

> To enable each voter to feel *really* represented by a council member who lives in that voter's district;
> To create neighborhoods to bring together people with common interests and problems;

To make each council member more responsible, and more responsive to the voters in their districts;
To increase interest in voter turnout because each vote *does* make a difference in district voting;
To more fairly represent voters in all areas of the City.[5]

In addition to these formally stated reasons, however, it seems clear that the petition drew upon resentment among some Anglo voters concerning the growing role of Latinos in city affairs. The rapid—and obviously continuing—growth of the City's Latino population seems, also, to have fueled resentment, even fear, among some older residents. Although such feelings were not publicly aired, several leaders of the Southern California Latino community saw the movement to district Colton as a racially-inspired effort to turn back the clock. Thus, civil rights attorney, Richard Fajardo, the lead attorney for MALDEF in the *Garza v. Los Angeles County* case, called the move "a ploy to dilute Latino voting strength."[6] Richard Rodriguez, a Latino political activist in the area, said districts represented "an attempt to shift the balance of power from Latinos to whites," emphasizing that three of the council's five current members were Latinos. "What they've done is cluster the Hispanic vote in two or three wards, making it unlikely that Hispanics will ever have a majority on the council again," he said.[7]

One of the few Latino voices in favor of the move to districts was that of John Aguilar. His support of the move, however, seems to have been based on irritation with the existing council rather than with any general concern for or against ethnic representation. Essentially, Aguilar seems to have seen districts as a way of assuring turnover and bringing in new council members: "We have to break up what's there now on the council and make the new people who run really feel the effect of the people's will to change."[8]

The petition that was circulated by the Fair Representation committee required that the six new districts would be decided upon and drawn by a committee of seven persons: six registered voters of the City, of which three would be proposed by the Fair Representation Committee, three by the City Council, together with a seventh member, "an impartial accredited mapping technician." Each of the seven individuals had to be approved by both a majority of the Fair Representation Committee and a majority of the City Council. The petition required that the districts be established "with the underlying purpose of creating neighborhoods to bring people together, not to tear people apart; . . . [and] to create neighborhood districts as nearly equal in population as possible."[9]

The "impartial accredited mapping technician," who was to be the seventh member of the boundary-drawing commission, proved to be the current writer, and the comments that follow are drawn from the experience of working with the commission and responding to the varied pressures of many different groups and individuals within the City. Obviously, the districts had to be drawn in conformity with the federal mandates regarding equal population and voting rights. In the consultant's formal statement before the Colton Council, when she presented the plans, she noted:

> I met on December 9 with three appointees from the city council, three appointees from the citizens group and the acting city manager, Ms. Leslie Stratton. We discussed the criteria that should be used in districting. First, two federal mandates, the first of which is equality of population . . . and the second of which is minority voting rights. . . . We also talked about criteria such as geographical and man-made barriers and respect for identifiable communities of interest and/or neighborhoods. The group then shared with me their sense of the various communities within the city. I returned on Thursday, December 12th, with maps and data for two concepts. After thoroughly discussing the two concepts, one concept was chosen to develop into a final plan. I returned on Friday with two ways of finalizing the chosen concept, and a map was prepared and presented to the Council on December 17.

The initial plan presented by the consultant (see figure 48 and table 29) provided for three majority Latino Districts: District 2 with 76.94 percent Latinos; District 3 with 67.16 percent; and District 4 with 72.17 percent. District 5, covering the area from which the Committee on Fair Representation had recruited much support, was only 17.33 percent Latino; District 6 was 22.60 percent Latino, while District 1 was 41.28 percent Latino. Plots of Colton's Latino population and Latino Voting Age population appear at figures 49 and 50. In the consultant's view, the three majority Latino districts fully met the Gingles tests and created viable Latino majorities without, however, over-concentrating them.[10]

The public comment on the district plan as presented was mostly from Anglos and focused on geographic detail with little evident

Figure 48. Colton, California, Initial Plan

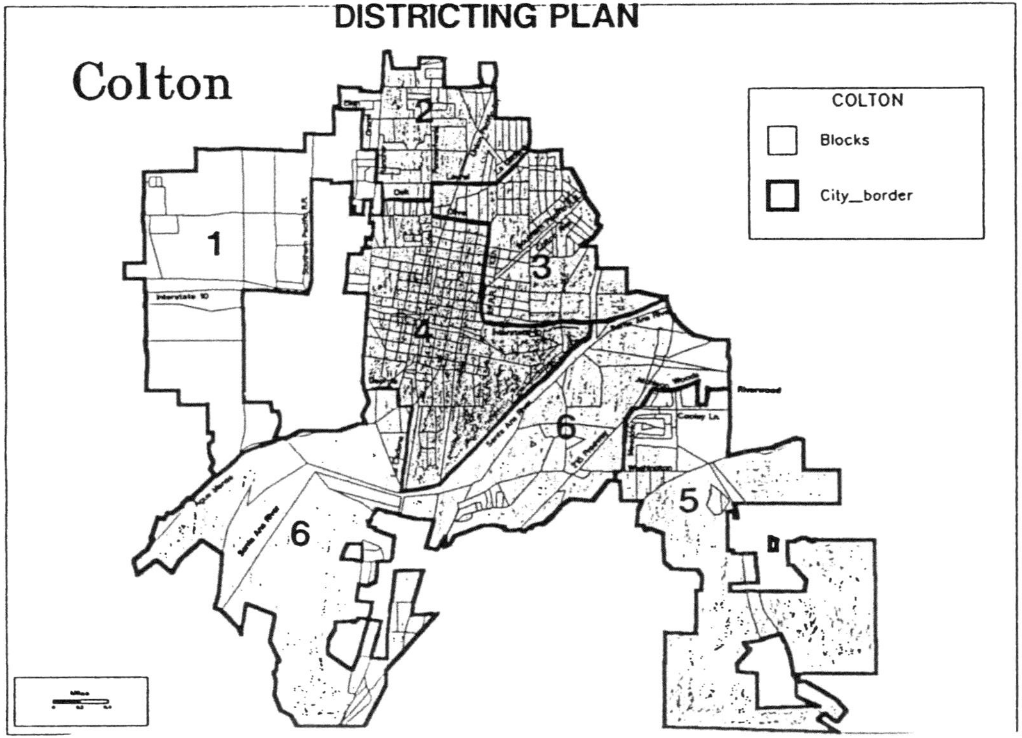

Table 29. Colton, California, Initial Plan

	District 1	%	District 2	%	District 3	%	District 4	%	District 5	%	District 6	%	Colton	%
Persons	6,664		6,734		6,750		6,756		6,629		6,680		40,213	
Hispanic	2751	41.28	5,181	76.94	4,533	67.16	4,876	72.17	1,149	17.33	1,510	22.60	20,000	49.74
NH White	2,445	36.69	1,121	16.65	1,782	26.40	1,534	22.71	4,326	65.26	3,729	55.82	14,937	37.14
NH Black	1017	15.26	338	5.02	260	3.85	133	1.97	788	11.89	845	12.65	3,381	8.41
NH Amer. Ind.	24	0.36	23	0.34	67	0.99	29	0.43	47	0.71	47	0.70	237	0.59
NH Asian	406	6.09	62	0.92	88	1.30	165	2.44	561	8.46	264	3.95	1,546	3.84
NH Other	21	0.32	9	0.13	20	0.30	19	0.28	24	0.36	19	0.28	112	0.28
Total 18+	4,441		4,300		4,417		4,425		5,086		4,509		27,178	
18+ Hispanic	1637	36.86	3,209	74.63	2,754	62.35	3,031	68.50	752	14.79	945	20.96	12,328	45.36
NH 18+ White	1,855	41.77	862	20.05	1,359	30.77	1,228	27.75	3,331	65.49	2,779	61.63	11,414	42.00
NH 18+ Black	644	14.50	157	3.65	180	4.08	64	1.45	531	10.44	547	12.13	2,123	7.81
NH 18+ Amer. Ind.	15	0.34	17	0.40	46	1.04	19	0.43	36	0.71	33	0.73	166	0.61
NH 18+ Asian	275	6.19	49	1.14	66	1.49	72	1.63	421	8.28	194	4.30	1,077	3.96
NH 18+ Other	15	0.34	6	0.14	12	0.27	11	0.25	15	0.29	11	0.24	70	0.26
Housing Units	2,343		1,887		2,349		2,216		3,043		2,929		14,767	

"NH" = "Not of Hispanic Origin"

Table 29 (continued)

District Deviations (Ideal District: 6,702)

	District 1	District 2	District 3	District 4	District 5	District 6
Population	6,664	6,734	6,750	6,756	6,629	6,680
Deviation	(38)	32	48	54	(73)	(22)
	-0.57%	0.48%	0.72%	0.81%	-1.09%	-0.33%

Figure 49. Colton, California, Plot of Hispanic Population

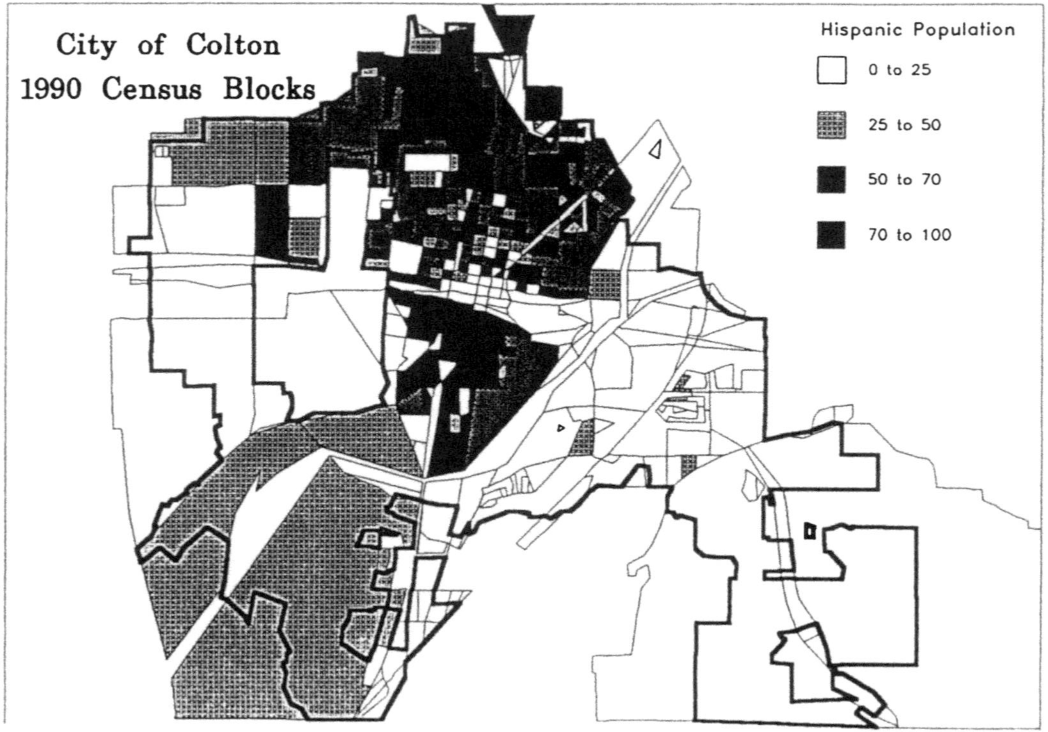

Figure 50. Colton, California, Plot of Hispanic Voting Age Population

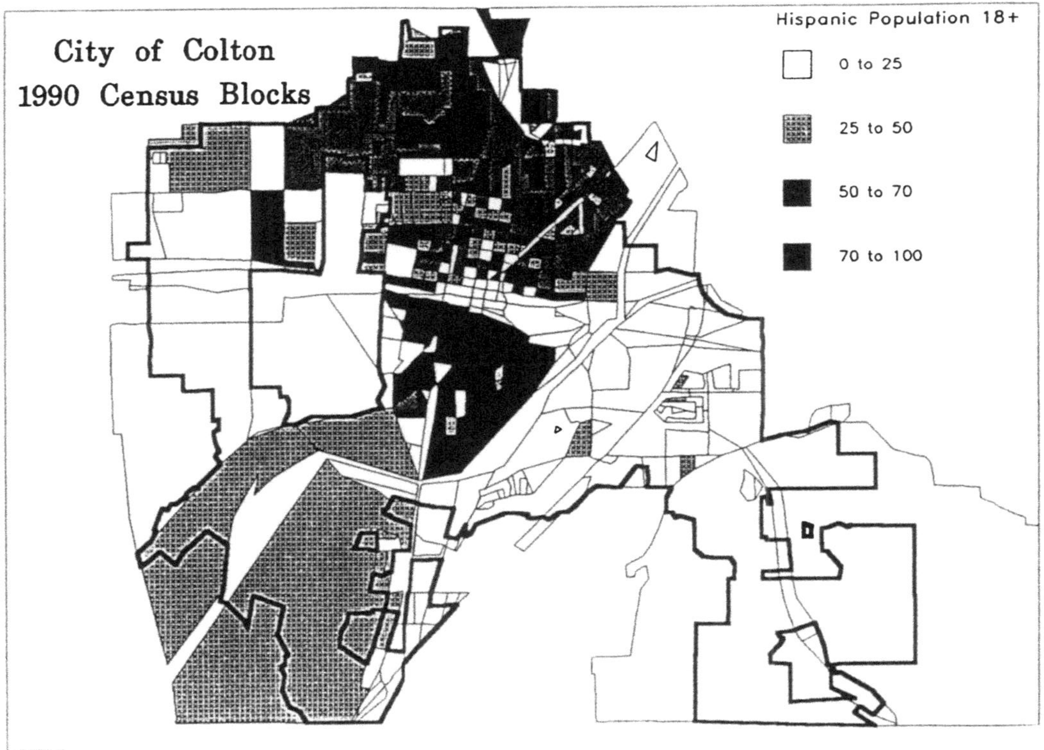

concern for issues of ethnic representation.[11] The revisions made in consequence of the comments primarily affected District 5: its population was increased slightly, but the changes left the Latino percentage of this and the other districts intact. The only organized opposition to the districting plan came from a group known as Citizens for Truth in Government Organization (CTGO). They submitted a statement, signed by Garland Fredrickson, the president and chairman of the group, complaining that the map failed to encompass all of the City's territory and urging that the boundary line between Districts 5 and 6 follow I-215 to permit District 5 "to control the industrial section at its north end." The latter change was made by the consultant and supported by the Commission and the Council. The final map and data set appear at figure 51 and table 30.

In the view of most members of the Commission and participants in the process with whom the consultant spoke, the districting plan, as accepted by the Council in 1992 and submitted for vote by the citizens, carried out the intent of the original citizen petition, while also fully conforming with the requirements of federal law.

In the primary election of 1992, Colton embraced the proposal that created six districts in the form of Measure W: A total of 2,541 voters, or 51.03 percent, voted for the Measure, and 2,438 voters or 48.97 percent, against. Although this verdict was hardly resounding, the Measure became law. Mayor Gonzalez, however, continued to oppose what he termed "community separation instead of cohesiveness." "I still don't feel a need for six council people and mayor." Gonzales said:

> The city could have been split into four quarters instead of these six wards, because the city is too small. And I believe everybody should vote for all the wards. Not just their own. Otherwise, the people don't have to care about overall Colton. Just their own area.[12]

Gonzales predicted that he would have to be the mediator for a lot of competition among the wards—assuming, of course, that he would be re-elected in November. He said:

> There's going to be a lot of ill feeling. Now what happens when people are fighting for a few more dollars for the programs in their areas? We used to spread what little resources we have all over the city and split the money evenly. Now some wards may be left out if their councilman doesn't try hard enough.[13]

Figure 51. Colton, California, Final Plan

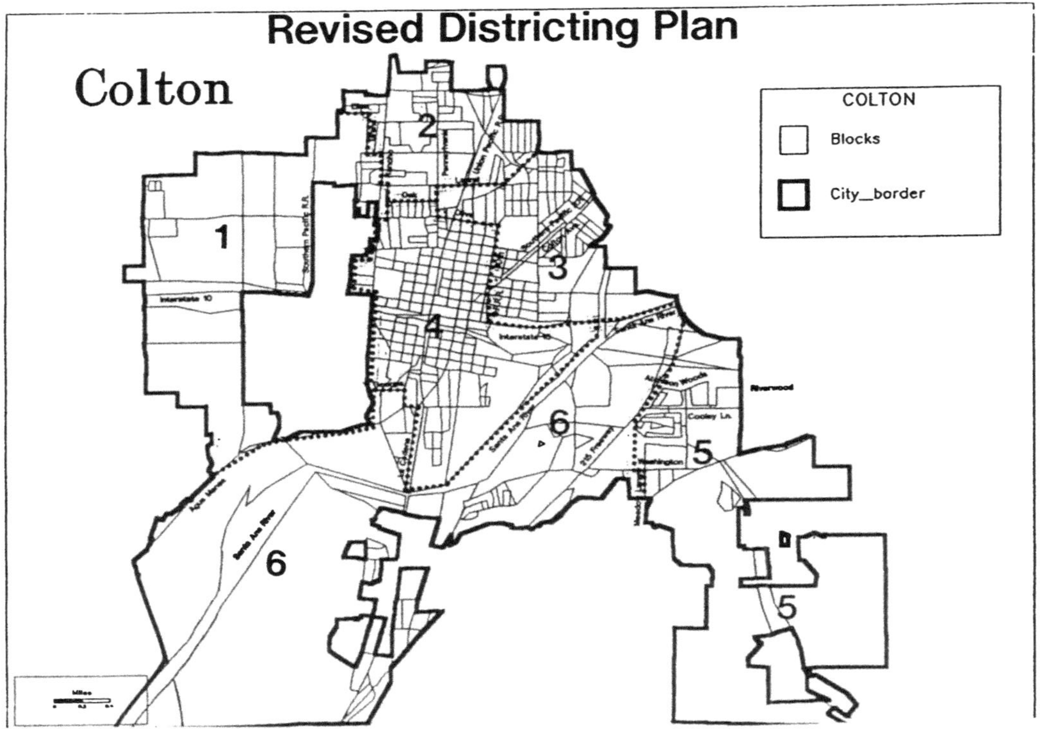

Table 30. Colton, California, Final Plan

	District 1	%	District 2	%	District 3	%	District 4	%	District 5	%	District 6	%	Colton	%
Persons	6,664		6,734		6,750		6,756		6,657		6,652		40,213	
Hispanic	2751	41.28	5,181	76.94	4,533	67.16	4,876	72.17	1,090	16.37	1,569	23.59	20,000	49.74
NH White	2,445	36.69	1,121	16.65	1,782	26.40	1,534	22.71	4,197	63.05	3,858	58.00	14,937	37.14
NH Black	1017	15.26	338	5.02	260	3.85	133	1.97	708	10.64	925	13.91	3,381	8.41
NH Amer. Ind.	24	0.36	23	0.34	67	0.99	29	0.43	41	0.62	53	0.80	237	0.59
NH Asian	406	6.09	62	0.92	88	1.30	165	2.44	601	9.03	224	3.37	1,546	3.84
NH Other	21	0.32	9	0.13	20	0.30	19	0.28	20	0.30	23	0.35	112	0.28
Total 18+	4,441		4,300		4,417		4,425		4,855		4,740		27,178	
18+ Hispanic	1637	36.86	3,209	74.63	2,754	62.35	3,031	68.50	705	14.52	992	20.93	12,328	45.36
NH 18+ White	1,855	41.77	862	20.05	1,359	30.77	1,228	27.75	3,200	65.91	2,910	61.39	11,414	42.00
NH 18+ Black	644	14.50	157	3.65	180	4.08	64	1.45	470	9.68	608	12.83	2,123	7.81
NH 18+ Amer. Ind.	15	0.34	17	0.40	46	1.04	19	0.43	31	0.64	38	0.80	166	0.61
NH 18+ Asian	275	6.19	49	1.14	66	1.49	72	1.63	438	9.02	177	3.73	1,077	3.96
NH 18+ Other	15	0.34	6	0.14	12	0.27	11	0.25	11	0.23	15	0.32	70	0.26
Housing Units	2,343		1,887		2,349		2,216		2,836		3,136		14,767	

"NH" = "Not of Hispanic Origin"

Table 30 (continued)

District Deviations (Ideal District: 6,702)

	District 1	District 2	District 3	District 4	District 5	District 6
Population	6,664	6,734	6,750	6,756	6,657	6,652
Deviation	(38)	32	48	54	(45)	(50)
	-0.57%	0.48%	0.72%	0.81%	-0.67%	-0.75%

A further indication that the line-drawing process for the new districts was in reality more contentious than the public process had suggested centered on the issue of how the existing incumbents would be treated under the new plan. Gonzales charged that councilman Roy Roman, a Latino colleague, was "in reality . . . being recalled" by the plan. Gonzales pointed out that although elected to serve a four-year term, and having already served two years, Roman's chance of representing a district for a further two years depended merely upon the luck of the draw.[14]

Nevertheless, although the charge that the districts would discriminate against Latinos continued to be made, the plan seemed to undercut much of the criticism: in addition to the three majority Latino districts, District 1 with its 41 percent Latino population, its 15.26 percent non-Hispanic black population and its 6.09 percent non-Hispanic Asian population, was generally considered a minority-dominated district.

The 1992 elections, moreover, seemed to offer conclusive rebuttal to charges by Rodriguez, Fajardo and others that the district plan was systemically anti-Latino, for five of the seven council members after the election proved to be Latino. District 1 voted for a Latino, as did District 6 (despite its tiny Latino population). Indeed, the only surprise was that District 4, with its huge Latino majority, failed to elect a Latino; but in this case, four Latino candidates were attracted to the contest, allowing the Anglo, Betty Cook, a marginal victory.

In the aftermath of the 1992 elections, the issue of an anti-Latino gerrymander in Colton seemed destined to fade altogether, and the memory of the charges made by Rodriguez and Fajardo concerning a reverse ethnic gerrymander seemed likely to dim. The 1994 elections, however, served abruptly to re-open the issue. In the wake of those elections only one Latino, Abe Beltran, served on the Council and he was quickly subjected to the threat of recall.

It is possible, of course, to explain this dramatic turnaround in terms of specific issues and the conflict of personalities. Frank Gonzales, the plan's principal opponent as Mayor, was defeated by George Fulp. Prior to Mayor Gonzales' defeat, Colton was reporting its worst deficit in history and was widely rumored to be on the verge of bankruptcy. Moreover, Gonzales certainly had alienated parts of his own home base, including some in the Latino community who abstained from voting, even if they did not support Fulp.[15] It is probable, as well, that many Latinos were unconvinced by the critique of the district system offered by Fajardo, Rodriguez and other Latino leaders: some in the Latino community may have believed that a district system would do for their community in Colton what Fajardo and many others claimed it had done for Latino communities in other jurisdictions; and Fulp may have benefited from his leadership of the district movement in parts of the Latino community.[16]

The 1994 election produced several other surprising results. One was the re-election of Betty Cook in District 4, despite its 69 percent Latino advantage. Her 1992 victory had been as a result of the competition of four Latino candidates dividing the vote. Two years later, her victory seems to have been due to the failure of Latino candidates to file: her opponents were Anglos, Linda Young and Lorraine June, and the race was conducted in issue terms without reference to concerns of ethnic representation. An equally surprising result occurred in District 2, where the Latino incumbent, Jerry Rios, was defeated by Anglo challenger, John Hutton, despite the 75 percent Latino majority in the district. Again, a principal cause of this outcome was division of the Latino vote: Hutton took 571 votes, Rios 529, but a second Latino, Edward Martinez, attracted 295 votes.

District 1 also produced a somewhat surprising result, the Latino incumbent, Connie Cisneros, lost her seat to Don Sanders, an African American, despite the relatively tiny proportion of African Americans to Latinos in the district. In this case, the Latino incumbent's demise seems to have been the result of a recall petition that had been circulated during 1992; although Cisneros defeated the recall, its effects weakened her and undermined her alliance with Fulp; thus Fulp's endorsement of Sanders proved sufficient to assure him the victory.

In District 6, a Latino, David Sandoval, won the 1994 election but quickly quarreled with Mayor Fulp, who supported a recall movement that succeeded in replacing Sandoval with John Hanson, an Anglo, in February of 1996. Interestingly, Sandoval and some Latino supporters noted that the single-member district system had made his recall easier: prior to the district system, recall petitions had to be circulated city-wide to receive a percentage of the signatures of the total city electorate at considerable cost either in volunteer effort or dollars; in 1995, Sandoval's recall was accomplished at a small fraction of the cost.

It is unclear whether the downfall of Latino candidates in 1994 is to be explained only in terms of specific circumstances and individual political problems or whether the district system itself played a role. Some Latinos have suggested to this writer that the recalls of Latino candidates were organized by Anglo business interests; and there have been charges that interests outside Colton are better able to manipulate district elections to their advantage and to the detriment of Latinos. Any final measure of the effects of the Colton districting on Latino candidacies, however, must await the outcomes of future elections. If we know the fate of Latino candidates in the 1996 and 1998 elections, we may have some better insight into whether the 1992 or the 1994 results are more representative of any built-in tendency to advantage or disadvantage Latino candidacies.

This writer is inclined to believe that even the millennium may not afford a definite proof one way or the other. Already, two major issues—a city-wide measure to establish a casino in Colton and a scandal over a waste contract—have heavily roiled Colton's politics and, while bringing new "reform" figures to the fore, seem destined to remove some leading figures, perhaps including Mayor Fulp, from the City Council. These issues, cutting across community lines, are likely to overshadow ethnic concerns or divisions for some time to come.

It is to the redistricting following the millennial census, perhaps, that we should look for answers. That census is likely to report a further increase in Colton's Latino population, and it will be a very interesting question whether an enlarged Latino majority will seek a return to a city-wide electoral scheme. To Richard Fajardo and other Latino activists, the Colton districting originated as an effort to undermine the electoral power of Latinos at the very moment when they were about to move into majority status. In their eyes—and it is the fundamental political logic of the Latino voting rights movement—it is axiomatic that districts aid the minority. Given an emerging Latino majority, however, districts may represent a retrogression to continued white domination of Colton's political process.

Colton is an appropriate case with which to conclude this study for it raises some interesting practical doubts about voting rights remedies. Not only in Colton, but in many communities in California, Arizona and elsewhere in the southwest, Latinos will soon be the majority group: if Colton's Latino activists correctly interpreted the political logic of districts, then the districts that have been imposed on many communities over the past decade may prove handicaps to the new majority. Ironically, this aspect of the voting rights movement may prove self- defeating.

At another, more practical level, however, the Colton case raises doubts about the commitment of today's voters to "ethnic representation." Colton's voters, whether Latino or Anglo, seem prepared to vote for candidates of their choice almost regardless of ethnicity. In late twentieth century suburban California, there may not be enough cohesion in the minority electorate to produce the representational results that voting rights theorists have predicted.

Indeed, the Colton case gives abundant illustrations of the obstacles of ethnically-represented districts: Latino candidates competing with one another in majority Latino districts can guarantee the election of an Anglo-minority candidate. Recalls can tarnish the credentials of even popular Latino incumbents, thrust them from office, and replace them with Anglo-minority candidates. The effects of scandals can outweigh ethnic ties.

Of course, to list these and other circumstances that can undo the best laid plans of districters—whether Latino or Anglo—is to emphasize the fact, often overlooked in the scholarly literature and judicial opinions, that districts are just one factor among many in local politics, and frequently not the most important one.

NOTES

1. Lynette Jueneman, "Measure W: For Better For Worse," *Colton Courier*, Vol. 116, No. 27, June 25, 1992.

2. In April of 1996, in discussion with Chris Rattay, a Claremont McKenna College undergraduate, Fulp gave an example of the lack of representation of the southeast "corner" of Colton. He charged that, under the old system, the representatives from downtown or the "flatlands" would impose the same building plans for the canyon portions of Colton to its southeast as for the urban areas. This required "cutting mountains and ruining the ranching community that was trying to settle there." In Fulp's view, the new geographic representation would assure that building would be more in accord with the desires of the residents of District 5 that now serves that area. In the same interview, Fulp countered the claim that districts would fragment the public interest in the good of the city as a whole: under the new system, he claimed, the budget of the city is not broken down by districts; there is one budget every year for the whole city; therefore, the council members have to think of the city at-large, because they have to vote on where the money goes; as a result, councilmembers compromise because they need votes from their colleagues; and, thus, in this way, all members, not only the mayor, must think about the city as a whole. Fulp also claimed as a further benefit of districting that one person from each district has an appointed seat on all commissions and

committees: in his view, this gives people a sense that their votes count and gives them a feeling of community participation.

3. Maria C. Hunt, "Battle Lines Drawn over Move to Divide City into Six Wards," *San Bernardino Sun*, December 4, 1991.

4. *Colton Courier*, June 25, 1992. In the course of the interview with Chris Rattay of April 1996, Fulp pointed out that one of the council members elected in 1994 under the district system had won on a campaign budget as low as $1,500. Fulp also cited District 4 as an example of the openness of the new district system: the first district election in 1992 had brought out seven challengers for that seat; and the winner, Betty Cook, had won with little more than 23 percent of the vote.

5. Petition from Colton Voters for Fair Representation Committee.

6. Maria C. Hunt, "Battle Lines Drawn over Move to Divide City into Six Wards," *San Bernardino Sun*, December 4, 1991.

7. Ibid.

8. Jueneman, *Colton Courier*, June 25, 1992. Aguilar seems to have been disgruntled principally because the existing Council had ignored requests to improve the youth boxing organization that he ran. He charged that a former member of the boxing organization, who was hostile to its new management, had successfully lobbied the council against support of the boxing club.

9. The Petition, in the form of a draft ordinance, dealt with the potentially inflammatory issue of the assignment to districts of incumbent council members as follows: "Upon establishment of the neighborhood district boundaries, and prior to the first day of candidate filing for the November 3, 1992 General Municipal Election, the City Clerk by lot shall assign each of the four (4) incumbent councilmembers to a district, regardless of the location of his/her residence (as defined by the State Elections Code), provided however that if an incumbent councilmember resides within the boundaries of a district and no other incumbent councilmember resides within that same district, said councilmember shall be assigned to that district. If more than one incumbent resides within a district, the district shall be assigned to one of the incumbent members residing within that district as determined by the casting of lots among those incumbents. Election to the office of Councilmember for the two (2) district offices assigned to incumbent councilmembers whose terms expire in 1992, and one (1) new district office, shall be held in November 1992 and every four (4) years thereafter to conform to current council terms. Election to the remaining open district office shall be in November 1992 as a Short Term seat to expire in November 1994. The term of the person elected to that seat to expire in November 1994. The term of the person elected to that seat in 1994 shall be for four (4) years and for every four (4) years thereafter. Election to the

office of Councilmember for the two (2) district offices whose terms shall expire in 1994, shall be held in November 1994 and every four (4) years thereafter. The Mayor shall continue to be elected as Mayor, separate and apart from the other members of the City Council."

10. It is important to note in this regard that the percentage of Hispanics of 18 years of age and older is significantly less in each of the districts than the percent of total Hispanic population (see plots at figures 49 and 50). Thus, District 2 is only 74.63 percent 18-plus Hispanic; District 3 is only 62.35 percent 18-plus Hispanic; and District 4 is only 68.50 percent 18-plus Hispanic. Of course, when non-citizens are deducted from the totals, these percentages fall even further. Even in Districts 2 and 4, it is far from certain that an Hispanic voting majority would always and reliably come to the polls.

11. Of twelve individuals who made presentations before the commission, only three had Hispanic last names, and no adverse comments were made from the perspective of Hispanic representation.

12. Hunt, *San Bernardino Sun*, December 4, 1991.

13. Ibid.

14. Responding to this criticism, Fulp pointed out that Roman would have the same chance as every other member of the existing council: he would draw a number corresponding to an open district, one of which would be District 2, where he lived; the district number that he would draw would be the one he would be allowed to serve in; and he would represent that district without competition and with a once-only exemption of not having to live in the district. Of course, it should be noted that if Roman did not wish to represent the district whose number he had drawn, then he could only opt to resign and run—but with the likelihood of competition—to represent another ward.

15. Sixty-three percent of registrants voted in the 1992 election; but, in 1994, the turnout dropped to 47 percent. The decline in turnout seems to have been particularly sharp in precincts with heavy Hispanic population.

16. In the previously quoted conversation with Rattay, George Fulp said that many in the Hispanic community had thanked him for his role in the passage into law of the district system.

CHAPTER 11

Conclusions

For more than three decades now, claims of representational unfairness have roiled American law and politics. The basis for the *Baker-Reynolds-Wesberry* reapportionment cases was the charge of unfairness against malapportioned legislatures that over-represented rural areas, and under-represented cities. At bottom, too, the impulse behind the Voting Rights Act and its amendments was the belief that racial and ethnic minorities are unfairly under-represented, white majorities over-represented.

Both the one-man-one-vote revolution and the voting rights revolution sought remedies through district lines. In the former case, the lines had to produce equipopulous districts, and in the latter, lines had to produce majority-minority districts.

Have districts produced fairness or have we asked too much from the districting process? Equipopulous districts broke the power of rural minorities, both in Congress and in the state legislatures. It is far from clear, however, that the principle of population equality has achieved full representational fairness. Even in the case of rural-urban-suburban representation, the original focus of concern in the reapportionment cases, it is unclear that equality of population necessarily produces "fair" results. We know that the lines of exactly equipopulous districts can be drawn to assure the over-representation of one area, the under-representation of others. Thus, for thirty years after 1964, urban areas got much more than their fair share of representation in Congress and in many state legislatures.[1] Moreover, the principle of population equality, by demoting older constraints on the districting process such as county boundaries, has unleashed partisan and bi-partisan gerrymanders.

Similarly, if the expectation of voting rights activists was that single-member districts would quickly produce minority electoral successes in proportion to minority populations, the result has been disappointing. One reason is that non-minority incumbents continue to control the design and re-design of district lines. More important, however, are the characteristics of the single-member district system itself.[2] Indeed, single-member districts produce the sad irony that minorities are elected proportionate to population only when they are residentially segregated. If minorities do not reside in numerical concentrations sufficient to become voting majorities, they cannot dominate district elections. Assimilation and its associated tendency to disperse the minority population, therefore, hamper minority electoral success in district systems.

Of course, an impressive increase has occurred in the number of black representatives in Congress, in state legislatures and in local governments.[3] In many cases, that increase arose directly from the replacement of multi-member and at-large arrangements with single-member districts; and in other cases, it was assisted by majority-minority districts.[4] These gains, however, have produced a backlash, both in the courts, where racially homogeneous single-member districts have come under strict scrutiny, and among Democratic leaders who think black seats lead to Republican gains.

Among voting rights activists, too, the gains have fallen short of expectations, producing another kind of backlash. Lani Guinier, for example, complains that the increase in the number of black elected officials has produced no visible improvement in the socioeconomic status of black voters. In her view, the problem rests in the districting solution itself:

> The districting strategy excludes the possibility of representation for those whose interests are not defined by, or consistent with, those in the geographically defined district. . . . Districting decisions may simply reflect the arbitrary preferences of incumbent politicians who prefer packed safe districts to ensure their reelection. Indeed, districting battles are often pitched between incumbents fighting to retain their seats, without regard to issues of voter representation. Because the choice of districts is so arbitrary, incumbents enjoy extraordinary leverage in self-perpetuation through gerrymandering. Thus, districting strategies often promote noncompetitive election contests which further reduce voter participation and interest.[5]

Dissatisfaction with the results, or the sharp contrast between political promise and actual political dividends, has driven many voting rights activists to suggest alternatives to single-member districts. Cumulative voting, for example, is now a leading alternative to racially homogeneous single-member districts. Charging that majority-minority districts preserve the racial divisions in society,[6] others have embraced one or another form of proportional representation.[7] To their supporters, these alternatives provide a means of increasing the numbers of minority candidates elected, but without the creation of racially homogeneous districts. The Court's recent rulings in *Shaw v. Reno*, *Johnson v. Miller* and *Bush v. Vera*, and their indictment of "racially segregated districts" or electoral "apartheid," have given additional impetus to this attempt to find alternatives to districts.

DISTRICTS AND THE ELECTION OF MINORITIES

What do the case studies in Chapters 3 through 10 suggest concerning the advantages and disadvantages of districting? We need to look, first, at the political dividends for minority representation, defined in terms of numbers of candidates elected. The districtings we have described produced few new elected minority group members.

Perhaps even more heroic efforts should have been made to maximize minority group concentrations. Sharper contortions of district shapes could have produced slightly higher minority concentrations in Colton, Hanford, Glendale, Peoria, Sanger Unified and Kerman Unified. Regardless of the Court's current opposition to such a course, however, the failure to elect minorities in the jurisdictions considered in this study was not attributable to a lack of aggressive line-drawing or insufficiently ingenious solutions. In many of these jurisdictions no district could have concentrated minority populations sufficient to elect minority candidates: the minorities were simply too widely dispersed. An equally important problem was the lack of political organization in the Hispanic community and its general alienation from the political process. Almost regardless of concentration levels, several of the Hispanic communities in these jurisdictions lacked levels of registration, turn out, and the experience in mobilization behind candidacies that would be required to win.

In all the communities studied, Hispanics had lower registration and lower turnout rates than Anglos or African Americans. In part, this phenomenon may stem from lack of political interest.[8] Hispanic studies[9] have suggested that only the clear potential for electing representative members of the Hispanic community will generate the enthusiasm that leads to political involvement; and majority-minority districts have been billed as the means for doing this. In the jurisdictions here, however, there is little evidence that districts have performed in such a role. In Glendale, for example, the Anglo incumbent, Bob Huffman, won the Hispanic influence district in 1990 with only 871 votes out of a total of 6,313 eligible voters in the district.[10] The failure to develop candidacies from Ocotillo District seems also to have been a sign of lack of interest and of undeveloped political organization. In the case of Hanford, the only reason a Hispanic won is that city officials persuaded him to run.

In other cases, however, the problem seems to have been less the Hispanics' lack of interest than a lack of unity. Deep divisions within the Hispanic community cropped up in Watsonville, Sanger and Colton. Moreover, the new majority-minority districts often fostered intense competition among Hispanic candidates. Thus, in Colton an Anglo was elected as a direct result of competition among several Hispanic candidates. Indeed, Betty Cook was twice elected in a Colton district that was 69 percent Hispanic: on the first occasion, she won because the Hispanic vote split among Hispanic candidates; and on the second occasion, she seems to have won the support of a significant majority of Hispanic voters.

In several other jurisdictions as well, at least some Hispanics seem to have been content with non-Hispanic representation. In Phoenix in 1995, Salomon Leija led two Anglo opponents with 42.54 percent of the vote in the primary election to replace popular Hispanic representative Mary Rose Wilcox; nevertheless, he lost to Doug Lingner in the runoff, 48.82 percent to 51.18 percent, in a district that is 50.8 percent Hispanic. Indeed, in several of the jurisdictions, race was not a dominant or even a prominent feature of local politics and, therefore, Hispanic voters had little reason to cast their ballots in those terms.

Still, do not underrate the positive results in those communities where Hispanics were elected. Certainly, the new Hispanic members of the Council in Watsonville succeeded in changing not only the tone and tenor of city politics but also the substance. As of this writing, although there is still only a minority of Hispanics on the Watsonville City Council, the strong pro-grower bias of city government no longer goes unchallenged and the Hispanic majority is no longer pushed to one side in city politics.

ETHNICITY OR IDEOLOGY?

If the goal is the election of a minority candidate, then majority-minority redistricting is not always the answer. We have described cases in which districting actually threatened the political survival of current and former minority incumbents. Tony Campos in Watsonville, who had won in the at-large system, lost to an Anglo in the new district system. Art Brieno, who had represented Hanford in the at-large system, does not live in the majority-minority district or in the "influence district;" and he did not attempt to run in the mostly Anglo district where he lives in north Hanford, for the concentration of Hispanic voters in the other districts left him to face a predominantly Anglo electorate. These are examples of Hispanics whose continued reelection was not a primary value of the Hispanic activists who dominated the districting process.[11]

District lines are manipulated by both Anglo and Hispanic groups to aid favored candidates. Corcoran's voters ultimately decided not to move to a district system; but districts were created for Corcoran, precleared by the Justice Department and placed on the June 1994 ballot. Rueben Quintanilla, who lives in one of the Hispanic districts created for the ballot initiative, was appointed to the City Council to fill the seat of Tony Beltran (also Hispanic), who resigned from the Council during the districting process. Mr. Quintanilla, who was perceived by the Council as someone more in line with the Council's views, was appointed over the protests of Hispanic activists who supported Ms. Toni Baltierra. Had the district system been imposed, Mr. Quintanilla would have faced opposition from Ms. Baltierra. The Corcoran case suggests that districting may be itself the cause of rifts within the Hispanic community, helping to promote multiple candidacies that pave the way for Anglo victories.

When lines are deliberately drawn to include the residence and political base of a chosen minority candidate, and equally deliberately to exclude the residence and political base of another minority candidate, districting promotes a factional cause. Perhaps the clearest case is Watsonville, where unionist organizers dominated the districting process in an attempt to oust the pro-grower city council. The redistricting placed two targeted councilmembers in the same district and cut another incumbent from his base and placed him instead in an overwhelmingly Hispanic district.

Our cases suggest that, to many activists, the major purpose of districting is less to open the door to Hispanic candidacies than to assure that the Hispanic community is represented by individuals who embrace an activist political agenda. The test for the success of a districting in this case is essentially ideological: a Tony Campos or a Rueben Quintanilla will not do.

DISTRICTING AND THE NON-MINORITY ELECTORATE

Districts seem to be widely accepted by electorates—minority and non-minority alike—in jurisdictions where they result from an electoral decision. This was the case, for example, in Pomona, Phoenix, Glendale and Peoria. Although the electorate divided over the ballot measure implementing districting, the election result seemed to validate and legitimize districts. By contrast, in jurisdictions where districts were imposed either by court order or as the result of a threat of litigation, districts remain a distinctly controversial institution. This was the case in Watsonville, Dinuba, Sanger and Hanford.

The lack of support for districts is often paralleled, also, by heightened tension between the minority and non-minority populations. Racially-based divisions, already evident prior to the districting in Watsonville, Sanger, and Dinuba were sharpened by the process. In Watsonville, Anglo citizens felt punished: because they had fought against districts, they were told that they could not have an at-large mayor as in Salinas. In Sanger, the primary concern of the all-Anglo Board was to build community-based districts around the elementary schools; but they instead had to make race the primary consideration. In Dinuba and Hanford, the huge costs resulting from litigation had a punitive aspect in the eyes of Anglo (and also some Hispanic) voters. Watsonville, Sanger and Dinuba were communities, of course, in which racial concerns were a primary reason for Hispanic agitation for districts in the first place;[12] and it may be argued that the gains were ultimately more important than any loss in inter-ethnic comity. Yet, there are other jurisdictions where the gains from districts were counter-balanced by the negative result of racially-based hostilities. Communities such as Hanford, where Hispanics had won under at-large arrangements, and where racial tensions had been relatively low, responded harshly to the imposition of districts. In such situations, the gains in minority representation, which are slight, hardly seem to justify the enormous upheaval.

BUILDING INTER-ETHNIC COALITIONS

In most California and Arizona jurisdictions few majority-minority districts can be formed; nor is there an impressive record of electing minorities in influence districts. In many combined Hispanic/African American districts, also, Hispanics often run second to an African American candidate. If large numbers of Hispanic candidates are to win in states such as California and Arizona, where the Hispanic population is increasingly dispersed, it will be because many non-minority voters support them. In most of the jurisdictions we have examined, election of Hispanic candidates with minority votes alone is unlikely: either insufficient concentrations of Hispanic voters or apathy and lack of political organization doom such candidacies. Only if Hispanic candidates can appeal across ethnic lines can they ever win in cities such as Glendale and Peoria. In such jurisdictions, no majority-minority districts can be formed to bring into being even 50 percent total Hispanic population, much less voting majorities of Hispanics; and, by definition, it is impossible to expect the election with minority votes alone of Hispanic candidates in the influence districts. Even in cities such as Phoenix, Pomona and Colton, with their large minority populations, Hispanic candidates typically need Anglo votes.

If the goal is the election of minorities, then, districts should be drawn to unify minority and non-minority voters. This, of course, is much easier said than done; and it may be impossible or even undesirable in cases where there are strong inter-ethnic tensions. Yet, it points attention to an important potential function of districts: the development of cross-racial coalitions—something the racially homogeneous district can only frustrate.

At the end of the day, the concern about constituencies such as those in Watsonville and Dinuba, where new districts excluded all but tiny percentages of non-minorities, is that the elected representative depends only on minority votes. Absent from such districts are the beneficent effects of grassroots politics in healing divisions between the communities and assisting development of a politics that rises above race.

PUNITIVE MEASURES

The goal of assisting the political progress of minorities has been supported by the U.S. Department of Justice with a number of strong, even punitive, measures. Take, for example, the imposition of district systems as a remedy for alleged minority vote dilution resulting from annexations. A district system was forced on Hanford even though it was impossible to create an effective majority-minority district. Districts were imposed even though Hispanic candidates had been elected at-large in Hanford, as well as in the school district and hospital district centered on Hanford.

The draconian character of imposed districts in this case is further underscored by the fact that the annexations dated back to 1972 and that, taken annexation by annexation, their contribution to minority vote dilution had been minuscule. The residents of Hanford's annexations had previously voted in city elections and, thus, had contributed to the election of several Hispanics in Hanford and the special districts containing Hanford. The imposition of districts divided the community along ethnic lines and with little counter-balancing gain in ethnic representation. Recent election results suggest, instead, a lack of interest on the part of the minority community. Dennis Sanchez, a candidate popular in both the Hispanic and Anglo communities, very well could have won in the at-large system had he run; and, from all reports, he was a most reluctant candidate in the recent district election. No other Hispanic candidates emerged in either the majority-minority district or in the "influence" district; nor did any Hispanic candidates—even Laura Yrigollen or Art Brieno—file in any of the other districts.

The requirement of non-retrogression, as enforced by the Justice Department, can also have a punitive aspect. Glendale made a self-conscious effort to go beyond the requirements of law: it enhanced minority access with a minority influence district, which it had then equipped with an especially high negative deviation. When, in 1991, the new census showed that the Hispanic percentage of Ocotillo District had increased (as a result of the district being severely underpopulated in relation to the rapidly growing northern districts), the Justice Department tried to hold the City to the higher percentage (rather than the percentage of the Ocotillo District as it had been created in 1988). The Department threatened to withhold preclearance unless the boundaries were contorted to capture this additional 4.62 percent, even though 3,500 persons needed to be added to the district in order to comply with the one-person one-vote mandate.

Retrogression standards are peculiarly inappropriate in the new suburban developments of Arizona and California. In such communities, barrio-like concentrations are losing population while up-scale areas are gaining population, both Anglo and Hispanic. The demographic movement in such cities is at odds with a standard that was developed in the much more stable societies of the South.

Equally troubling are situations where enforcement of the non-retrogression standard adds Hispanic population to a district that is already securely represented by an Hispanic, while preventing the addition of Hispanics to other districts where their votes could elect new Hispanic candidates. This was clearly the case in Peoria where Councilman Osuna would have been secure in a district with a reduced Hispanic percentage.

The litigation bill submitted to Dinuba is an example of a different punitive measure. The charge to every resident of Dinuba, of $60.00 per person for contesting the imposition of districts, suggests the huge burden that voting rights litigation can impose on small communities. Unlike states and large cities, small communities such as Dinuba can be brought to the verge of bankruptcy by such costs. Associated with such costs, the litigation process itself becomes a means of intimidating jurisdictions into the use of district arrangements. An even more extreme example may be Hanford which had already committed to a district system when a suit was thrown at it, resulting in hundreds of thousands of dollars in legal costs.

RULES FOR DISTRICTS

To rehearse the disadvantages of districts, as we have done above, is to run the risk of forgetting how the Voting Rights Act ended anti-minority gerrymanders. Jurisdictions with established districts must now take greater care before cutting through concentrations of minority voters or improperly packing them. Since 1965, black communities have had the protection of law against such racially motivated gerrymanders; and for the past quarter century, Hispanics have shared in that protection. Today it is hard to find districts in the legislative or municipal maps of California or Arizona where Hispanics are disadvantaged by blatant gerrymanders.[13]

CONCLUSION

By building on the achievement of the Voting Rights Act, how can the United States continue to advance minority participation? In the eyes of many civil rights leaders, the single-member district has exhausted its contribution. They see many of the same difficulties with the districting process as appeared in our case histories: the problem of building majority-minority districts for dispersed minority populations; the frequent failure (whether as a result of low minority turnout or a divided minority vote) of such districts to elect minority candidates; and the ever-present threat of incumbent gerrymanders. Moreover, in the line of cases beginning with *Shaw v. Reno*, the U.S. Supreme Court has made increasingly clear its opposition to the use of race or ethnicity as the primary basis for drawing district lines.

Districts, however their lines are contorted, simply will not produce minority incumbents in proportion to minority population unless residential segregation again becomes the norm. Nor will cumulative voting or any of the forms of proportional representation achieve such a result—unless, tragically, race becomes the single, dominant issue of our politics. After all, the only purpose of these voting arrangements is that they will give an advantage to a group or groups that self-consciously form around an issue or issues that are of paramount importance to them. Do we, then, hope for a politics in which racial issues are the paramount concerns of minority groups? How long will it be before white majorities begin to counter-organize along racial lines? It is easy to predict that the civil rights community will react to the Court's decisions on the Georgia, North Carolina and Texas districts by urging the use of non-district-based solutions such as proportional representation (PR); yet, the failure of such solutions is equally predictable. If a party organizes around race—the Hispanic Party, the African American Party, and so forth—it may win something approaching a racially proportionate share of votes;[14] but, to do so, would be to encourage the organization of opposed racial coalitions.

The better course is to improve the ways in which districts are drawn, not only to prevent minority vote dilution but to improve their representational functions in such a way as to enhance minority representation and involvement. At one level, this course involves preventing racial gerrymanders: packing and cracking of minority concentrations whether by individual incumbents or by legislative majorities (and whether by Anglo or minority incumbents) should continue to be unlawful.[15] In turn, courts should continue to enforce the provisions of Section 2.

The task of reviving effective district representation, however, involves more than concern with minority vote dilution. As several of the cases in this study have demonstrated, the development of district lines places extraordinary power in the hands of the line-drawing authority. The Court has recently limited line drawers' discretion by restoring traditional districting criteria—in particular, compactness, respect for jurisdictional lines and attention to the facts of physical and manmade geography. Although scorned by many critics, these criteria are not intrinsically harder to implement than the concept of "fair representation" for minorities. The charge is made that they lack definition or cannot be quantified. In response we may ask: How easily defined is fair minority representation? We have seen that there is no direct quantitative correlation between racial percentages and the likelihood of electing a minority representative; and the quantitative rigor of voting rights concepts is largely the product of statistical measures that apply to different aspects of vote dilution, not to the effectiveness of the remedies that are applied.[16] Complaints that the traditional criteria are always potentially in conflict are also made: for example, districts cannot be compact, it is said, if they are also to follow traditional jurisdictional lines.[17] Yet, this objection is no more than to say that wherever more than one rule applies to any process, there may be conflict among rules. Thus, as we have seen in some of our case histories, there is inherent tension between the two federal mandates of equality of population and appropriate concentration of minority voters.

It is even charged, as well, that there is little substantial public interest content to concepts such as compactness, respect for jurisdictional lines and attention to facts of physical and manmade geography. Yet, as several of our case histories revealed, many voters, both minority and non-minority, put a very high value on district lines that follow other jurisdictional boundaries, that provide them with easy access to voting places, and that make for recognizable districts. Indeed, it is apparent, on the basis of districting processes in cities such as Glendale and Peoria, that federal requirements that result in irregular district lines are fueling resentment against Justice Department bureaucracies and federal administration of local electoral arrangements.

Many of the most serious problems associated with districting today trace back to the efforts by Congress and the Court to solve problems in unfairness in representation through new regulations on district line drawing. When the Court declared that districts must be equipopulous, it weakened the older criteria, especially the importance of existing jurisdictional boundaries.[18] The result at every level of government has been the proliferation of ever more bizarrely shaped districts that have become progressively more remote from political geography. It is now time to restore the traditional criteria to a fuller role in the process.

A first step is to end the cynical abuse of the criterion of equal population by incumbents and legislative majorities. The Court's insistence on exact equality in congressional redistricting has been so blatantly abused that it is now obvious that exact equality of numbers produces little beyond an excuse for extreme gerrymandering. It would be far more constructive if the Court accepted substantial deviations from the ideal, perhaps as much as 20 percent (or twice the maximum deviation of 10 percent that has emerged from court rulings on local districtings), but with the requirement that such deviations be justified in terms either of respect for minority concentrations or any of the traditional criteria of compactness, traditional jurisdictional boundaries and natural and manmade geography.[19] Exact equality in districts is a chimera: after all, as voting rights specialists are the first to acknowledge, the census count is never exact; moreover (and this is especially true in the West and Southwest) populations are ever shifting and show no respect for district boundaries when they move. Clearly, there should be a hierarchy among the acceptable justifications for deviations from equality: minority representation should have priority, followed by existing jurisdictional lines, followed by natural and manmade geography, with compactness bringing up the rear.

One traditional criterion to which the Court seems willing to give respect—protection of incumbents and party majorities—should be removed from the list of acceptable reasons for deviations from equality: the incentive to manipulation is already great enough without giving it legal status.[20] It is insufficiently recognized, for example, that minority incumbents typically push for the overconcentration of minorities in their districts in order not only to assure re-election but to ease the task of working their constituencies. The proposed rules for districting would undoubtedly work best if overseen and implemented by independent redistricting boards and commissions.

The dramatic increase in the numbers of jurisdictions that now use district lines has been largely the responsibility of the Voting Rights Act and litigation under it. Many of the newly districted jurisdictions include significant minority populations. Surely, we need better rules to produce not only representational fairness but also to achieve the kind of community-based politics that well-drawn districts can achieve. After all, districting is a process that profoundly affects the "political and racial landscape of this nation."[21]

NOTES

1. It is impossible to understand the domination of Congress by urban Democrats in the 1970s and 1980s absent manipulation of district lines. The Democrats learned to center districts in urban areas while picking up a lesser balance of population from suburban and rural areas. A good example of this technique at work is the treatment of the Los Angeles metropolitan area in the districtings masterminded by Phil Burton in 1981-82. See Leroy Hardy and Alan Heslop, *Redistricting Reform: An ACTION Program* (1989), *The Gerrymander: Origin, Conception, and Re-emergence* (1990) and *The Westside Story: A Murder in Four Acts* (1990) published by the Rose Institute of State and Local Government, Claremont, CA.

2. Single member district systems will not yield proportional representation of any group. See, for example, Taagepera, Rein, and Matthew Soberg Sugart, *Seats and Votes: The Effects and Determinants of Electoral Systems* (New Haven: Yale University Press, 1989); and Edward R. Tufte, "The Relationship between Seats and Votes in Two Party Systems," *American Political Science Review 67 (1973)*: 540-547. Also see Bernard Grofman and Lisa Handley, "Minority Population Proportion and Black and Hispanic Congressional Success in the 1970s and 1980s," *American Politics Quarterly* 17 (1989): 436-445.

3. An increase occurred from 1,500 black elected officials in 1970 to more than 7,300 black elected officials in 1990. See Harold W. Stanley and Richard G. Niemi, *Vital Statistics on American Politics*. Third Edition, (Washington, D.C.: CQ Press, 1992).

4. Some of this increase, of course, is now under challenge: legally, because of the court's new rulings against "affirmative action gerrymandering," and politically, because of the discovery that Republicans have been the primary gainers from the enlargement of the black caucus within a shrunken House Democratic caucus.

5. Lani Guinier, "No two seats: the Illusive quest for Political Equality, *Virginia Law Review* 77 (1991): 1413-1455 at 1454. See also, Lani Guinier, "The Triumph of Tokenism: The Voting Rights Act and the Theory of Black Electoral Success," *Michigan Law Review* 89 (1991): 1077-1139.

6. That is, by making it unnecessary for candidates to appeal outside their own racial group, racially homogenous districts force development of compromise in the legislature at the policy making level, instead of encouraging interactive compromise among the voting public itself. In cumulative voting, however, candidates of all races are said to have a reason to appeal to voters of all races, and bi-racial and multi-racial coalitions can form at the grassroots level. See Edward Still and Pamela Karlin, "Cumulative Voting as a Remedy in Voting Rights Cases," *National Civic Review*, 84 No. 4 (Fall-Winter 1995): 337-347; Richard L. Engstrom et. al, "Cumulative Voting as a Remedy for Minority Vote Dilution," *Journal of Law and Politics* 5 (1989):469-497; Richard L. Cole et al., "Alternatives to Single-Member Districts," *Western Political Quarterly*, (March 1990), 191-199; Edward Still, "Alternatives to Single Member Districts," In Chandler Davidson, ed., *Minority Vote Dilution* (Washington D.C.: Howard University Press, 1984) 253-258; Wilma Rule and Joseph F. Zimmerman, eds., *United States Electoral Systems: Their Impact on Minorities and Women* (Westport: Greenwood Press, 1992).

7. See, for example, Douglas J. Amy, *Real Choices/New Voices: The Case For Proportional Representation Elections in the United States* (New York: Columbia University Press, 1993); Stephen J. Mulroy, "Limited, Cumulative Evidence: Divining Justice Department Positions on Alternative Electoral System," *National Civic Review* 84 No. 1 (Winter 1995): 61-69; and Joseph F. Zimmerman, supra, 302-303.

8. It is well known, of course, that Hispanic political involvement is handicapped by disproportionate numbers of persons under 18 years of age and by large numbers of non-citizens. There is also a disproportionate number of Hispanics in the 18 to 30 age group, which includes many non-registrants and infrequent voters in all ethnic groups.

9. See Richard Santillan, ed., *The Hispanic Community and Redistricting*, Volumes 1 (1981) and 2 (1984), the Rose Institute of State and Local Government, Claremont, CA.

10. Ocotillo District has one-third to nearly one-half fewer voters than the other districts in the City of Glendale, leading to complaints from a councilmember who needed 1,956 votes to win his district.

11. Perhaps the best known example of the phenomenon of the "wrong Hispanic" is Sara Flores, the Republican who emerged as the primary winner in the existing county-drawn district in Los Angeles in 1990. Her election did not

prevent MALDEF, the ACLU and the U.S. Department of Justice from proceeding with a packed Hispanic district of Rorschach test dimensions, to secure the election of Gloria Molina, a prominent member of the liberal wing of the California Democratic Party.

12. In Watsonville, the tensions between the Anglo growers and the Hispanic workers were already at the breaking point. An equally bitter sense of estrangement was evident in the Hispanic community in Sanger: one Hispanic citizen told the Board that they lacked "sensitivity" to the needs of the Hispanic community. One can contrast these cities with Hanford, where there was virtually no interest in districts prior to the Justice Department's letter to the City.

13. The examples from the 1980s were mostly "affirmative action gerrymanders," drawn to the advantage of African Americans, that, over time, and with development of the Hispanic population, had come to protect the African American incumbent at the expense of the Hispanics.

14. Although even this is unlikely, not only because of the reasons given above, but also because significant numbers of Hispanics and African Americans are deeply opposed to using race as a basis for political organization.

15. It needs to be emphasized, I believe, that racial gerrymanders may be conducted by minority incumbents who over-concentrate minority voters in order to provide themselves with additional security for reelection.

16. The voting rights literature, for example, is filled with controversy over the threshold level at which a majority-minority district will elect a minority member. Is it 65 percent (as the court required in *Gomillion v. Lightfoot*) or is it 60 percent or only 55 percent? The truth is that the percentage varies from area to area, from time to time, from election to election. There is no true quantitative definition of a majority-minority district.

17. *Garza v. Los Angeles County Board of Supervisors*, CV 88-5143 KN, 918 F.2d 763 (9th Cir. 1990).

18. At the level of Congress and the state legislatures, county boundaries lost their status as the fundamental constraints on partisan and incumbent gerrymanders. Something of the same sort happened in local jurisdictions when the emphasis on population equality opened the door to decennial redistrictings: district lines could be redrawn, sometimes dramatically, and neighborhoods exchanged from one district to another all with an eye to political advantage.

19. One may note here that the malapportionment cases would surely never have reached the United States Supreme Court if the districts in Illinois or Tennessee had been only 20 percent deviant from an ideal. Citizens could well understand the inequity of a legislature that gave two or three times as

many representatives to rural areas as their numbers deserved. No one can seriously mind if they live in a district that has 20 percent more population than its neighbor. After all no one seems to be concerned that some U.S. reps are elected with only 50,000 votes, while others in districts with higher turnout levels need 150,000 votes.

20. The Court's language in *Bandemer v. Davis* suggests that, at least at one point, the Court was near to understanding the constitutional problems of the partisan gerrymander.

21. The phrase is Justice Stevens's in his dissent in *Bush v. Vera*. The truth, of course, is that the rules required by the Court from *Reynolds v. Sims* forward have, themselves, profoundly affected politics and race in this nation. The complete quote follows: "I cannot profess to know how the Court's developing jurisprudence of racial gerrymandering will alter the political and racial landscape in this Nation—although it certainly will alter that landscape. As the Court's law in this area has developed, it has become ever more apparent to me that the Court's approach to these cases creates certain perverse incentives and (I presume) unanticipated effects that serve to highlight the essentially unknown territory into which it strides. Because I believe that the social and political risks created by the Court's decisions are not required by the Constitution, my first choice would be to avoid the preceding analysis altogether, and leave these considerations to the political branches of our Government." The Supreme Court of the United States, Nos. 94-805, and 94-988. *Bush v. Vera*, On Appeals from the United States District Court for the Southern District of Texas, June 13, 1996.

Bibliography

Abrams, K. "'Raising Politics Up': Minority Political Participation and Section 2 of the Voting Rights Act." *New York University Law Review* 63 (June 1988): 449-531.

Adams, Florence. *Local Representation: Problems and Prospects.* Prepared for conference, The Rose Institute of State and Local Government and The Institute for Social Justice, Claremont, CA, November 2, 1989.

"Affirmative Racial Gerrymandering: Fair Representation for Minorities or a Dangerous Recognition of Group Rights?" *Rutgers Law Journal* 26 (Spring 1995): 595-624.

Aleinikoff, T. Alexander, and Samuel Issacharoff. "Race and Redistricting: Drawing Constitutional Lines After Shaw V. Reno." *Michigan Law Review* 92, no. 3 (December 1993): 588.

"Alternative Voting Systems as Remedies for Unlawful At-Large Systems." *The Yale Law Journal* (1982): 144-160.

Baker, Gordon E. "Judicial Determination of Political Gerrymandering: A'Totality of Circumstances' Approach." *Journal of Law and Politics* 3 (Winter 1986): 1-19.

Ball Howard, Dale Krane, and Thomas P. Lauth. *Compromised Compliance: Implementation of the 1965 Voting Rights Act.* Westport, CT: Greenwood Press, 1982.

Bartlett, John L. "Reapportionment of the California County Central Committees." *Stanford Law Review* 18 (February 1966): 742-749.

Berri, Brett W. "Annexation and Municipal Voting Rights." *Washington University Journal of Urban and Contemporary Law* 35 (Spring 1989): 237-48.

Beeman, Mary P. "Implementing Equality: The Voting Rights Act and Its Impact on Municipal Government," Paper delivered at Southwestern Political Science Association Annual Meeting, Dallas, March 1987.

Bierstein, Andrea. "Millennium Approaches: The Future of the Voting Rights Act After Shaw (Shaw v. Reno, 113 S. Ct. 2816 (1993), De Grandy (Johnson v. De Grandy, 114 S. Ct. 2647 (1994), and Holder (Holder v. Hall, 114 S. Ct. 2581 (1994))." *The Hastings Law Journal* 46 (July 1995): 1457-531.

Bilzin, Marsha D. "Reapportionment on the Sub-State Level of Government: Equal Representation or Equal Vote?" *Boston University Law Review* 50 (Spring 1970): 231-270.

Bledsoe, Timothy, and Susan Welch. "The Effect of Political Structures on the Socioeconomic Characteristics of Urban City Council Members." *American Politics Quarterly* (November 1985): 467-483.

Blumstein, James F. "Racial Gerrymandering and Vote Dilution: Shaw v. Reno (113 S. Ct. 2816 (1993)) in Doctrinal Context." *Rutgers Law Journal* 26 (Spring 1995): 517-93.

Blumstein, James F. "Shaw v. Reno (113 S. Ct. 2816 (1993)) and Miller v. Johnson (115 S. Ct. 2475 (1995)): Where We Are and Where We Are Still Headed. (Discussion of Still Hazy After All These Years: Voting Rights in the Post-Shaw Era. P.S. Karlan. 26 Cumb. L. Rev. 287-311 '95/'96)." *Cumberland Law Review* 26 (1995/1996): 503-13.

Boyd, William. "Local Electoral Systems: Is there a Best Way?," *National Civic Review* 65 (March 1976): 135.

Brace, Kimball, et. Al. "Minority Voting Equality [In the U.S.]: The 65 Percent Rule in Theory and Practice." *Law and Policy* 10 (January 1988): 43-62.

Brischetto, Robert R. "Latino Representation and the 1990 Census." William P. O'Hare. Redistricting in the 1990s.

Brouthers, L.E., and D.L. McClure. "The Effect of Council Size and District Elections on City Council Representation." *Aztlan* 15 (Fall 1984): 263-276.

Browning, Rufus P., Marshall, Dale Rogers, David H. Tabb. "Blacks and Hispanics in California City Politics: Changes in Representation." *Public Affairs Report* 20 (June 1979): 1-9.

Bullock, Charles S. III, and Charles M. Lamb, eds. *Implementation of Civil Rights Policy.* Monterey, CA: Brooks/Cole, 1984.

Bullock, Charles S. "Section 2 of the Voting Rights Act, Districting Formats, and the Election of African Americans." *The Journal of Politics* 56, no. 4 (November 1994): 1098. Southern Political Science Association Proceedings.

Burns, Jerry. "How Barbagelata Lost His Heart in San Francisco." *California Journal* 8 (September 1977): 303-305.

Butler, Katharine Inglis. "Affirmative Racial Gerrymandering: Rhetoric and Reality." *Cumberland Law Review* 26 (1995/1996): 313-63.

Cabeza, Aide Cristina. "Total Population: A Constitutional Basis for Apportionment Reaffirmed in Garza v. Los Angeles County (918 F.2d 763 (1990))." *Chicano-Latino Law Review* 13 (Summer 1993): 74-95.

"California Redistricting Studies at County Level." *National Civic Review* 50 (June 1961): 331-332.

"Constitutional Law - Discriminating Vote Dilution - Purposeful Discrimination May be Inferred from the Totality of Circumstances." *Mississippi Law Journal* 57 (September/December 1987): 865-81.

"Congressional Reaction to Judicial Construction of Section 5 of the Voting Rights Act of 1965." *Columbia Journal of Law and Social Problems* 29, no. 3 (Spring 1996): 337.

"Constitutional Limits on Racial Redistricting: Miller v. Johnson, 115 S. Ct. 2475 (1995)." *Harvard Journal of Law and Public Policy* 19, no. 1 (1995): 188.

Cooper, Matthew. "Beware of Republicans Bearing Voting Rights Suits." *Washington Monthly Review* (February 11-15, 1987).

Cotrell, Charles L., and Arnold Fleishmann. "The Change from At-Large Representation and Political Participation of Minority Groups in Fort Worth and San Antonio Texas." *Urban Affairs Quarterly* 10 (September 1974): 17-39.

"County Districting Passed in California," *National Civic Review* 53 (September 1964): 446.

Davidson, Chandler. *Minority Vote Dilution.* Washington, D.C.: Howard University Press, 1984.

Days, Drew S. III, and Lani Guinier. *Enforcement of Section 5 of the Voting Rights Act.* 1984 167-79.

De La Garza, Rodolfo, and Louis Desipio. *Making Latino Numbers Add Up to Increased Representation: The Road to the 1990 Census, Reapportionment and Redistricting.* Austin, TX: Texas Population Research Center Papers, Series 11: 1989.

De la Garza, Rodolfo O., and Louis Desipio. "Save the Baby, Change the Bathwater, and Scrub the Tub: Latino Electoral Participation After Seventeen Years of Voting Rights Act Coverage." *Texas Law Review* 71 (June 1993): 1479-539.

DeLeon, Richard E. *Race and Politics in San Francisco.* Prepared for delivery at the 1988 Annual Meeting of the Western Political Science Association, San Francisco, CA, March 10-12, 1988.

Din, Grant. "An Analysis of Asian/Pacific American Registration and Voting Patterns in San Francisco." Masters Thesis, Claremont Graduate School, 1984.

Dixon, Robert G. "Local Representation: Constitutional Mandates and Apportionment Options," *The George Washington Law Review* 36 (May 1968): 693-712.

Dixon, Robert G. *Democratic Representation: Reapportionment in Law and Politics.* New York: Oxford University Press, 1968.

Dixon, Jr., Robert G. "Rebuilding the Urban Political System: Some Heresies Concerning Citizen Participation, Community Actions, Metros, and One Man-One Vote." *Georgetown Law Journal* 58 (March-May 1970): 955-958.

Dixon, Robert G. "Local Government and Reapportionment;" Paper delivered at the 73rd National Conference on Government of the National Municipal League, November 12-15 1967 Milwaukee, Wisconsin.

Dutton, William H., and Alana Northrop. "Municipal Reform and the Changing Pattern of Urban Party Politics," *American Politics Quarterly* (October 1978): 429-52.

Eichenthal, D.R. "Voting Rights, Political Gerrymandering, and Proportional Representation." *Annual Survey of American Law* 1987 (June 1988): 93-116.

Eisenberg, Ralph. *Guide to County Redistricting.* Charlottesville, VA: University of Virginia, Institute of Government, 1970.

Engstrom, Richard L., and Michael D. McDonald. "The Effects of At-Large Vs. District Elections on Racial Representation in U.S. Municipalities: Electoral Laws and Their Political Consequences." Bernard Grofman, and Arend C. Lijphart, Editors. New York: Agathon Press, 1986.

Engstrom, Richard L., and Michael D. McDonald. "The Effects of At-Large VS. District Elections on Racial Representation in U.S. Municipalities: Electoral Laws and Their Political Consequences." Bernard Grofman, and Arend C. Lijphart, Editors. New York: Agathon Press, 1986.

Engstrom, Richard, and Michael D. McDonald. "The Underrepresentation of Blacks on City Councils: Comparing the Structural and Socioeconomic Explanations of South/Non-South Differences." *Journal of Politics* 44 (November 1982): 1088-99.

Engstrom, Richard, and Michael McDonald. "Quantitative Evidence in Vote Dilution Litigation, Part II: Minority Coalitions and Multivariate Analysis." *The Urban Lawyer* 19 (1987): 65-75.

Engstrom, R.L., and Michael McDonald. "Quantitative Evidence in Vote Dilution Litigation. Political Participation and Polarized Voting. Minority Coalitions and Multivariate Analysis." *Urban Law* 17 (Summer 1985): 369-377 and *Urban Law* 19 (Winter 1987): 65-75.

Ervin, Sam J. "The Truth Respecting the Highly Praised and Constitutionally Devious Voting Rights Act." *Cumberland Law Review* 12 (1981/1982): 261-81.

Esposito, John A. "Impact of 'One Person, One Vote' Reapportionment Concept on Government of New York City," *Brooklyn Barrister* 16 (May 1965): 235-242.

"Fair and Effective Voting Strength Under Section 2 of the Voting Rights Act: The Impact of Thornburg V. Gingles [106 S.CT. 2752] on Minority Vote Dilution Litigation." *Wayne Law Review*34 (Fall 1987): 303-329.

Fleischman, Arnold, and Lana Stein. "Minority and Female Success in Municipal Run-Off Elections." *Social Science Quartely* 68 (June 1987): 378-385.

Flores, Bill. "At-Large Elections: California Cities Should Follow Salinas' Example." *San Jose Mercury News*, February 12, 1989 1C.

Freeberg, Louis. "Latinos: Building Power From the Ground Up." *California Journal* (1987): 12-17.

"The Future of Voting Rights After Shaw v. Reno (113 S. Ct. 2816 (1993)): Symposium." *Michigan Law Review* 92 (December 1993): 482-682.

Gallagher, John F. "Apportionment in California Counties." *State Government* 37(Winter 1964): 36-41.

Gallagher, John F. *Apportionment in California Counties: The Impact of Judicial Decisions*. Davis, CA: University of California, Davis, Institute of Government Affairs, 1964.

Garcia, John. "Election Reform and Hispanic Political Participation." Paper delivered at Western Political Science Association Annual Meeting, Anaheim, March 1987.

Gelman, Andrew, and Gary King. "Enhancing Democracy Through Legislative Redistricting." *The American Political Science Review* 88, no. 3 (September 1994): 541.

"Geometry and Geography: Racial Gerrymandering and the Voting Rights Act." *The Yale Law Journal* 94 (November 1984): 189-208.

"Gerrymandering and the Courts: a Symposium." *UCLA Law Review* 33 (October 1985): i-ii, 1-281.

Gilbert, Charles E. "Electoral Competition and Electoral Systems in Large Cities," *Journal of Politics* 24 (1962): 323-347.

Gluck, Scott. "Congressional Reaction to Judicial Construction of Section 5 of the Voting Rights Act of 1965." *Columbia Journal of Law and Social Problems* 29 (Spring 1996): 337-84.

Greene, Kenneth R. "Race, Party, and Constituency in a Local Legislature," *Social Science Legislature* 56 (December 1975): 492-501.

Grofman, Bernard. "Would Vince Lombardi Have Been Right If He Said: "When it Comes to Redistricting, Race Isn't Everything, It's the Only Thing?" *Cardozo Law Review* 14 (April 1993): 1237-76.

Grofman, Bernard N., Michael Migalski, and Nicholas Noviello. "The Totality of Circumstances' Test in Section 2 of the Voting Rights Act: A Social Science Perspective." *Law and Policy* Vol. 7, No. 2 (April 1985): 209-233.

Grofman, Bernard, and Lisa Handley. "Black Representation: Making Sense of Electoral Geography at Different Levels of Government," *Legislative Studies Quarterly* 14 (May 1989) 265-79.

Grofman, Bernard, and Lisa Handley. "Identifying and Remedying Racial Gerrymandering." *The Journal of Law & Politics* 8 (Winter 1992): 345-404.

Grofman, Bernard M., Arend Lijphart, Robert McKay, and Howard Scarrow, eds. *Representation and Redistricting Issues.* Lexington Books, 1982, 107-128.

Gross, Ronald S., and Leonard V. Kaplan. "Legal Problems of Ward Realignment in Philadelphia," *Temple Law Quarterly* 38 (Winter 1965): 174-226.

Guerra, Fernando. "Black, Jewish and Latino Representation in Los Angeles." Paper delivered at Western Political Science Association Annual Meeting, Anaheim, March, 1987.

Guinier, Lani. "Comment: [E]racing Democracy: The Voting Rights Cases." *Harvard Law Review* 108, no. 1 (November 1994): 109.

Guinier, Lani. "Groups Representation, and Race-Conscious Districting: A Case of the Emperor's Clothes." *Texas Law Review* 71 (June 1993): 1589-642.

Hall, Stuart C. "Supervisorial Districting in California: The Shape of the Counties." (MA thesis, Dept. of Political Science, Stanford University, 1961.

Hall, Stuart C. *County Supervisorial Districts in California.* Berkeley, CA: University of California, Bureau of Public Administration, 1961.

Halpin, Stanley A., Jr. "Waves and Backwashes in Voting Rights Law: Recognition Without Implementation of a New Principle Opposing

Gerrymandering." *Southern University Law Review* 22 (Spring 1995): 255-73.

Hamilton, Howard D. "Legislative Constituencies: Single-member Districts, Multi-member Districts, and Floterial Districts," *Western Political Quarterly* 20 (June 1967): 321-340.

Hero, Rodney. "The Election of Hispanics in City Government: An Examination of the Election of Federico Pena as Mayor of Denver." *Western Political Quarterly* 40 (March 1987): 93-105.

Hero, R.E. "Mexican Americans and Urban Politics: A Consideration of Governmental Structure and Policy." *Aztlan* 17 (Spring 1986): 131-147.

"In Search of Empowerment: San Francisco's Chinese Community Strives for a Voice in City Hall." *San Francisco Business* (July 6-11, 1985).

Jacobs, Paul W. II, and Timothy G. O'Rourke. "Racial Polarization in Vote Dilution Cases Under Section 2 of the Voting Rights Act: The Impact of Thornburg v. Gingles (106 S. Ct. 2752) / by P.W. Jacobs, II, T.G. O'Rourke." *The Journal of Law and Politics* 3 (Fall 1986): 295-353.

Jewell, Malcolm E. "Local Systems of Representation: Political Consequences and Judicial Choices," *George Washington Law Review* 36 (May 1968): 790-807.

Jones, Murel Mathews. "The Impact of Annexation—Related City Council Reapportionment on Black Political Influence: The Cities of Richmond and Petersburgh, Virginia." Ph.D. diss., Howard University, 1977.

Karlan, Pamela. "Maps and Misreadings: The Role of Geographic Compactness in Racial Vote Dilution Litigation." *Harv Civ R&CLL Rev*24 (1989): 173.

Karlan, Pamela S. "All Over the Map: The Supreme Court's Voting Rights Trilogy." *The Supreme Court Review* 1993 (1993): 245-87.

Karnig, Albert K. "Local Elections in the U.S.: Separate and Unequal," *National Civic Review* 66 (April 1977): 182-185.

Karnig, Albert. "Black Resources and City Council Representation," *Journal of Politics* 41 (February 1979): 134-149.

Karnig, Albert. "Black Representation on City Councils: The Impact of District Elections and Socioeconomic Factors," *Urban Affairs Quarterly* 12 (December 1976): 223-242.

Kousser, J. Morgan. "Beyond Gingles: Influence Districts and the Pragmatic Tradition in Voting Rights Law. *University of San Francisco Law Review* 27, no. 3 (Spring 1993): 551.

"Latinos and Redistricting." Conference packet, Rose Institute of State and Local Government and The Institute for Social Justice, Claremont McKenna College, June 3, 1989.

Lamar, Cynthia Grace. "The Resolution of Post-Election Challenges Under Section 5 of the Voting Rights Act." *Yale Law Journal* 97 (July 1989): 1765-1782.

Latimer, Aimee D. "Miller v. Johnson (115 S. Ct. 2475 (1995)): The Supreme Court Eases the Burden of Proving Racial Gerrymandering. *Loyola University Chicago Law Journal* 27 (Fall 1995): 97-148.

Lee, Eugene C., and Jonathan S. Rothman. "San Francisco's District System Alters Electoral Politics." *National Civic Review* 67 (April 1978): 173-178.

Leeson, Susan Marg "Briar in the Thicket: 'One Man, One Vote' and Local Government," Ph.D. diss., Claremont Graduate School, 1971.

Levenson, Rosaline. "San Francisco Voters Repeal Districts." *National Civic Review* 69 (October 1980): 504.

Levenson, Rosaline. "San Francisco Voters Uphold District Elections." *National Civic Review* 66 (October 1977): 461-462.

Lyons, W.E., and M.E. Jewell. "Minority Representation and the Drawing of City Council Districts." *Urban Affairs Quarterly* 23 (March 1988): 432-447.

Machiarola, Frank J., and Joseph G. Diaz. "The 1990 New York City Districting Commission: Renewed Opportunity for Participation in Local Government or Race-Biased Gerrymandering?" *Cardozo Law Review* 14 (April 1993): 1175-235.

MacManus, Susan A. "City Council Elections Procedures and Minority Representation: Are they Related?" *Social Science Quartely* 59 (June 1978): 153-161.

MacManus , Susan A., and Charles S. Bullock, III. "Minorities and Women Do Win At-Large!" *National Civic Review.*

MacManus, Susan A. "Mixed Electoral Systems: The Newest Reform Structure," *National Civic Review* 74 (November 1985): 484-490.

McClain, Paula D., Bernard Grofman and Chandler Davidson, eds. "Controversies in Minority Voting: The Voting Rights Act in Perspective." *Contemporary Sociology* 22, no. 3.

McKaskie, Paul L. "The Voting Rights Act and the "Conscientious Redistricter." *University of San Francisco Law Review* 30 (Fall 1995): 1-94.

Martin, P.L. "'One Person, One Vote' and California's Water Districts," *Natural Resources Law Review* 8 (1975): 9.

Martin, Philip L. "The Supreme Court and Local Government Reapportionment: The First Phase." *Tennessee Law Review* 35 (Winter 1968): 313-317.

Martin, Philip L. "The Supreme Court and Local Government Reapportionment: The Second Phase." *Baylor Law Review* 21 (Winter 1969): 5-17.

Martin, Philip L. "The Supreme Court and Local Government Reapportionment: The Third Phase." *George Washington Law Review* 39 (October 1970): 102-122.

Martin, Philip L. "The Supreme Court and Local Government Reapportionment: Voter Inequality in Special-Purpose Units." *William and Mary Law Review* 15 (Spring 1974): 601-614.

Martin, Philip L. "Local Reapportionment," *Journal of Urban Law* 47 (1969-1970): 345-365.

Martin, P.L. "Local Reapportionment: The Exemption of Water Management Districts," *Santa Clara Lawyer* (Fall 1973): 31-45.

Martinez, Douglas. "How Local-Election Laws Keep Chicanos Out of Office." *California Journal* 6 (April 1975): 121-122.

"Metro Improves its Representation," *National Civic Review* 68 (May 1979): 261-262.

McDermott, John E., and Bernard Grofman. "Pro/Con: Should City Councils be Elected by District?" *Western City* (March 1987): 4-8, 24-31, 44.

McKaskie, Paul L. "The Voting Rights Act and the 'Conscientious Redistricter.'" *University of San Francisco Law Review* 30 (Fall 1995): 1-94.

McKay, Robert B. "Reapportionment and Local Government." *George Washington Law Review* 36 (May 1968): 713-740.

Miller, A.P., and M.A. Packman. "Amended Section 2 of the Voting Rights Act: What is the Intent of the Results Test?" *Emory Law Journal* 36 (Winter 1987): 1-74.

Miller, Binny. "Who Shall Rule and Govern? Local Legislative Delegations, Racial Politics, and the Voting Rights Act." *The Yale Law Journal* 102 (October 1992): 105-203.

Mireles, Valerie. "Surging Toward a Latino State." *California Journal* (January 1987): 19-21.

Neighbor, Howard. "Dilution of the Chicano Vote in El Paso." Western Political Science Association Meeting, Tempe, Arizona, April 29, 1976.

O'Hare, William P. "The Changing Hispanic Political Landscape." Redistricting in the 1990s.

"One Man, Less Than One Vote; How Certain Methods of Electing City Councilmen Result in Significant Under-Representation of Minorities in Major California Cities." Sacramento, CA: Senate Majority Caucus, June 1971.

O'Rourke, Timothy G. "City and County At-large Elections and the Problem of Minority Representation," *University of Virginia Newsletter* 55 (February 1979): No. 5 Charlottsville, VA: Univ. of VA, Institute of Government, 1979.

Peterson, Joyce. "L.A.'s Political Scramble." *Golden State Report* 3 [Los Angeles City Districts] (January 1987): 7-12.

Peterson, Paul E., ed. *Classifying by Race.* United States: Princeton University Press, 1995.

Pildes, Richard H. "The Politics of Race." *Harvard Law Review* 108 (April 1995): 1359-92.

Polinard, J.L. and Robert D. Wrinkle. "Mexican Americans and Education Policy: The Impact of Change to District Elections." Paper delivered at the Annual Meeting of the American Political Science Association, Washington, D.C. September 1-4, 1988.

Political Participation of Mexican Americans in California. Washington, D.C.: Government Printing Office, 1971.

Polsby, Daniel D., and Robert D. Popper. "Ugly: An Inquiry Into the Problem of Racial Gerrymandering Under the Voting Rights Act." *Michigan Law Review* 92 (December 1993): 652-82.

Reader, Scot A. "One Person, One Vote Revisited: Choosing a Population Basis to Form Political Districts." *Harvard Journal of Law and Public Policy* 17 (Spring 1994): 521-65.

(Redistricting Symposium). *Cumberland Law Review* 26 (1995/1996): 287-536. United States: H.W. Wilson Co., 1995.

Regalado, James A. "Council Wars and Minority Representation in Los Angeles and Chicago." Paper delivered at Western Political Science Association Annual Meeting, Anaheim, March 1987.

Regalado, James A. "Latino Political Empowerment: The Dilemma of Representation in Los Angeles, California." A paper presented at the Political Agenda for Latino Empowerment Symposium. University of Texas, El Paso. September 19, 1986.

Regalado, James A. "Racial Gerrymandering in Los Angeles, California? Redistricting and the Question of Latino Representation." A paper presented at the Western Political Science Association Annual Meeting, Eugene, Oregon, March 2-5, 1986.

Regalado, James A. "Vote Dilution in America's Biggest Cities: 1980 Councilmanic Reapportionments, Coalition Politics, and Minority Representation in Los Angeles, Chicago and New York." Prepared for delivery at the 1988 Annual Meeting of the Western Political Science Association, San Franciso, California, March 10-12, 1988.

Rehfuss, John. "Are At-large Elections Best for Council-Manager Cities?," *National Civic Review* 61 (May 1972): 236-241.

Renner, Tari. "Municipal Election Process: The Impact on Minority Representation,:" Base Line Report 19 1-11.

"The Results Test of Amended Action of the Voting Rights Act: An Examination of the Senate Report Factors." *Mississippi Law Journal* 54 (June 1984): 289-318.

Robinson, Ted P., Robert E. England, and Kenneth J. Meier. "Black Resources and Black School Board Representation: Does Political Structure Matter?," *Social Science Quarterly* 66 (December 1985): 976-982.

Romero, Gloria. "The Challenge to At-Large Elections in California: Romero, Et Al. V. The City of Pomona." Paper delivered at Western Political Science Association Annual Meeting, Anaheim, March 1987.

Rush, Mark E. "The Supreme Court's Approach to Gerrymandering and Representation." *The Journal of Law & Politics* 6 (Summer 1990): 683-722.

Salces, Luis M., and Peter W. Colby. "Mañana Will be Better: Spanish-American Politics in Chicago." *Illinois Issues* 6 (February 1980): 19-21.

Sample, Herbert. "Black Political Power: As Asian and Latino Populations Expand, Will Black Political Power Fade?" *California Journal* (May 1987): 232-239.

Salzman, Ed. "Bent Boards? A New One-Man, One-Vote Court Decision Casts a Shadow on Regional Government Agencies." *Golden State Report* (November 1989).

Silbaugh, Timothy W. "Apportionment Problems in Local Government," *Notre Dame Lawyer* 49 (February 1974): 671-685.

Simmons, Charlene. "Ethnics and Theories of the Representation." Western Political Science Conference paper, March 1990.

Simmons, Lee. "Constitutional Apportionment of Local Government in Montana," *Montana Law Review* 30 (Fall 1968): 35-45.

Skerry, Peter. "Not Much Cooking." *The Brookings Review* 11, no. 3 (Summer 1993): 42. Brookings Bulletin (Washington, D.C.: 1962).

Smith, Glenn P. "Interest Exceptions to One-Resident, One-Vote: Better Results From the Voting Rights Act?" *Texas Law Review* 74 (April 1996): 1153-94.

Stewart, Joseph. "In Search of Rainbow Coalitions: Racial/Ethnic Representation on Public School Boards," Paper at American Political Science Association, Atlanta, GA: September 1989.

Stoffers, William H. "Reapportionment in California Counties." *Santa Clara Lawyer* 4 (Spring 1964): 201-211.

The Supreme Court, Racial Politics, and the Right to Vote: Shaw v. Reno (113 S. Ct. 2816 (1993)) and the Future of the Voting Rights Act (conference)." *The American University Law Review* 44 (October 1994): 1-126.

"Symposium: Voting Rights Law." *University of San Francisco Law Review* 27 (Spring 1993): 549-652.

Tachibana, Judy. "California's Asians: Power From a Growing Population." *California Journal* (November 1986): 534-543.

Taebel, Delbert. "Minority Representation on City Councils: The Impact of Structure on Black's and Hispanics." *Social Science Quarterly* 59 (June 1978): 142-152.

Thernstrom, Abigail M. "The Odd Evolution of the Voting Rights Act." *Public Interest* (Spring 1979): 49-76.

Thermstrom, Abigail M. "Voting Rights: Another Affirmative Action Mess." *UCLA Law Review* 43, no. 6 : 2031.

Thernstrom, Abigail M. *Whose Vote Counts? Affirmative Action and Minority Voting Rights.* Cambridge, MA: Harvard University Press, 1987.

"Thornburg V. Gingles [106 ST.CT. 2752]: The Supreme Court's New Test for Analyzing Minority Vote Dilution." *University Law Review* 36 (Winter 1987): 531-563.

Tinley, Gervase. "Voting Rights and the Constitution: The Disenfranchisement of Non-English Speaking Citizens." *Yale Law Journal* 97 (June 1988): 1419-1437.

Uhlaner, Carole, Bruce Cain, and D. Roderick Kiewiet. "Patterns of Political Participation Among Ethnic Minorities in California." Paper delivered at WPSA, March 1986.

"Unapportioned Justice: Local Elections, Social Science, and the Evolution of the Voting Rights Act." *Cornell Journal of Law and Public Policy* 4 (Fall 1994): 199-271.

"United Jewish Organizations V. Carey and The Need to Recognize Aggregate Voting Rights." *Yale Law Journal* 87 (January 1978): 571-602.

Valle-Riestra, Paul. "At-Large Elections Declared Invalid." *Western City* (September 1988): 6-7"Voting Rights and the Democratic Process: Where Do We Stand Today?—special conference issue." *The Urban Lawyer* 17 (Summer 1985): 333-528.

Voting Rights After *Shaw v. Reno* (113 S. Ct. 2816 (1993)): symposium. *Rutgers Law Journal* 26 (Spring 1995): 517-773.

"Voting Rights and Elections." *University of Chicago Legal Forum* (1995): 1 -599.

"Voting Rights and the Democratic Process: Where Do We Stand Today?—special conference issue." *The Urban Lawyer* 17 (Summer 1985): 333-528.

"Voting Rights Law: Symposium." *University of San Francisco Law Review* 27 (Summer 1993): 737-872.

"Voting Rights Symposium." *Howard Law Journal* 28 (1985): 393-601.

"Voting Rights Symposium." *Stetson Law Review* 21 (Summer 1992): 707-869.

"Voting Rights Symposium." *Mississippi Law Journal* 65 (Winter 1995): 205-461.

Wasby, Stephen L. *Vote Dilution, Minority Voting Rights, and the Courts.* Washington, D.C.: Joint Center for Political Studies, 1982.

Way, Frank. Malcolm E. Jewell, ed. "California: 'Brutal Butchery of the Two-Party System'?" *The Politics of Reapportionment*: 249-264Weber, Ronald E. "Redistricting and the Courts: Judicial Activism in the 1990s." *American Political Quarterly* 23, no. 2 (April 1995): 204.

Way, Heather K. "A Shield or a Sword? Section 5 of the Voting Rights Act and the Argument for the Incorporation of Section 2." *Texas Law Review* 74 (May 1996): 1439-83.

Weber, Ronald E. "Redistricting and the Courts: Judicial Activism in the 1990s." *American Political Quarterly* 23, no. 2 (April 1995): 204.

Weinstein, Jack B. "The Effect of the Federal Reapportionment Decisions on Counties and Other Forms of Municipal Government." *Columbia Law Review* 65 (January 1965): 21-54.

Young, Charles Edward. "The Politics of Political Boundary Making." Ph.D. diss., University of California, Los Angeles, 1959.

Zimmerman, Joseph F. "A 'Fair' Voting System for Local Governments," *National Civic Review* 68 (October 1979): 481-487.

Zimmerman, Joseph F. "A Proportional Representation System; and New York City School Boards.," *National Civic Review* 63 (October 1974): 472-474, 493.

Zimmerman, Joseph F. "The Federal Voting Right Act and Alternative Election Systems." *William and Mary Law Review* 19 (Summer 1978): 621-660.

Table of Cases

Allen v. State Board of Elections, 393 U.S. 544 (1969).
American Continental Corporation v. Donna Culbertson, Superior Court, Division II, Arizona, No. C-479271.
Baker v. Carr, 369 U.S. 186 (1962).
Beer v. United States, 425 U.S. 130 (1976).
Breedlove v. Suttles, 302 U.S. 277 (1937).
Bush v. Vera, Docket No. 94–805, June 1996 (U.S. Reports citation not yet available).
City of Mobile v. Bolden, 446 U.S. 55 (1980).
City of Petersburg, Virginia v. United States, 354 F.Supp. 1021 (1972).
City of Richmond v. United States, 376 F.Supp 1344 @ 1351 (1974).
City of Richmond v. United States, 422 U.S. @ 358 (1975).
Connor v. Johnson, 402 U.S. 690 (1971).
Connor v. Finch, 431 U.S. 407 (1977).
Garza v. Los Angeles County Board of Supervisors, Slip opinion no. CV 88–5143 KN, 918 F.2d 763 (9th Cir. 1990).
Gomez v. City of Watsonville, 863 F.2d 1407 (9th Cir. 1988), *cert. denied* 489 U.S. 1080 (1989).
Gomillion v. Lightfoot, 364 U.S. 339 (1960).
Grovey v. Townsend, 295 U.S. 45 (1935).
Guinn v. United States, 238 U.S. 347 (1915).
Holt v. City of Richmond, 459 F.2d 1093 @ 1099 (4th cir., 1972, *cert. denied*, 408 U.S. 931 (1972).
Lane v. Wilson, 307 U.S. 268 (1939).
Miller v. Johnson, 115 S.Ct. 2475 (1995).
Mississippi v. United States, 490 F.Supp. 569 (D.D.C. 1979), *aff'd* 451 U.S. 934 (1981).

Perkins v. Matthews, 400 U.S. 379 (1971).
Reynolds v. Sims, 377 U.S. 533 (1964).
Romero v. City of Pomona, 883 F.2d 1418 (9th cr. 1989).
Shaw v. Hunt, Docket No. 94–923, June 1996 (U.S. Reports citation not yet available).
Shaw v. Reno, 113 U.S. 2816 (1993).
Smith v. Allwright, 321 U.S. 649 (1944).
South Carolina v. Katzenbach, 383 U.S. 301 (1966).
Thornburg v. Gingles, 478 U.S. 30 (1986).
United Jewish Organizations of Williamsburgh v. Carey, 430 U.S. 144 (1977).
United States v. Cruikshank, 92 U.S. 542 (1876).
United States v. Reese, 92 U.S. 214 (1876).
Wesberry v. Sanders, 376 U.S. 1 (1964).
White v. Regester, 412 U.S. 755 (1973).
Wilkes County v. United States, 450 F.Supp. 1171 @ 1178 (D.D.C. 1978).
Yrigollen v. City of Hanford, CV-F-93 5303–OWW/NEW, June 3, 1994.
Zimmer v. McKeithen, 485 F.2d 1297 (5th cir. 1973), *aff'd on other grounds sub nom East Carroll Parish School Board v. Marshall*, 424 U.S. 636 (1976).

Index

For Product Safety Concerns and Information please contact our EU
representative GPSR@taylorandfrancis.com
Taylor & Francis Verlag GmbH, Kaufingerstraße 24, 80331 München, Germany

www.ingramcontent.com/pod-product-compliance
Ingram Content Group UK Ltd.
Pitfield, Milton Keynes, MK11 3LW, UK
UKHW022111190926
475702UK00013B/1373
9781138979444